Desktop Marketing with the Macintosh

**Stacy Gasteiger and
Tracy Emerick**

Brady Publishing

Published by Brady Publishing
a Division of Prentice Hall
Computer Publishing

Manufactured in the United States of America

2   3   4   5   6   7   8   9   10

Library of Congress Cataloging-in-Publication Data

Gasteiger, Stacy.
    Desktop marketing with the Macintosh / Stacy Gasteiger and Tracy
Emerick.
        p.   cm. – – (Lotus books)
    Includes index.
    ISBN 0-13-203613-4 : $34.95
    1. Direct marketing – – Data processing.   2. Macintosh (Computer)
I. Emerick, Tracy.   II. Title.   III. Series.
HF5415.126.G37   1992
658.8'4– –dc20

Acknowledgments

The authors extend thanks to Mel Berger for initially coming up with the idea for this book; to Susan Hunt for making the idea a reality; to Winnie Davis for her copy edit of the manuscript; and to Bettina Versaci for her skilled management of production.

Dedication

Stacy would like to dedicate this book to Daniel, who, somehow or other, turned her into a writer.

Trademarks

All brand and product names mentioned herein are trademarks or registered trademarks of their respective holders.

Limits of Liability and Disclaimer

Contents

---

5   Define Your Prospective Customers 75

What This Book Can Do for You

This book is oriented toward the sales-and-marketing person in a small business. In most cases, this person and the owner are one and the same. This book can also be helpful to someone in the branch office of a large company who may want to take control of his or her own marketing efforts without waiting for the main office to take action.

Promoting and marketing a small business is a challenge, particularly in these competitive times. Everyone is after an ever-shrinking portion of the pie. Anything you can do to increase the visibility and viability of your company is important.

This book introduces you to direct marketing—direct marketing the way the big companies do it. Up until recently, if you wanted to create powerful, directed direct marketing campaigns, you had to turn to outside vendors to do almost everything—design brochures, print mailers, select lists, and handle follow-ups.

Now, with the increased power of the Macintosh, the quality of software, and new methods of delivering information to the Macintosh, you can have the same power of the big companies right on your desktop.

You don't have to be a computer pro to make these software packages and techniques work for you. The authors of this book are not computer programmers; we're marketers who use this same software to accomplish *our* marketing tasks. With a little practice, anyone should be able to control marketing campaigns from the Macintosh.

Using This Book

This book guides you through the essential steps of creating a direct marketing campaign, from the first consideration to the analysis of results. For each stage of the plan, it explains how you can perform the steps on your Macintosh using a wide range of software and software tools.

In most cases, the book will refer to one specific brand of software when explaining how to perform the step. However, there are usually many comparable software packages available. For example, when we explain how to do something with MacWrite II, you usually can do it with any other Macintosh word processor as well.

Because you may have a wide variety of software, our explanations of how to use the software tend to be more descriptive than specific. Use the general description to convert the concepts to your specific software.

1

What Is Desktop Marketing?

Every business needs customers, and it's your job to find and keep those customers. With the help of your Macintosh and some special software, you can find and keep customers while selling more product and increasing your market share.

In the past 10 years, sales-and-marketing personnel in large businesses have come to depend on computers. Analysts pore over immense reports created by gigantic databases sitting on company mainframes looking for market advantages. Businesses have turned their static customer lists into continuous sales transactions through the use of direct mail. Niche marketing has exploded as computer analysis of customers and potential customers has been enhanced.

Somehow, this blitz of computerized marketing efficiency continues to bypass smaller companies and even the branch offices of large businesses. Although personal computers are now tremendously powerful with a wide variety of available software, they just haven't made significant inroads into sales and marketing departments. It hasn't been clear how to make personal computers work *for* the average sales-and-marketing person, helping them find new customers and bringing those customers knocking on the door. You can use the Macintosh to generate new leads, convert them to sales, and keep them as customers.

Desktop marketing can change all this. But what is desktop marketing?

Desktop Marketing Definition

Desktop marketing is the active pursuit, targeting, and maintenance of customers using a personal computer and a wide selection of software tools such as lead generation, word processors, database management, lead-tracking tools, spreadsheets, and desktop publishing.

By using a Macintosh to do marketing, you'll gain several benefits:

- *Control:* You don't need to use outside sources to create your marketing programs; instead you can get professional-looking results doing it yourself.

- *Flexibility:* With a Macintosh, you can change any aspect of your marketing program simply and easily, allowing you to respond more quickly to market changes.

- *Time saving:* If you're controlling the entire marketing process, you can make things happen when *you* want them to happen. You no longer have to wait for other vendors to get around to your job.

■ *Cost savings:* By using the tools on your desk, you don't have to use expensive outside services as often. In addition, powerful analytical tools can save you from wasted and costly efforts trying to sell to the wrong market.

Direct Marketing

For the purpose of this book, desktop marketing refers to the process of doing direct marketing with a Macintosh—everything from initial market analysis to the final tallying of sales. With desktop marketing, everyone, from the most sophisticated direct marketer to a first-timer, can create an entire direct marketing campaign with a Macintosh, printer, CD drive (optional), modem (optional), and the appropriate software tools. To understand desktop marketing, you should understand exactly what direct marketing is.

Definition of Direct Marketing

Direct marketing is the process of gaining new customers and maintaining existing customers without you or a salesperson ever having to see the customer. Direct marketing requires four key ingredients:

1) *Target Customers*—Targets are either existing customers or prospects you would *like* to become customers.

2) *Contact*—A method to make and continue communication with the target customers.

3) *Offer*—An item, service, or intangible you can offer target customers to create sales now or in the future.

4) *Information base*—A collection of information about each target customer and all contacts your company has with each target customer. The information base is the key difference between direct marketing and other forms of marketing.

Direct marketing is more than putting a flyer in the mail. It is a combination of marketing strategy, powerful methods of communication, and data processing that works together to keep your company's products and services in front of potential customers. The goal is a dialogue that will lead to sales.

Best of all, direct marketing is measurable in both costs and results. With direct marketing, you know exactly how much money you earn— or lose.

There are seven steps in traditional direct marketing:

Step 1—Prepare yourself.

Step 2—Develop an offer.

Step 3—Find prospective customers.

Step 4—Create a direct mail package.

Step 5—Create a telemarketing plan.

Step 6—Analyze results.

Step 7—Maintain ongoing marketing.

Chapter 2 goes into the direct marketing process in much more detail.

Desktop Marketing Tools

Through the power of technology, you can now use hardware and software tools for all parts of the direct marketing process. You may already use some of the tools of desktop marketing for entirely different purposes—word-processing software, database management, spreadsheets. You can use these tools to contact and track customers or to do analysis. There are other tools that are more specifically targeted to your marketing needs.

Word-Processing Software

You can use word-processing software to write copy, to compose offer letters, or to create telemarketing scripts. With word-processing software, you can easily modify and change your copy until you get exactly what you want. With most word processors, you can create personalized offers by combining names from electronic lists with your offer letter.

Desktop Publishing

Desktop publishing software is designed to create publishable pieces such as newsletters, brochures, and catalogs. The software allows you to combine both text and graphics and gives you powerful layout capabilities. Because you are working in the Macintosh WYSIWYG (What You See Is What You Get) environment, you can see exactly what a piece will look like after it's printed.

Database Management

This type of software helps you to maintain customer and prospect lists. If you already have a customer database, you can transfer it to a database management software package in order to do customer analysis and to make follow-up marketing much easier.

Financial Management

With spreadsheet software or specialized accounting software, you can do the accounting and cash management you need to support the administrative functions of desktop marketing. You can use spreadsheets to examine the status of your own business, to analyze the results of your desktop marketing programs, and to assist in your analysis of new markets. Once you're finished with all your number crunching, use their graphing features to make the presentation of your findings more persuasive.

Lead-Generation

Lead-generation tools generally combine marketing information about a large collection of potential customers with the software tools you need to narrow that list down to your best possible targets. The marketing information either resides on a mainframe computer you access remotely or on CD-ROM. The powerful combination of data and software lets you put your target customers right where you want them—on your desktop

---

What is CD-ROM?

A CD-ROM is very much like the CDs you can listen to on your stereo. Instead of holding music, a CD-ROM disc holds data. A single CD-ROM can hold 650 megabytes of information—the same amount of information as 200,000 typewritten pages. CD-ROM is an extremely efficient method of making vast quantities of information available on your Macintosh.

To access a CD-ROM disc, you must have a CD-ROM drive, which connects to the Macintosh through a standard SCSI connection. Once you connect the CD-ROM drive, it acts just like a hard disk, only more slowly.

Other Specialized Software

Several different types of software can help you with the more specialized aspects of desktop marketing. Mapping software can help you to analyze information in a geographic context. Label-generation software can aid in the creation and enhancement of mailing materials. Use clip-art packages to find graphics to jazz up your creative efforts. For more comprehensive customer tracking, you can use lead tracking software, which is database management software enhanced specifically for the purpose of tracking leads and customers.

The Desktop Marketing Difference

The following brief example should illuminate the difference between marketing with and without desktop marketing tools.

All-American Insurance Before Desktop Marketing

Maria Ferrara is an insurance representative for All-American Insurance in Minnesota. Her current goal is to sell liability insurance to small businesses. Maria will use direct marketing to find new customers, but she'll do it the old-fashioned way.

Step 1—Prepare yourself: Maria decides she is selling peace of mind; with liability insurance, her customers will not lose a business or home if a huge claim should arise. Before she begins her direct marketing effort, she gets all her insurance applications prepared and sets up a method to track new applicants. She also does an evaluation of the current state of her business so that she'll know if her direct marketing efforts are successful.

Step 2—Develop an offer: Maria develops an offer she feels will appeal to small businesses and will motivate them to buy from her.

Step 3—Find prospective customers: Maria calls the head office for any leads they may have received for her territory. They send her a handful of leads, but most of them are six to nine months old—and there's no indication of which type of insurance each lead expressed interest in.

Next, she calls a list broker to try to rent a mailing list. The broker wants to know the type of businesses Maria would like to target. When Maria describes what she wants, the list broker isn't sure how many names he can get to fit her descriptions but promises to call Maria back the next day.

When she gets the list counts from the broker, Maria decides she wants to do small mailings to five different types of businesses to find out which is the most promising. However, the list owners insist on a minimum purchase of names from each list, which makes the purchase of five segments too expensive. When she asks to take a look at the lists to help her choose, the broker refuses. Purely on gut instincts, Maria chooses two lists. It will now take the broker 10 days to deliver the lists, *and* he wants to approve her mailing materials even before he begins to process the lists.

Step 4—Create a direct mail package: Maria begins to work on the pieces of her direct mail package. She hires a designer to help create the brochure. Unfortunately, the designer gets a bigger, rush job and postpones working on Maria's relatively small job. Maria also hires a lettershop to handle the production of her direct mail piece. The lettershop will personalize her letters by putting the name and address of the recipient on each letter. It will also stuff the envelopes and do the actual mailing.

Step 5—Create a telemarketing plan: Maria prepares her secretary for the phone calls that will come in. Maria describes the types of questions people may ask and gives the secretary lots of miscellaneous backup material.

Step 6—Analyze results: As the calls begin to roll in, Maria and her secretary track them all in a ledger book. They mark down how many interested calls come in and how many result in actual sales. As the decision process drags on and more variables are added, it becomes more and more difficult to track the progress and the record keeping becomes spotty. After three months, it's almost impossible for Maria to calculate how much money she earned from her initial offer.

Step 7—Maintain ongoing marketing: Maria calls her clients once a year to make sure they plan to renew their liability insurance. Her secretary goes through the files each month to find clients whose policies will expire in the next two months. In the note she sends about the renewal, Maria also asks clients if they would like to change any of their other insurance policies to her company.

Maria's direct marketing efforts did work, but they worked haphazardly. She was never certain whether the direct mailing had been a good idea, because she wasn't able to evaluate it fairly. In addition, she always felt nervous about passing control of her marketing programs over to someone who didn't feel as much concern for its success as she did.

All-American After Desktop Marketing

After her frustrating early attempts, Maria decides to take control of her marketing efforts with a Macintosh, CD-ROM drive, and a LaserWriter printer.

Step 1—Prepare yourself: Maria is still selling peace of mind, and her financial review process is very similar. However, instead of ordering lots of blank insurance forms and getting them ready for incoming orders, she duplicates the layout with her desktop publishing software. Now she'll be able to fill out the forms on the Macintosh, which will make corrections and additions a breeze.

Step 2—Develop an offer: Maria feels comfortable with the offer she created prior to her entry into the desktop marketing world, so she decides to keep it.

Step 3—Find prospective customers: Maria now turns to MarketPlace Business, a CD-ROM-based lead-generation package to find her prospects. She begins by using the Analysis feature to get a better understanding of her potential markets. MarketPlace gives her market sizes, market comparisons, and the ability to examine many different targeting possibilities in a short period of time.

After spending some time poring over the analysis reports, Maria decides to do test mailings to five different business segments, something she couldn't afford with the broker's list-minimums. She creates lists for each of the five segments and looks them over. Because she just wants to test the different lists, she pulls out a 10 percent random sample for each list. She transfers the sample lists onto the hard disk of her Macintosh, so that she'll be able to use the names with her other software.

Step 4—Create a direct mail package: Maria uses her new word processor to experiment with several different letters for her direct mail package. Once she is satisfied with the letter, she combines the body of the letter with the names and addresses from the

MarketPlace list to create personalized letters. She then prints those letters on company letterhead using her LaserWriter.

Maria decides to create a targeted brochure by herself. She uses her desktop publishing software to create a simple but powerful brochure spelling out all the benefits liability insurance can give to a small business. She creates the master brochure on the laser printer and hands it over to a printer to do the mass printing.

Step 5—Create telemarketing plan: Because she can't afford an outside service to receive telephone responses, Maria still plans to use her secretary to handle most of the incoming calls. However, instead of the ad hoc method she used before, Maria uses her word processing software to create a standard script for the secretary to follow, complete with the most common questions and their answers.

Step 6—Manage results: Instead of her paper ledger book, Maria transfers her MarketPlace leads with all their associated information to a database management program. Now, as soon as her secretary gets a call or a response comes through the mail, the secretary can match the response with the appropriate record. In three month's time, Maria used the database software to analyze what type of company was most likely to respond to her offer.

She also uses a spreadsheet to do some in-depth numerical analysis of the desktop marketing campaign—and most important, its profitability. Maria learns which of her five lists has the greatest potential, so that she can prioritize her future efforts. She can even use the spreadsheet to create presentation-quality graphs to use when discussing her results with her regional sales director.

Step 7—Maintain ongoing marketing: With her new database, Maria now has a simple way to track all her clients and prospects. She uses the database to track any and all client information, even taking notes about every customer phone call. With this new easy access to clients, Maria decides to use her desktop publishing software to put together a quarterly newsletter to send to all her customers and contacts. By discussing new policies, laws, and insurance news on a regular basis, Maria hopes All-American will be in the forefront of her clients' thoughts whenever any new insurance need occurs.

She can also use the database as a source for future marketing efforts, since her current customer will be her most likely future customers. And, with MarketPlace's quarterly updates, Maria will be kept apprised of any changes in address, contact, or phone numbers.

The Benefits

Of course, you don't have to do everything yourself as Maria did in the above example. The Macintosh and the desktop marketing tools give you a tremendous flexibility to control those aspects of a direct marketing campaign that you want to control. If your sense of design is decidedly lacking, feel free to use a graphic designer to create your brochures. But you may choose to create and manage a Macintosh-based customer database that lets you sell more because you understand your customers' needs more.

The Macintosh and its software tools give you the power to create a more level playing field with the big corporations that surround you.

2

Basics of Direct Marketing

It's difficult to be unaware of direct marketing. You receive evidence of it almost every day with mail or phone calls trying to sell you products or services. Direct marketing has become a large part of American business, with $10 trillion worth of goods sold directly per year (*Direct Marketing Magazine*).

However, you may be unaware of the exacting nature of direct marketing. This chapter is designed to give you an overview of the direct marketing process, before we discuss how you can use desktop marketing tools to do it yourself.

An In-Depth Definition of Direct Marketing

We already briefly described direct marketing as the process of gaining new customers and maintaining existing customers without you or a sales person ever having to see the customer. Direct marketing may be oriented to making an immediate sale, like most of the direct mail you receive at home, or to generating leads for big-ticket items that may need additional selling, like a lot of business-to-business direct mail. A more detailed definition of direct marketing is:

Direct Marketing:

1) Seeks to gain or maintain a customer.

2) Is a structured system of contacts.

3) Measures inputs and outputs.

4) Complements, supplements, or substitutes current selling methods.

5) Requires shared information base.

6) Is a basis for continuing contact.

7) Uses any media.

Direct marketing is a process—not an event. It's a process that uses all available methods of communication to make a contact with a customer or a target prospect in order to generate a lead or make a sale. People often describe direct marketing as a mailing or a series of phone calls. Those are just the communication parts of direct marketing, not the entire process. Direct marketing includes all the phases of contact that creates the relationship between a company and its customers. Direct marketing includes advertising, order taking, delivering a good or performing a service, collecting money, and so on.

To help you understand direct marketing more thoroughly, we'll expand on each part of the definition.

1) Seeks to Gain or Maintain a Customer

This first aspect of direct marketing encompasses the overall responsibility of marketing: to gain and keep customers. Direct marketing is a marketing process focused on the growth of a business through continual and valuable contacts with customers and potential customers. The key word is *valuable*. There's a distinct difference between staying in touch and making valuable contact. A valuable contact delivers some form of benefit to the target customers.

For example, sending a price increase notice to your customers may generate some orders, but it doesn't deliver value to the customer. When he gets value, a customer wants to receive communications from you. If all of your communications are administrative or are company-focused, rather than customer-focused, the value of the communication is reduced.

Think of the value relationship as a customer capital account. As you bring value to your customers, you make deposits in the account. As you ask for orders, you make withdrawals from the account. If all contacts are withdrawals, the customer account will eventually dry up. Keeping value in the relationship is what keeps customers coming back. Once your withdrawals outweigh your value contributions, the account will close.

Remember, direct marketing doesn't require a lead or a sale every time you make a contact. Often you make a contact to keep the relationship moving forward until the next order. Staying on your customer's mind is a way to stay on the order list and keep your competitors from taking your place.

2) Structured System of Contacts

Successful direct marketing is not a series of accidental events that might lead to a sale. Direct marketing is a planned series of contacts that are each geared to move a target through to the next step in the closing process.

Travel with successful salespeople, and you'll find they tend to do the same things over and over with a prospect. Each move the sales rep makes is calculated to set the stage for the next step in the process. For current customers, this process can be abbreviated because there is less time spent developing rapport. The key is that there are a series of steps involved in creating initial sales and in creating more sales and upgrades with customers.

3) Measures Inputs and Outputs

Direct marketing measures the process in order to evaluate the profitability of an approach. Just because a series of steps is employed to create a sale doesn't mean the sale is profitable. New salespeople will often sacrifice markup to create a sale. The same can be true with direct marketing—the cost of making a sale can be greater than the gross margin of the sale. Sometimes it's better to lose money on a sale if customers can be gained or maintained for long-term profitability.

The most difficult task you'll have is keeping track of marketing programs and tying together the results to the program. Measurements can be assessed on the investment made in a program (Inputs) and on the results of the program (Outputs). Even if you can't get all the information, measure what you can in the time available so that you'll have some guidance to make future marketing decisions.

4) Complements, Supplements, or Substitutes for Current Selling Methods

Direct marketing can and should support current selling approaches. If salespeople are your primary method for making contact with customers, direct marketing can substitute for some portion of their time so that they can spend more time looking for new business. Direct marketing can allow the reps to concentrate their time on those customers who are most valuable to your business.

5) Requires Shared Information Base

Direct marketing cannot be successful unless there is a shared information base. Every person in the circuit needs to have information to do his/her job. Without common information between the phone center and the field representative, there's no chance a structured marketing approach can be achieved.

Another term for a shared information base is *database*. The term database, however, gives the impression of accumulated data sitting there waiting for decision makers to analyze it. An information base, on the other hand, provides not only data but some type of analysis to indicate what actions should be taken.

One type of information might include a scoring system that guides specific actions by different people in the company. The scoring system and the associated actions are all defined in the structured phase of setting up the program.

6) Basis for Continuing Contact

Direct marketing is a continual process that feeds contact information into the information base. This information is in turn used to create new contacts. The dynamics of the direct marketing process are neverending. Many programs can be underway at the same time to different segments of the base. And the information base can be profitably promoted all the time.

7) Uses Any Media

Direct marketing can use any media to generate a response or a sale. You're not constrained to use direct mail or telephone, even though these are the workhorses of direct marketing. You can use any media to generate a response—even a sales rep. If you use a structured approach with effective measurement, you'll learn what media sells the most for your business.

Direct Mail and Telemarketing: Direct Marketing's Two Most Effective Methods

 lthough the last defining step of direct marketing says you can use any media, direct marketers have learned through experience that two techniques—direct mail and telemarketing—are the most effective.

Direct Mail

With direct mail, you send mail to your prospect or customer in order to produce a response, a lead, or an order. Once you have created any marketing program that sells your product, you can use direct mail to put this proposition in front of tens, hundreds, or thousands of prospects, using a postal worker to deliver your message.

Direct mail can range from a picture postcard to a beautiful catalog. Mailings are limited only by your imagination. We have known people to put postage and an address on a 2 x 4 or on a coconut, both of which the post office quickly delivered. The type of direct mail you create can be as varied as your imagination.

Direct mail is a very flexible marketing medium, and it can be even more so with your Macintosh and desktop marketing tools. You can deliver different messages tailored to each target market you select. You can test a product with different prices or special coupons, all at the same time, by sending the different offers to different prospects. No other marketing method makes it so easy to test and analyze so many variables at the same time.

Your best source for understanding direct mail is your own mailbox. Begin saving direct mail pieces that catch your eye. Look for graphics you find appealing. Save letters with copy you like. Keep a lookout for offers you might be able to replicate. You can use these materials as a guide when you begin to create your own direct mail pieces.

Telemarketing

The telephone has grown as a direct marketing tool over the last several years. Today, the telephone is being used as an active marketing tool, not just as a convenient way to communicate. The use of the telephone in direct marketing falls into three separate categories:

1) **Outbound telemarketing**—Telemarketers use a detailed script to deliver a consistent message to every customer or prospect they call. The script provides for answers to the basic questions and objections that might come up during a phone contact. This form of phone use is equivalent to direct mail on the telephone.

2) **Telesales**—Telesales reps may use a call guideline, but the flow of the conversation with the prospect or customer is based on the skill of the telesales rep. This form of phone use mimics field sales on the telephone.

3) **Inbound**—This is usually an 800 telephone number offered to customers or prospects to contact *you* via the telephone. This form of phone use can be either telemarketing or telesales, depending on the freedom you give the people taking the calls.

Seven Steps for Direct Marketing

As we mentioned in Chapter 1, there are seven basic steps to direct marketing. They are:

Step 1—Prepare yourself.

Step 2—Develop an offer.

Step 3—Find prospective customers.

Step 4—Create a direct mail package.

Step 5—Create a telemarketing plan.

Step 6—Analyze results.

Step 7—Maintain ongoing marketing.

When setting out to do direct marketing, you shouldn't plan to divide your time evenly among the seven steps, because time spent on some steps will generate a better payoff. Ideally, you should allocate your time as follows:

Market identification and selection (Steps 1 and 3)—50 percent of your time. If you do not properly identify and select your target market, everything else you do will fail. Selecting the right market will help even a poorly executed program succeed.

Offer development (Step 2)—25 percent of your time. Developing the right proposition to get your prospective customers to take action is crucial to direct marketing. If your offer is appealing, target customers will act, even if the mail piece isn't elaborate or your phone script isn't elegant.

Format (phone or mail) (Step 4 or 5)—15 percent of your time. You must strategically plan the best way to deliver your offer by deciding whether your prospects will respond best to phone or mail— or a combination of both.

Copy/Graphics (Step 4 or 5)—10 percent of your time. Many people fall into the trap of expending most of their effort on the actual creation of mailing pieces or telemarketing scripts. Most prospects won't read every word of the copy you send them and telemarketers will not read exactly what you have written. Therefore, there is no such thing as the perfect letter or perfect script— don't waste your time trying to achieve it.

With an understanding of how you should spend your time, the following are brief explanations of the steps you should follow. Each step will be described in greater depth in subsequent chapters.

Step 1: Prepare Yourself

Preparation consists of five different steps to ensure you're ready to use direct marketing. You have to A) evaluate and prepare your current marketing systems, B) define your product or service, C) position your product, D) prepare to fulfill promises, and E) consider financial matters.

A) Evaluate and Prepare Your Current Marketing Systems

If you've never done direct marketing, one of your biggest challenges will be to adjust to this new marketing method. Start by evaluating your current marketing efforts and results. Define your goals. Because the results of direct marketing are measurable, you need to know what you want to measure and be able to compare the results with your current programs. To accomplish this, you should take a financial overview of your current marketing programs and your customer acquisition procedures. Without learning your current costs, you'll have no way to know what results you'll need to make your direct marketing a success.

Once you are set to go ahead, you must prepare yourself and your staff for the changes direct marketing will bring to your regular routine. For example, when you do direct marketing, prospects will begin contacting your company. It is vital that everyone on your staff knows how to speak with and handle a customer. Even the bookkeeper must be prepared to take charge of a customer on the phone.

You must also decide how to explain your direct marketing efforts to your current distributors, whether they are wholesalers, retailers, or your own sales force. Traditionally, people within these distribution systems complain and threaten if you begin to contact potential customers directly. There are several ways to handle their reactions. The simplest way is to not sell your products or services directly; instead, let your desktop marketing program generate qualified leads which you pass on for fulfillment. If you choose to sell directly, reassure your distributors that any direct marketing efforts you make will increase customer interest in your products. Many people will still buy from their usual supplier rather than buy direct, making both you and your distribution network happy.

In addition to more sales, there is a major advantage to contacting your market directly. By going direct, you can gain market information you will never learn from your distribution channel. Your distributors are interested in exchanging your goods for money, not gathering information for you. The market information you learn from direct marketing can be used to improve all your future marketing efforts.

B) Define Your Product and Service

You will hear this maxim in almost every marketing course you take—you have to know what you're selling. For example, in the previous chapter, Maria could have defined her service as liability insurance. But she realized she was really selling the peace of mind that comes with knowing you are protected if a mistake or accident occurs. If you can't explain your product or service without a demonstration or face-to-face contact, your direct marketing program should be oriented to generating sales leads or store traffic to make the in-person pitch. Many people won't buy complex products, such as computer networking, without seeing exactly how it works. Therefore, direct marketing for computer networks should concentrate on lead generation.

C) Position Your Product

It's tempting to describe how wonderful your product or service is and what a great company you are. However, it's crucial to position your product or service to emphasize how it will benefit the buyer. You must give prospects a reason to want what you're selling—something that is directly related to the customers' needs.

D) Prepare to Fulfill Promises

The fastest way to lose a new customer is to make an offer and not fulfill it. Not only have you lost that customer, you may also lose everyone the customer complains to about your service. Before making any promises, make sure your organization is capable of responding to the demand created by your direct marketing efforts.

E) Financial Considerations

In addition to examining the potential profits and losses for your direct marketing effort, you must be sure all the financial controls are in place. Your accounting department should be prepared to send invoices and to track sales. You should decide the types of payments you can accept and how you will qualify a customer's ability to pay.

To properly analyze your results, you will need accurate records of sales, receivables, and the like.

Step 2: Develop an Offer

Just letting people know you have something to sell will seldom move them to action: you must develop a selling proposition that creates action. Your current customers will usually respond to a good offer, because they know you and your products. Potential customers don't know you and are therefore more reluctant to take action. Prospects must see a clear benefit *plus* some reward for taking action.

Because Step 2 and Step 3 are closely related to each other, you don't have to do one before the other. You're likely to go back and forth between developing your offer and finding prospective customers until you create the best possible offer for the most promising list of prospects you can get.

Step 3: Find Prospective Customers

The best place to begin looking for prospective customers is your current customer base. If you continue to sell the same products or services, it's likely that future customers will resemble the customers you have now. Think about your customers and ask yourself questions about what they are like. Concentrate on defining your top 20 percent of customers. If you can find more customers like them, your business is bound to grow.

When you look at the top 20 percent, you may find that although your customers come from a wide range of business types, the ones that buy the most from you are manufacturing companies. Or, the customers who spend the most money per order are in rural areas, where they don't have great access to stores.

With the answers to these descriptive questions, you can define the type of prospects you want. With this definition in hand, you can explore electronic databases such as MarketPlace, on-line links to mainframe databases, or contact a list broker about commercially available lists.

Step 4: Create a Direct Mail Package

The elements of the direct mail package are straightforward:

Letter: To extol your product and extend the offer

Brochure: To explain your product and extend the offer

Response device: To extend the offer and ask for action

Reply envelope: To carry your response device

Effective copy coordinated with graphics can make a direct mail package fun to read. If it is not enjoyable for the reader, it won't be read. Remember to focus on the benefit to the reader, not the wonders of your product.

Before going ahead with a full-blown direct mail campaign, it is important to test. Test your direct mail effort on a small section of the target market to find out what works before you make a big investment. Try not to be impatient when starting a program and bypass the testing step. For example, you may find that prospects respond better if the offer describes the price as a 20 percent discount, instead of simply offering the low price with no explanation.

Step 5: Create a Telemarketing Plan

You can use the telephone as a marketing tool either in conjunction with your direct mail campaign or on its own. If you decide to use the phone, you should develop a script or a call program for your telemarketers. If you are going to take inbound calls, you need to prepare your staff to handle those calls. To insure measurability, you need to create a system for the use of the telephone, so that your marketers know who to call, when to call them, and what to say.

Step 6: Analyze Results

Once the leads and orders start pouring in, your office can easily turn to chaos, and this can cause you to lose track of what's happening. Establish tracking procedures *before* the marketing program begins so as to avoid losing track of each prospect and the final outcome of your relationship with the prospect.

To accurately evaluate your results when the program is finished, you will need to know how many sales you need (from your up-front planning) and how many you have made to date. The numbers and information you gather will also help you to pick out the most successful parts of any direct mail effort, so you can then apply them to future attempts.

Step 7: Maintain Ongoing Marketing

Your job is only beginning with the first sale. You should think of each sale as the start of a long-term customer relationship. It is the ongoing value of a newly found customer that makes prospecting by direct marketing pay off. Direct marketing is most effective when your new customer becomes a recurring customer. The tools of desktop marketing can help you with the job of finding and *keeping* customers.

All seven steps can be done using the Macintosh on your desk and the proper selection of software. With desktop marketing, you can develop and control your own campaigns from beginning to end.

3

Prepare Yourself

You have some good customers, some average customers, and some poor customers, for a customer base that looks something like Figure 3.1. If you continue with your regular marketing methods, it is likely you will continue to grow these three groups of customers in the same proportion (Figure 3.2).

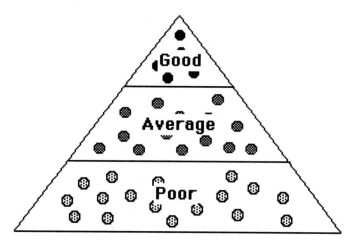

Figure 3.1: The customer base of a typical company.

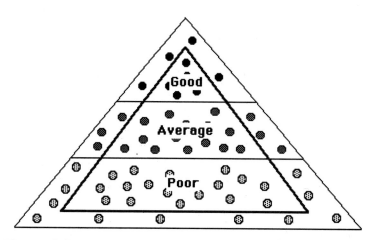

Figure 3.2: Customer base growth without desktop marketing.

The goal of desktop marketing is to create a customer base that looks more like Figure 3.3. You want to add more good customers, but just as importantly, you want fewer poor customers. With desktop marketing, you'll learn how to focus on your good customers and stop marketing to poor customers whose new order cost is greater than the profit from the order.

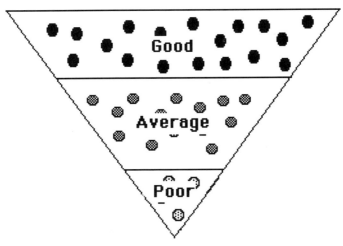

Figure 3.3: An ideal customer base is heavy with top-buying customers.

This chapter will show you the five planning steps you should take to establish the groundwork on which to build your desktop marketing programs.

Evaluate and Prepare Your Current Marketing Systems

T he first planning question you need to ask yourself is a matter of attitude and resources. You need to decide if desktop marketing is for you and, if necessary, persuade others in your organization to your way of thinking. To help you make your decision, go over your current and future sales goals in a detailed manner. Without evaluating your current status and where you want to go, it will be difficult to judge the feasibility of any desktop marketing program.

Think Through Your Sales Process

In every business, there's a series of steps that leads to a sale. If you're not sure what the series of steps is for *your* business, think back to a typical recent sale and try to visualize the point of sale. Ask yourself these questions about the scene:

- What does the target customer have in his hands: catalogs, contracts, proposals, sales collateral, demonstration disks, video, etc.?

- Who was involved: a sales rep, other company staff, other staff at the customer's company, etc.?

- Where was the sale taking place: the customer's office, the customer's home, your office or store, a fourth location?

- How did the order take place: in person, phone, mail, fax, overnight mail, etc.?

Once you answer these questions, you can begin to discover how desktop marketing can make a difference in your business. Now that you've visualized the close of sale, think back one step. What happened to create the proper environment for closing a sale? What had you or your company done to create that environment?

For example, if a proposal was in the hands of the target customer, someone must have created the proposal and delivered it to the target. If the target was holding product collateral at the time of sale, it had to have been delivered to the target customer somehow.

Keep thinking backward to visualize each step that led to the sale. For each step you remember, write down all the elements involved in that step. Once you've written all the elements, go over all of them to figure out exactly what the customer needs from you. Then, think of how these steps and customer needs can be accomplished without face-to-face contact.

Generally, the steps to purchase are more complex when selling to other businesses than when selling to consumers. This isn't surprising, considering that many business sales have to go through a complex approval process and may involve several contacts. However, it's still important that you spell out the steps involved in a typical sale.

Let's look at a scenario of a company that's trying to generate business leads:

1) Prospect visits booth at a trade show and discusses product options with company staff. Prospect leaves business card and takes product brochures.

2) Salesperson is given the prospect's name for follow-up.

3) Sales representative makes contact over the phone and questions the prospect. If the prospect sounds qualified, the rep sends additional information and makes an appointment.

4) Sales rep visits the company only to discover that the contact person is the wrong person to make the decision. The rep seeks out the right person and the contact person makes introductions.

5) The sales rep sends a follow-up letter and product information to the right person.

6) The rep calls the right person to answer questions and to set an appointment.

7) The rep makes a personal visit that includes a discussion of the product application and specifications, as well as a demonstration.

8) The rep supplies a proposal to the prospect.

9) The rep contacts the prospect for a meeting.

10) This last meeting results in a sale.

Once the marketing manager has written out all the steps of a typical sale, he or she can evaluate them for the real customer needs. After reviewing all 10 steps, it's clear a new customer needs the following before deciding to buy:

- A proposal based on specific needs

- Product collateral

- Product demonstration

- Influence to make the decision

After making this evaluation, the manager develops a direct marketing approach for the same trade show:

1) Prospect visits booth at trade show and discusses needs with company staff. He leaves his name and information on his needs and buying influence. The company staff doesn't give him any product collateral.

2) Telemarketer calls the prospect to reconfirm the product needs and specifications. The telemarketer asks for the names of the other people involved in the decision and makes a tentative appointment for all the people involved to see a product briefing and demonstration.

3) Marketing staff sends appointment confirmation letters and product information to all involved parties at the target company.

4) A sales rep makes a presentation to the team and presents a proposal based on the specifications given at the trade show and over the phone.

5) A final proposal, reflecting any changes discussed at the meeting, is delivered via overnight courier.

6) The sales rep closes on the phone, making another personal visit only if it's required.

The key difference between these two sample sequences is the role of the sales representative. In the direct marketing approach, the sales rep is used as a closing tool and not an information tool. In the direct marketing approach, the company asks for more information earlier in order to build an information base to increase the effectiveness and efficiency of the rep. This allows the sales rep to focus on the most qualified targets and use direct marketing to keep track of the potential market.

Once you understand the steps involved in creating a sale, you can decide whether direct marketing can fulfill some of your sales and marketing needs.

Make Your Goals More Concrete

It's also useful to put some numbers on your expectations. Wanting to make "lots more" sales or to get "greater" market share is vague. Use Worksheets 1–4 in Appendix A to help you calculate some numbers to make your planning easier. The four worksheets are titled:

- Value and Worth of Customers
- Salesperson Cost and Closing
- New Customer Planning
- Market Size Requirements

Once you complete these worksheets, you will have a series of standard measurements you can use for any marketing program, including: marketing cost per order, customer's acquisition cost, and sales contact cost. To fill out the worksheets, you'll need to know or estimate:

- Your total sales for the past year
- Your total number of customers
- The number of customers who order each year
- The number of sales or orders each year
- Your gross margin percentage
- The number of years a customer continues to order
- Total annual marketing expenses (including salaries)
- Number of salespeople
- Average number of sales contacts per day per sales rep
- Available sales days per year per sales rep
- Your desired sales forecast for next year
- Number of new customer programs planned for next year

Value and Worth of a Customer

These calculations tell you how much money you make, on average, on every customer. Not only does it tell you what each customer is worth annually, it also tells you the lifetime worth of the customer. Knowing the worth of each customer will make it easier for you to evaluate the costs of different marketing programs. If the cost of gaining a new customer is higher than the profit gained from the acquisition, you don't have a good marketing program.

In the example in the Appendix, James Roberts runs a window-cleaning service for office buildings. In James' case, he calculated that each new customer he gains is worth $5,128 in sales and $1,692 worth of profit each year. Because James believes customers continue to order for an average of three-and-a-half years, the lifetime worth of each new customer is $5,923.

Salesperson Cost and Closing Rates

In order to evaluate your new desktop marketing efforts, it is useful to figure out how much your current sales process is costing you. If you have never done these calculations before, you may be amazed at how high your sales costs actually are. By using the worksheet, James discovered that it is costing him $74 for every sales contact his sales representatives make. And, because the reps only close on 42 percent of their sales calls, it costs him $176 per order.

At this point, it is important to compare the cost of getting an order with the profit you gain with each order. If the costs outweigh the profit, you are in big trouble. James is comfortable, because he makes $580 on his average order, which outweighs his sales cost of $176.

Your goal with desktop marketing should be to create an alternative sales channel that costs you less or decreases your salesperson cost by generating better leads.

New Customer Planning

If you want to grow your business and your revenues, you must figure out how many customers you need to fulfill your goals. Not only do you want new customers to fuel growth but you need new customers to replace customers who stop buying. If you learn that you'll need a lot of new customers to sustain your growth goals, you should consider a broad-based desktop marketing plan to find sufficient numbers of prospects. If your needs are smaller, you can be more selective in your targeting efforts.

To reach his goal of 5 percent growth, James will need 2,080 new prospects for his sales reps, and his sales reps will need to spend 20 percent of their time contacting potential customers instead of new customers.

Market Size Requirements

Finally, you need to do a reality check on your growth plans. You should check out the overall market size you need to sustain your prospect and customer needs. It is possible that the actual size of the market is smaller than the number of prospects you calculated in New Customer Planning. You can use Lotus MarketPlace to examine the size of your different target markets to judge whether your goals are realistic. We will explain how to do this in more detail in Chapter 6.

In James' case, he calculated a market size of at least 117,067 businesses is necessary to get the qualified prospects he wants to increase his revenues. With MarketPlace, he learned the actual market size is much larger, so that he can grow with confidence.

With these four measurements of your current status and future goals, you are ready to measure the success of any desktop marketing program. Each aspect of the process (target market, direct mail, telephone selling, trade shows, sales calls) should be measured and analyzed for its contribution to the overall results. If you can decrease customer acquisition costs, your direct marketing program is coming out ahead.

Define Your Product or Service

You probably have multiple products or services you can offer your prospects. The difficult task is deciding which to sell with the desktop marketing approach. Although it may be tempting to combine everything you sell into one marketing effort, it is usually a mistake. It can be successfully done via cataloging, but in most cases, multiplying the offers only succeeds in losing the message. It is far better to choose one product or service and target it toward the people with the highest potential for purchase.

Of course, you can still offer multiple products at the same time by creating a series of desktop marketing programs, each targeted to a different market. For example, a cosmetics firm could offer antiaging creams and lotions to women over 50, neon-colored makeup to young women between the ages of 16 and 24, and expensive, neutrally-shaded cosmetics to career women of all ages. You simply divide your target market into subcategories and offer different products to each category.

When you are choosing a product for a desktop marketing program, don't select an overly complex product. Select the product that will give the most user benefits with the least explanation. If a prospect needs a more complicated version, it will be easier to explain and upgrade the prospect once the selling process has begun.

Don't select a product that is currently unsuccessful. Desktop marketing isn't a method for getting rid of overstock or unwanted merchandise. If the product doesn't sell via your regular channels, it isn't going to sell directly. You will only be setting yourself up for failure if you choose unsuccessful products.

Position Your Product

There is only one certainty in a desktop marketing program. Your prospect is asking "What's in it for me?" (WIIFM). To help the prospect determine what's in it for him or her, you should focus on the benefits, not the features, of your product.

The best method for developing product benefits is to list the features of your product or services down the left-hand side of a piece of paper. Then, write "What this means to you is…" on the top of the page and answer the question on the right-hand side of the page opposite each feature. For example, Cheryl Curran is the owner of a computer store. She would like to sell more portable computers. To help her position the portables, she wrote out the following list:

	What this means to you is….
Weighs 9 pounds	You can easily carry the computer on the road with you so that you won't lose work time.
20 megabyte hard disk	You can store your major applications in the computer, so that you don't need to carry a lot of diskettes.

	What this means to you is….
Five-hour battery	You can work even when there isn't an electrical power source, as on an airplane or in a car.
Portable	You can easily bring work home and spend more time with your family.
Built-in modem	You can communicate more easily with your office, even when you're on the road.
Gas plasma display	You will be able to easily see everything on the computer screen without straining your eyes.

With this list completed, Cheryl knows she should emphasize the ease of doing work away from the office, not weight or modems. As a bonus, Cheryl also has an initial clue to who her best targets are—travellers and people who already use computers. By making a simple list of user benefits, you too can characterize your target customers.

The key to good positioning is plucking an emotional string in the mind of the target. With a little imagination, you can find an emotional benefit for virtually any product. Look at tires. Years ago, most people thought of them as a commodity product, with no emotional context. Then, along comes a company that ties the purchase of tires to the safety of your children. Suddenly, people see tires in an entirely different context. Your emotional tie-in can be much subtler; but remember, even purchasing agents have feelings.

Prepare to Fulfill Your Desktop Marketing Programs

All businesses have a conflict between what is sold and what can be delivered—the eternal conflict between marketing and fulfillment.

Every time you deliver a piece of mail to customers or prospects, you are communicating a set of expectations in their minds. These expectations become the yardstick by which customers will measure you; don't make the mistake of overstating your case. It's crucial for you to deliver on any promises you may make.

Fulfillment ranges from answering the telephone to taking an order and sending a product. You must have your fulfillment steps in place *before* you begin your desktop program. It is better to plan for more fulfillment than you think you'll need, because you're likely to lose customers if you can't keep up with demand.

Plan your actual fulfillment process carefully. If your process is oriented to immediately selling products, as with a catalog, your fulfillment is focused entirely on quickly sending out products once an order is received. In a more complex selling process, where your prospects may be requesting more information or a sample, your fulfillment process may be more difficult.

It's important to "qualify" your respondents when you are involved in a more complex selling process. Many people may respond to your offer, but only a certain percentage will have the requirements needed to buy your product or service—either the necessary budget, purchasing authority, or equipment. You want to make sure you spend your time and effort concentrating only on those who are qualified to buy. For example, someone may respond to an offer about a videotape subscription. But if he doesn't have a VCR, he isn't "qualified" to buy—and you shouldn't spend valuable time going after him.

When someone responds to your initial contact, the next thing she hears or receives should be designed to produce a more qualified lead or an order. Sending out standard product sheets or your company brochures will not lead to an improved inquiry or sale, because the materials were not designed with desktop marketing in mind. For the most effective desktop marketing program, your fulfillment materials should reinforce your offer and the reasons for the respondent to take the next step. For example, mailings for the Prodigy on-line computer service pushes the service, but it pushes a demonstration disk even more. However, when Prodigy sends the second mailing with the demo disk, everything is focused on signing you up for Prodigy.

The worst fulfillment process you can set up is your own sales force. You shouldn't be using their expensive time to qualify respondents as potential buyers. Only about 12 percent of all sales leads are followed up by salespeople, which means you will not have fulfilled your promise to 88 percent of your respondents. You also lose control of the program, because your sales reps will rarely follow the same offer you have made. Sales reps want to make sales and will do anything they need to make those sales. Therefore, it's difficult to track your leads or to duplicate results on later efforts, because the results will depend so strongly on individual personalities.

However, don't abandon your sales force. They are extremely valuable for closing sales—just don't use them for your initial fulfillment process. Design your fulfillment contacts so that you can give your sales reps the nearly closed, "qualified" contacts. Then they can do what they do best—close sales.

Consider Financial Matters

 ou need to make sure all your accounting systems are prepared and ready to handle the responses. Plan out payment possibilities and have your staff ready to handle them. Are you accepting credit cards, purchase orders, checks, etc?

If you are new to desktop marketing and plan to allow customers to buy directly, you should discuss the implications with your accounting staff and prepare them for the upcoming orders. They should be prepared to send out invoices in a timely manner and know how to go about collecting late payments. They should also be ready on the supply side, making sure there's enough money available to buy or make all the product.

Other Financial Considerations

You should also do some early thinking about three financial variables that will be key to measuring your ultimate success at desktop marketing.

- Marketing campaign cost
- Gross margin
- Response rate

Ideally, you would like to break even on acquisition of a new customer with the gross margin equalling marketing campaign costs. If you calculate the cost of your direct marketing campaign to be $158 per sale, the money you make on each sale should be at least $158. Profit will come from the lifetime value of a customer, since it is usually less expensive to sell to an established customer than to a new one.

Marketing Campaign Cost

Before actually beginning your desktop marketing efforts, you should decide on an overall budget for your desktop marketing program. As you plan your offer and campaign, you can use the budgeting worksheets in Appendix A to help estimate the total cost of whichever marketing formats you have chosen. These will be vital to measuring whether your programs are successful, as a successful campaign should always pay for its own marketing costs.

Gross Margin

For our purposes, gross margin is the price of your product or service minus the cost of manufacturing or performing it. You can also get it directly from your profit and loss statement by dividing the cost of goods by total sales. You will have to use gross margin to calculate whether the money you earn with the acquisition of a new order covers the marketing costs of gaining that order. With gross margin in mind, you can calculate marketing break-even costs, not including the absorption of overhead costs or your primary objective, profit.

Let's say you sell your product for $49, and it costs you $20 to manufacture it.

Sales price − Cost of product/service = Gross margin

$49 − $20 = $29

You will need to spend $29 or less on your marketing costs in order to break even.

You may find you have different gross margins for different products. Generally, you can have higher margins on those products that are exclusive to your company or are more difficult for customers to buy. One goal of desktop marketing should be to increase sales of your high-margin items and reduce dependence on lower-margin goods. If you have a choice, you should focus on selling products with a 45 percent margin over those with a 15 percent margin. When you are planning a desktop marketing program, you should use the gross margin specific to the product you are selling, not the average gross margin of several products. Otherwise, your break-even calculations will not be accurate.

Response Rate

Response rate is the percentage of people who respond to an offer you make. To calculate a response rate, you divide the number of offers you make by the number of responses you receive.

No. of offers made/no. of responses   = response rate

10,000 telephone contacts made/150 responses   = 1.5 percent response rate

Response rate is the most "controversial" of the three variables. People are always saying, "What will my response rate be?" "We shouldn't get less than 5 percent response rate," "I can't live with anything less than a 2 percent response." The actual response rate you get is not important as long as you get enough responses to break even. Anything above the break-even point is gravy.

During the planning stages, there's no way for you to know the actual response rate you will get. Instead, using your estimated campaign costs and gross margin, you should calculate the response rate you'll need to break even. Treat this as a reality check. If you need a 25 percent response rate to break-even, you're not likely to be successful unless you have an unbelievably good offer.

When you calculate your needed response rate, keep in mind the number of steps in your marketing process. The percent of people who request literature doesn't tell you how many orders you'll ultimately get. Each step along the fulfillment process needs to be quantified so you can calculate the response rate you need for success.

For example, Larry Quinn is planning a desktop marketing campaign to 25,000 prospects. In the past, he has found that eight out of ten inquiries for his home burglary alarm service are qualified to buy and one in four actually buy. After estimating his desktop marketing campaign costs, he realizes he will need to generate 100 new sales to break even. To calculate the response rate he needs to make 100 sales, Larry divides the number of required sales by 25 percent (one in four buy) and divides the resulting number by 80 percent (eight in ten are qualified). The final number is the number of responses he will need.

100 needed sales/.25 (one in four buy)   = 400

400 qualified prospects/.80   = 500 responses
(eight in ten are qualified)   needed

Larry can now use the number of responses needed to calculate the response rate he needs from his mailing to break even.

500 responses needed/25,000 mailing   = 2 percent
                                                    needed response rate

Since 2 percent is not an unreasonable rate, Larry feels comfortable moving to the next step of the desktop marketing process.

All the numbers you obtain in the planning stages of a desktop marketing campaign will give you the vital controls you need to measure the success of your program. You know the value of your customer, so that you know how much you can spend to acquire a new one. The salesperson cost and closing rate gives you a level to beat with your direct marketing efforts. The number of customers you need to meet your growth objectives can help plan the scope of your direct marketing programs, and the market requirements insure your goals are feasible. Finally, a combination of your campaign cost, response rate, and gross margin will determine if you've made enough money to break even on your direct marketing program. Without these numbers, it would be difficult to evaluate whether a particular desktop marketing program makes sense or not.

4

Develop an Offer

An offer is the proposition you make to a prospect in order to generate a response. This response can be an order, a request for more information, or a visit to your store or office. If your target is a business person, you need to make an offer attractive enough to get past the mail room or past the assistant or administrator who screens out "nonessential" mail. If your targets are households, your offer has to catch their attention over all the other offers they receive in a day. You can have the greatest product or service, but unless you move someone to take the next step in your sales process, you will not achieve your goals.

Developing your offer is key to generating responses. Although offer development is the second step in your desktop marketing efforts, it is closely integrated with finding the best prospective customers (described in Chapters 5 and 6). You'll probably find yourself planning your offer based on target-market assumptions, and then returning to fine-tune your offer, once you have actually chosen your prospects.

How to Make an Offer

Your offer must be in line with your desktop marketing program goals and with your company's ability to follow up on responses. You mustn't create an offer that will totally overwhelm your fulfillment capabilities. If the objective is lead generation, make an offer that will generate only as many leads as you can effectively handle. Too many leads can be more destructive to your desktop marketing program than not enough leads, because you won't be able to follow up on all the leads, and you will have no idea which leads to focus on. Quantity is not as important as quality.

Whether the offer is for leads or actual orders, make the offer only as enticing as you can afford. It makes no sense to give away money to generate a response. There are exceptions when you might be willing to make no money on an initial order if the potential for future orders can make a customer profitable. When the Book-of-the-Month Club offers three books for $1 with no future commitment required, they're counting on making their money on later offers.

You should also consider whether your offer is *so* good that the quality of your respondents will be lowered. For example, if you offer a free phone and calculator to anyone who subscribes to your service, many respondents may only want the gifts. Because they have no intrinsic interest in your service, you may lose them as customers before you can turn a profit with them.

To create a response, your offer must contain three key elements:

- *Credibility:* Why should the prospect believe in you and your products?

- *Benefits:* What will this product do for the prospect?
- *Motivation:* Why should the prospect take advantage of your offer?

Credibility

Few people like to take a risk with a company they've never done business with before. You must reassure them that you are a respectable company and are worth their trust. There are five ways you can gain credibility with a prospect; you can use one or more of these techniques with any desktop marketing program.

1) *Years in business:* If you've been around for a while, you can use this fact to establish credibility. When you're marketing in a close geographic area, the length of time you've been in business can establish you as a "long-term" member of the community. Your prospects will assume you plan to be around for many years to come, and that in turn makes them feel you would be a trustworthy business partner.

2) *Product/service lines:* The actual products and services you're selling can add to your aura of credibility. If your products are well-known brands, people assume you have an acceptable business.

3) *Guarantees:* Guarantees reassure prospects. Guarantees spell out the rules that you will honor and how you will honor them. Giving a guarantee makes you more credible, because you're putting yourself on the line to satisfy your prospects and customers. People assume you wouldn't give a guarantee if you weren't sure very few customers would use it. Guarantees can eliminate a lot of a prospect's concerns about doing business with an unknown company. Of course, be sure you only give guarantees you *are* certain you can uphold and maintain.

4) *Testimonials/references:* Prospects may not trust your assurances about your own products, because they know you want to sell them something. This explains the power of testimonials. By using the words of a satisfied customer or allowing a prospect to speak directly with one of your customers, you let the prospect hear about your product or service from a less biased source. If you use references, be sure to list only satisfied customers and only with

their permission. Giving the names of unsatisfied customers is the quickest way to lose a prospect.

5) *Reputation:* It may sound corny, but a good reputation can give your business a tremendous amount of credibility. If you consistently conduct your business in a questionable manner, the word will get around and your potential market will begin to shrink. The smaller your market, the quicker the word will spread and the quicker your business will go downhill. On the other hand, businesses that obtain a good reputation find that word-of-mouth brings customers to them with little effort.

Benefits

No one cares about what you are selling. They only care about what your product or service can do for them. As mentioned in Chapter 2, it's easy to fall into the trap of extolling the features of your product. Instead, you have to describe what these features mean to the prospect.

Generally, your prospects don't really "need" what you're selling. They already have the basic essentials of life—food, water, and a roof over their heads. The goal of any offer is to make them want what you're selling and then convert that want into a need. Use benefit-selling to make this conversion happen.

Motivation

For any type of marketing, advertising, sales calls, etc., you have to establish the credibility of your company and the benefits of your products or services. The third part of your offer, motivation, differentiates desktop marketing from other types of marketing. Motivation is key to a successful desktop marketing campaign, because motivation makes your prospect take action. Without action, your campaign is a failure. There are several basic motivators you can use to create an effective offer:

1) *Price:* A low price can create action in buyers who have already made the decision to buy what you're selling. However, too low a

price can affect your credibility and reputation. People tend to suspect the long-term viability of discount providers. Although your prospects may be driven to action because of an unbelievable deal, they'll remain suspicious about your credibility.

You also need to be sure that the price you're offering isn't so low that you'll go bankrupt selling at that price. Most products sold by mail must be marked up three times over cost to be profitable.

2) *Time:* When you give your prospects a limited time to make a decision, they will focus on your offer more closely. Time limits can build excitement and increase response. The thought of running out of time creates an expectation that the prospect may lose out on a good deal.

3) *Hassle reduction:* Hassle reduction can be a particularly effective motivator for corporate employees. Because their primary goal is to keep their jobs and get promoted, corporate employees want as much time as possible to do the type of work that will increase their chances—and that means decreasing busywork and hassles. Hassle reduction can also be a powerful motivator in a family with two workers and dozens of responsibilities.

4) *Free trial:* Whether you allow prospects to try your complete product or service for a limited period of time or give them a sample, people are frequently motivated by the opportunity to try things out for themselves. There is also a general concern that shopping by mail or by phone is risky, because the buyer doesn't have a chance to see and try the product before paying money. Trial offers can eliminate this concern.

5) *Gifts and premiums:* Gifts have motivated people for years and have made them do things they might otherwise hesitate to do. By offering gifts, you can give prospects the extra incentive they need to take action. When deciding about a gift-related offer, most people will look at the free item to decide if it's something they want. So, if you are using a premium-supported offer, you should actually sell the premium more strongly than you sell your principal product.

Types of Offers

With the three parts of a successful offer in mind—credibility, benefits, and motivator—you're ready to develop an offer of your own. The type of offer you create can be straightforward or can use a variety of approaches and gimmicks that have proved successful to others. Be sure your offer includes your product, price, payment terms, and any motivators you are willing to include, along with any special conditions you attach to the offer.

In his book, *Profitable Direct Marketing*, Jim Kobs listed 99 direct response offers which are paraphrased here. You can base your offer on any combination of these, or create one entirely on your own.

Basic Payment Offers

1) *Right price:* The right price is the starting point for any product or service being sold by mail. Consider your market and what's being charged for competitive products; make sure when you set your price that you have sufficient margin to be profitable.

2) *Cash with order:* This is the basic payment option used with a money-back guarantee or it is used as a choice with other payment options. Incentives (such as paying the postage and handling charges) are often used to encourage the customer to send a check when ordering.

3) *Bill me later:* This is the payment option used with free trial offers. The bill is usually enclosed with the merchandise or follows a few days later, calling for a single payment. Because no front-end payment is required by the customer, your response rate can be as much as double the response rate you get with a cash offer.

4) *Installment terms:* This payment options works like the one above, except it usually involves a bigger sales price. The installment terms are usually set up to keep the payments around $10 to $20 per month. Installment terms are usually necessary to sell big

ticket items to households. Encyclopedias are often sold with installment terms, since the total outlay is usually more than families can handle at one time.

5) *Credit card privileges:* Charging purchases offers the same advantages of "bill me later" and installment plans, but you don't have to worry about collecting the money yourself.

6) *C.O.D.:* This is the Postal Service acronym for Cash-On-Delivery. The mailman collects when delivering the package. C.O.D. is rarely used because of the added cost and effort required to handle C.O.D. orders.

Free Gift Offers

7) *Free gift for an inquiry:* Provides an incentive to request more information about a product or service. It usually increases inquiries, but the inquirers tend to be less qualified.

8) *Free gift for a trial order:* Commonly called a "keeper" gift, because the consumer gets to keep the gift just for agreeing to try the product.

9) *Free gift for buying:* Similar to the above, except the customer only gets to keep the gift if he or she buys the product or service. The gift can be given free with any order or tied to a minimum purchase. During the holidays, *Sports Illustrated* usually offers some type of sports videotape if the customer subscribes to the magazine. They position the offer as a way to get two separate presents for the purchaser's favorite sports fans, just by making one purchase.

10) *Multiple free gifts with a single order:* If one gift works for you, consider offering two or more. You may be able to offer two inexpensive gifts at the same cost as one expensive item. Fingerhut Corporation is the biggest user of multiple gifts we are aware of. At last count, it was up to four free gifts for a single order. Multiple free gifts are also common with direct-response television ads in which the customer get lots and lots of attachments or pieces with each order.

Figure 4.1: Even if the recipient returns the book, he or she can keep the bonus audiocassette that comes with the order.

11) *Your choice of free gifts:* Giving a choice can be a quick way to test the relative appeal of different gift items, but a choice of gifts will seldom work as well as the best gift offered on its own. If you give a choice of gifts, the respondent must make a decision, which only adds complexity to the decision to order. A good gift will compel a person to order, whereas making a gift decision may postpone the process.

12) *Free gifts based on size of order:* Often used with catalogs or with merchandise that lends itself to quantity purchases. You offer an inexpensive gift for orders under $25; a better gift for orders running between $25 and $50; and a deluxe gift for orders over $50.

13) *Two-step gift offer:* Offer an inexpensive gift if a prospect takes the first step and a better gift if he takes the second step. For example, you may offer a free record album for trying a new stereo set and a deluxe headset if the prospect elects to buy it.

14) *Continuing incentive gifts:* Continuing incentives are used to keep customers coming back. For example, book clubs often give Bonus Points you can save to buy additional books.

Figure 4.2: Eddie Bauer will give a customer a free smoked salmon with any purchase.

15) *Mystery gift offer:* This sometimes works better than offering a specific gift. The offer is improved if you give some indication of the gift's retail value. A catalog will show a box with a $50 price tag over it. If the prospect orders, he or she will get the something worth $50. This offer works, because it is much like the surprise gifts for birthdays or holidays, and people love to be surprised.

Other Free Offers

16) *Free information:* This is one of the most inexpensive offers you can make, but it is often one of the weakest. The type of information you provide can range from a simple product sheet to a full-blown series of mailings, but you should try to have the information focused on your desktop marketing goals.

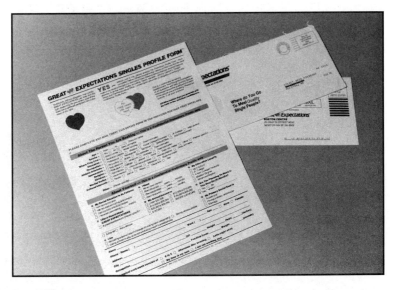

Figure 4.3: This singles club will give the prospect free information about where to find his or her perfect mate if he or she fills out a preliminary questionnaire.

17) *Free catalog:* This can be an attractive offer for both the consumer and the business market. In business, catalogs are often used as buying guides and saved for future reference. If dealing with households, you can often attach a nominal charge for postage and handling... or offer a full year's catalog subscription.

18) *Free booklet:* The booklet can help establish your company's expertise and know-how about specific problems in your industry. Booklets are most effective if they contain helpful editorial material—not just a commercial for your product or service. The booklet should have an appealing title, such as "How to Save Money on Heating Costs" or "29 Ways to Improve Your Quality Control System."

19) *Free fact kit/idea kit:* You can include a variety of enclosures in your fact kit—from booklets to trade paper articles to ad reprints—all put together in an attractive file folder.

20) *Free trial:* This offer is widely used for book and merchandise promotions. Free trial relieves a prospect's fears that you are trying to

cheat. By giving prospects the opportunity to examine your product or service, they know that they won't be stuck with an unsatisfactory purchase. Most free trial periods are 10 or 15 days, but the length of time should fit the type of product or service being offered. Time/Life Books usually offers 15 days to review the first book in one of its book series. If prospects don't like it, they can send it back.

21) *Free demonstration:* A lot of business equipment cannot be fully appreciated until it has been seen, so that offering an opportunity to view the equipment in action is an important offer. If the equipment is small enough, you can bring it to the prospect's plant or office. If not, you can arrange a private showing or group demonstration at your facilities.

22) *Free "Survey of Your Needs":* Offering a free survey by a sales representative or technical expert is appealing and gives you an opportunity to qualify a prospect. The offer can be ideal for some industrial products and services.

23) *Free cost estimate:* Many large industrial sales are only made after considerable study and cost analysis. The offer of a free estimate can be the first step in triggering such a sale.

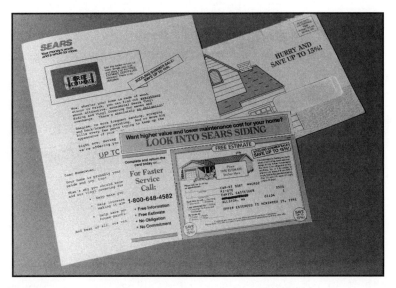

Figure 4.4: Consumers can get free estimates, too; Sears will give a free estimate on vinyl siding needs.

24) *Free dinner (breakfast or lunch):* Like the last five offers in this section, the free dinner offer is particularly suited to certain types of companies. Free dinners are widely used by real-estate and land companies who include it with a sales presentation on the property. If you've ever been on vacation in a resort area, you've probably seen the offers to get a free meal in exchange for listening to a sales pitch for a time-sharing condominium or a condo complex. This is the classic use of the Free Dinner offer.

25) *Free film offer:* Many mail-order film-processing companies have been built with some variation of this offer. Either the customer gets a new roll of film when sending in film for processing or the first roll is offered free, in hopes the customer will send it back to the same company for processing.

26) *Free house organ subscription:* Many companies create elaborate magazines or newsletters (called house organs), with helpful editorial material, to send to their customers and prospects. You can offer a free sample issue or a year's subscription.

27) *Free talent test:* Talent tests are popular with home-study schools, especially those that offer a skilled course such as writing or painting. Legal restrictions require that any such test be used to measure real talent or ability, not just as a door-opener for sales reps.

28) *Gift shipment service:* This is one of the basic offers used by virtually all mail order firms. Customers send their gift lists, and the firm ships packages directly to the recipients at no extra cost.

Discount Offers

29) *Cash discount:* This is the basic type of discount. It's often dramatized by including a discount certificate in the ad or mailing. However, a discount offer will not do as well as an attractive free gift of the same value. If someone wants a product, a free gift is seen as icing on the cake. The perceived value is usually much higher than the actual cost of the item. A cash discount does not have the same bonus value as a gift does.

30) *Short-term introductory offer:* This has become a popular type of discount to let your prospect try the product or service for a short

period at a reduced price. Examples include, "Try 10 weeks of the Wall Street Journal for only $5.97" and "30 days of accident insurance for only $.25." The goal is to convert the respondents to long-term subscribers or policyholders once they have experienced your service.

31) *Refund certificate:* Technically speaking, it's a delayed discount. You might ask somebody to send $1 for your catalog and include a $1 refund certificate good on the first order. The certificate is like an uncashed check—it can be difficult to resist the urge to use it.

32) *Introductory order discount:* A special discount used to bring in new customers. This type of offer can sometimes cause complaints from old customers, if they aren't offered the same discount.

33) *Trade discount:* This is usually extended to certain clubs, institutions, or types of businesses. Be careful of restraint of trade when you limit offers to certain groups. For example, some health clubs will offer discounts to employees of nearby companies.

34) *Early-bird discount:* The early-bird discount is designed to get customers to stock up before the normal buying season. Companies have sold a great many Christmas cards and gifts in the summer with this type of offer.

35) *Quantity discount:* This discount is tied to a certain quantity or order volume. Long-term subscriptions offered by magazines are really a quantity discount.

36) *Sliding scale discount:* In this case, the amount of the discount depends on the size of the order or the date ordered. For example, a 2 percent discount for orders up to $50, a 5 percent discount between $50 and $100, and a 10 percent discount for orders over $100.

37) *Selected discounts:* You can sprinkle selected discounts throughout a catalog to emphasize items you want to push or to give the appearance that everything is on sale. A lot of major catalogs list their special discounts in the black-and-white order-form section of the catalog. Because it does not take as much time to print these pages as the glossy, four-color pages, the firms can focus on discounting items that are currently overstocked in inventory.

Figure 4.5: Victoria's Secret varies the discount based on the amount of the purchase.

Sale Offers

38) *Seasonal sales:* Pre-Christmas sales or Summer Vacation sales are examples. If the sale is successful, you can repeat it every year at the same time.

39) *Reason-why sales:* This category includes Inventory Reduction, Clearance Sales, and similar titles. These explanatory terms help make the reason for the sale more believable to the prospect.

40) *Price increase notice:* A special type of offer that's like a limited time sale. It gives customers a chance to order at old prices before increases become effective.

41) *Auction-by-mail:* This is an unusual type of sale. It has been used to sell such items as lithographs and electronic calculators with limited quantities. Prospects send in a "sealed bid," and the companies sell the merchandise to the highest bidders.

Sample Offers

42) *Free samples:* If your product lends itself to sampling, this is a strong offer. Sometimes you can offer a sample made with or by your product—as does the steel company that uses take-apart puzzles made from its steel wire. Or, a printer who offers samples of helpful printed material produced for other customers.

43) *Nominal charge samples:* In many cases, charging a nominal fee for a sample—such as 10 cents, 25 cents, or $1.00—will get a better response than a free sample offer. The charges help establish a value for the item and screen out some of the curiosity seekers.

44) *Sample offer with tentative commitment:* This is also known as the "complimentary copy" offer used by many magazines. In requesting the sample, the prospect is also making a tentative commitment for a subscription. If the prospect doesn't like the first issue, he or she writes "cancel" on the bill and sends it back. Because legalities are involved, your lawyer should review this offer before you actually make it.

45) *Quantity sample offer:* A specialized offer that can work well for business services and newsletters. For example, a sales-training company may ask a sales manager to "tell us how many sales reps you have, and we'll send a free sample bulletin for each of them."

46) *Free sample lesson:* This has been widely used by home-study schools, which offer a sample lesson to demonstrate the scope and content of their courses.

Time Limit Offers

47) *Limited-time offers:* Any limited-time offer tends to force a quick decision and avoid procrastination. It's usually best to mention a specific date, such as, "This special offer expires November 20th," rather than "This offer expires in 10 days."

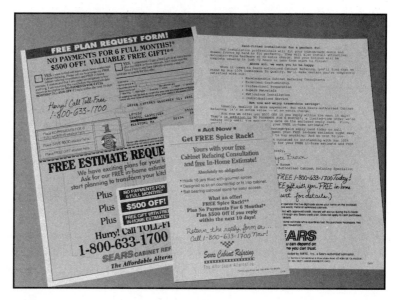

Figure 4.6: Sears will give a $500 discount to those who respond within 10 days.

48) *Enrollment periods:* Mail-order insurance companies use this type of offer widely, giving a specific cutoff date for an enrollment period. The cutoff implies that there are savings involved by processing an entire group of enrollments at one time.

49) *Prepublication offer:* This has been a long-time favorite with publishers, who offer a special discount or savings before the official publication date of a new book.

50) *Charter membership (or subscription) offer:* This offer is ideal for introducing new clubs, publications, and other subscription services. It usually includes a special price, gift, or other incentive for charter members or subscribers. It tends to appeal to those who like to be among the first to try new things.

51) *Limited-edition offer:* It is a relatively new direct response offer, but has proven to work for selling coins, art prints, and other collectable items. Franklin Mint bases its entire business on the limited-edition offer.

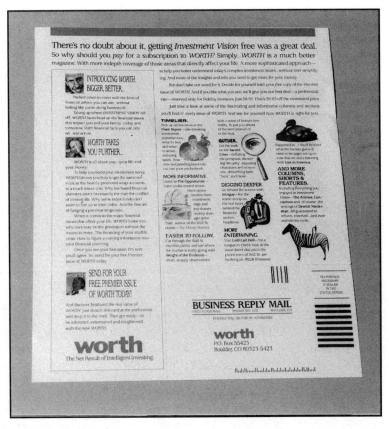

Figure 4.7: Subscribers can get in on the ground floor of *Worth* with this offer.

Guarantee Offers

52) *Money-back guarantee:* If for some reason you can't use a free trial offer, this is the next best thing. If you are offering a perishable such as food or plants, people can not return the products after use. But you can still guarantee freshness, or their money back. The main difference is that you ask the customers to pay part or all of the purchase price before you let them try your product. This offer puts the inertia of customers on your side; they are unlikely to take the time and effort to send a product back unless they are really unhappy with it.

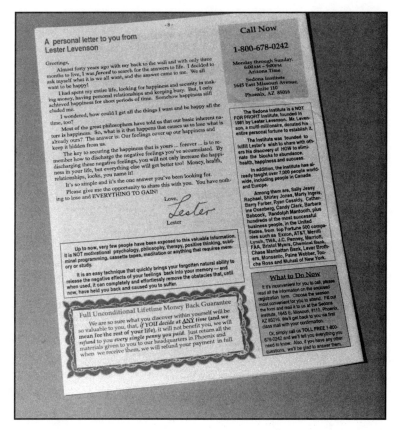

Figure 4.8: A prospect should be more willing to invest in this seminar, because it will give anyone his/her money back if not satisfied.

53) *Extended guarantee:* It includes letting a customer return a book up to a year later or offering to refund the unexpired portion of a subscription at any time before it runs out.

54) *Double-your-money-back guarantee:* This really dramatizes your confidence in your product—but you had better be sure the product lives up to your claims if you make an offer like this. This type of offer is rarely made these days, because it is perceived as unbelievable. As a result, most direct marketers have toned it down.

55) *Guaranteed buy-back agreement:* Although it's similar to the extended guarantee, this specialized version is often used with limited-edition offers on coins and art objects. To convince the prospect

of the value, the advertiser offers to buy back the objects at full price during a specified period that may last as long as five years.

56) *Guaranteed acceptance offer:* This specialized offer is used by insurance firms with certain types of policies that require no health questions or underwriting. It's especially appealing to those who might not otherwise qualify. You hear direct response advertising on television offering medical insurance with no medical history required and for which no one can be turned down.

Build-Up-the-Sale Offer

57) *Multiproduct offers:* You feature two or more products or services in one ad or mailing. The best-known type of multiproduct offer is a catalog, which can feature a hundred or more items.

58) *Piggyback offers:* It's similar to a multiproduct offer, except that one product is strongly featured. The other items ride along, or "piggyback," in hope of picking up additional sales.

59) *The deluxe offer:* Offer your standard item with an option to purchase a more deluxe version for an additional fee. For example, a publisher might offer a book in its standard binding for $9.95. The order form gives the customer the option of ordering a deluxe edition for only $2.00 more. It's not unusual for 10 percent or more of those ordering to select the deluxe alternative.

60) *Good–Better–Best offer:* This offer goes a step further by offering three choices. The mail-order mints, for example, sometimes offer their medals in a choice of bronze, sterling silver, or 24K gold.

61) *Add-on offer:* A low-cost item that's related to the featured product can be great for generating impulse orders. You could offer a wallet for $7.95, with a matching key case for only $1.00 extra.

62) *Write-your-own-ticket offer:* Some magazines have used this with good success to build up a sale. Instead of offering 17 weeks for $4.93—which is 29 cents per issue—the magazines give the subscriber the 29 cents-an-issue price and let the subscriber fill in the number of weeks the subscription should run.

63) *Bounce-back offer:* This approach tries to build onto the original sale by enclosing an additional offer with the product shipment or invoice.

64) *Increase an extension offer:* These are also follow-ups to the original sale. Mail-order insurance firms often give policy holders a chance to get increased coverage with a higher-priced version of the same policy. Magazines often use an advance renewal offer to get subscribers to extend their current subscriptions.

Sweepstakes Offers

Note: Sweepstakes and chance promotions to consumers are heavily regulated by the FTC. In particular, you must be certain that purchasers and nonpurchasers have an equal opportunity to win the prize. Always be sure your offer is within legal guidelines and definitely have your lawyer review your offer. Sweepstakes to businesses are not regulated in the same fashion, but it still would be wise to have your lawyer review them.

65) *Drawing-type sweepstakes:* The majority of sweepstakes contests are set up this way. The prospect gets one or more chances to win, but all winners are selected by a random drawing.

66) *Lucky number sweepstakes:* With this type of contest, winning numbers are preselected before making the mailing or running the ad. Copy strategy emphasizes, "You may have already won." A drawing is held for the unclaimed prizes. Clearinghouse Sweepstakes is probably the best-known version of this offer.

67) *"Everybody Wins" sweepstakes:* It is no longer widely used, but the "Everybody Wins" sweepstakes was a real bonanza when it was first introduced. It is set up so that everyone who doesn't win a big prize is still awarded an inexpensive or nominal prize.

68) *Involvement sweepstakes:* This type of sweepstakes requires the prospect to open a mystery envelope, play a game, or match a number against an eligible number list. In doing so, the prospect determines the value of the grand prize won if his or her entry is drawn as the winner. Some of these involvement devices have been highly effective in boosting results.

Figure 4.9: You probably get sweepstakes offerings like this in the mail all the time.

69) *Talent contests:* These are not really sweepstakes, but can be effective for some types of direct marketing situations, such as mail-order puzzle clubs or home-study art schools.

Club and Continuity Offers

70) *Positive option:* The customer joins a club and is notified monthly of new selections. To order, the customer must take some positive action, such as sending back an order card.

71) *Negative option:* The customer is still notified in advance of new selections, but the new selection is shipped *unless* the customer returns a rejection card by a specific date. Many book and record clubs operate on a negative-option basis. Customers will be sent the book or record of the month, unless they send back a form saying they don't want it.

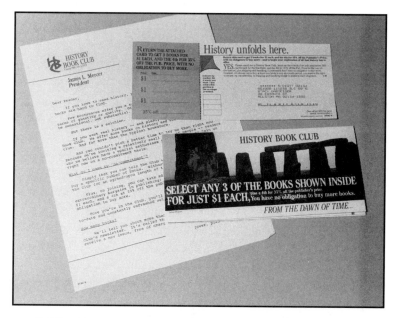

Figure 4.10: The History Book Club takes the chance that the prospect will get hooked on its products and continue to order.

72) *Automatic shipments:* This variation eliminates the advance notice of new selections. When the customer signs up, the customer gives the publisher permission to ship each selection automatically until the customer says to stop. It's commonly called a "Till Forbid" offer. The Time/Life Books series operates on an automatic shipment basis, with the customers getting the next book in the series every four to six weeks until they cancel their order.

73) *Continuity load-up offer:* It is usually used for continuity book series, such as a 20-volume encyclopedia. The first book is offered free. After the customer receives and pays for the next couple of monthly volumes, the balance of the series is sent in one load-up shipment. However, the customer continues to pay at the rate of one volume per month.

74) *Front-end load-ups:* This is where a record club gives a prospect four records for $1.00, if the prospect agrees to buy at least four more selections during the next year. The attractive front-end offer gets the prospect to make a minimum purchase commitment, usually to buy the remaining purchases within a fixed time period.

75) *Open-ended commitment:* It's like the front-end load-up, except there is no time limit for purchasing the additional selections.

76) *"No Strings Attached" commitment:* In this case, the offer is more generous because the customer is not committed to any future purchases. You gamble that you will make the future selections enticing enough to encourage the customer to make a certain number of purchases.

77) *Lifetime membership fee:* You offer the prospect a one-time fee to join—usually $5 or $10—and they will receive a monthly announcement of new selections. There is no minimum commitment and all ordering is done on a positive option basis.

78) *Annual membership fee:* Here, you offer the prospect an annual fee for club membership. It's often used for travel clubs where you get a whole range of benefits, including travel insurance. It is also used for fund-raising, where a choice of membership levels based on donation amounts is often effective.

79) *The philanthropic privilege:* This is the basis of all fund-raising offers. The donor's contribution usually brings nothing tangible in return but helps make the world a better place in which to live. Sometimes the offer is enhanced by giving a membership card, gummed stamps, or other tokens of appreciation.

80) *Blank-check offer:* It was first used in the McGovern fund-raising campaign. Supporters filled out blank, postdated checks that were cashed once-a-month to provide installment contributions. It was later adapted for extending credit to bank charge-card customers.

81) *Executive preview charge:* This offer can be successful for such things as sales training films. An executive agrees to pay $25 to preview the film, and if she or he decides to buy or rent it, the preview price is credited against the full price.

82) *Yes/No offers:* This offer asks a prospect to let you know the decision either way. In most cases, the negative responses have little or no value. But, by forcing a decision, you often end up with more "yes" responses. Several computer magazines have begun using the "Yes/No" offer in an attempt to increase subscriptions.

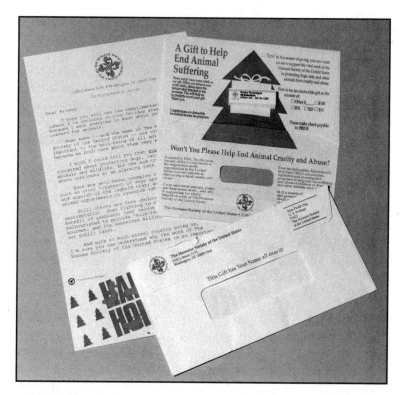

Figure 4.11: The Humane Society adds to the philanthropic privilege by giving return address labels with the prospect's name on it.

83) *Self-qualification offer:* It uses a choice of options to get the prospect to indicate the degree of interest in your product or service. For example, you can offer either a free booklet or a free demonstration. Those who request the demonstration qualify themselves as serious prospects and should get more immediate attention.

84) *Send me a sales rep:* If this is the only choice, responses will be decreased dramatically. However, the few who will check, "Have your representative phone me for an appointment" are normally more highly qualified inquirers than either those who request a free booklet or free demonstration. Those who respond are probably ready to order or seriously considering it.

85) *Exclusive rights for your trading area:* This offer can be ideal for selling certain business services to firms who are in a competitive business. Let's say you sell a syndicated banking newsletter to

banks and the banks then send the newsletter to their customers. When you market into one territory, you give the first bank that responds an exclusive for the trading area. Generally, you will find you seldom have to turn anybody down.

86) *The dramatic offer:* It's an offer like, "Smoke my new kind of pipe for 30 days. If you don't like it, smash it up with a hammer and send me back the pieces."

87) *Trade-in offer:* This offer allows prospects to easily get rid of what they're using now and replace it with your product. An offer such as, "We'll give you $10 for your old slide rule when you buy a new electronic calculator," can be very effective.

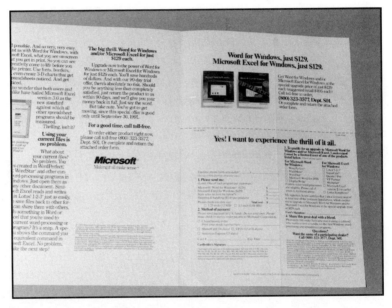

Figure 4.12: Microsoft will sell its products for less money if the prospect owns any products it lists as competitive.

88) *Third-party referral offer:* Instead of renting somebody's list, you get the list owner to make the mailing for you. Although you pay for the mailing, they use their own letterhead and recommend your product or service. It usually works better than your own promotion because of the rapport the company has with its own customers.

89) *Member-get-a-member offer:* This is often used to get customers to send in the names of friends who might be interested. It's widely used by book and record clubs, who give their members a free gift if the person they recommend signs up.

90) *Name-getter offers:* These offers are usually designed to build your own prospect list. You can offer a low-cost premium at an attractive self-liquidating price, just to get names for your list.

91) *Purchase-with-purchase:* You offer an attractive gift set at a special price whenever a customer makes a regular purchase. Cosmetic firms and departments stores use this type of offer frequently. For example, buy $25 worth of cosmetics and get a travel cosmetics bag for $8.88.

92) *Delayed billing offer:* The appeal is "Order now and we won't bill you until next month." It is especially effective before the holidays, when people have lots of other expenses.

93) *Reduced down payment:* It is frequently used as a follow-up in an extended mailing series. If the customer does not respond to the regular offer in the first mailings, you reduce the down payment to make it easier to buy.

94) *Stripped-down products:* This is also used in an extended mailing series. A home-study school, for example, that doesn't get the prospect to order the full course will come back with a starter course at a lower price.

95) *Secret bonus gift:* The bonus gift is usually used with TV support. The commercial offers an extra bonus gift not mentioned in the ad or mailing being supported. For example, you might offer a bonus record if the prospect writes the album number in the "secret gold box" on the order form.

96) *Rush shipping service:* The capability to use rush shipping services is appealing for customers ordering things such as seasonal gifts and film processing. Sometimes you ask the customer to pay an extra charge for this rush service.

97) *The competitive offer:* It can be a strong way to dramatize your selling story, like Diner's Club offering to pay prospects $5.00 to turn in their American Express cards.

98) *The nominal reimbursement offer:* You offer a token payment to get somebody to fulfill your request. Many research mailings use a crisp one-dollar bill to encourage respondents to fill out and return a questionnaire.

99) *Establish-the-value offer:* If you have an attractive free gift, you can build up its value and establish credibility by offering an extra one for a friend at the regular price.

Excerpted and paraphrased from *Profitable Direct Marketing*, by Jim Kobs, published by Crain Books, 740 Rush Street, Chicago, IL 60611

Here's the 100th item on this list:

100) *The perpetual offer:* The perpetual offer enables the customer to build up points toward gifts or awards every time the customer makes use of your products or services. You send regular reminders to your customers of their current "use" status, showing how much more they'll have to buy to be eligible to receive an award. In business, the offer usually provides personal benefit to a buyer when spending company money. One example of the perpetual offer is the airlines' frequent-flyer programs. Similar programs have been implemented by car-rental, hotel, and even catalog companies. The perpetual offer can work for consumers as well, even though consumers are spending their own money. This is the basic concept behind S&H, Goldbond, and other stamp companies that were so successful in the last few decades. Nowadays, many companies are encouraging frequent use of their credit cards by offering perpetual offers and many retail operations are exploring frequent-buyer options.

The primary drawback to this type of program comes when you want to curtail or eliminate it. Although you may have the legal right to do so, it can cause a great deal of hard feeling among your best customers. The plus of this type of program is the database of loyal and happy customers it creates.

These frequent users will be less expensive to promote to in the future, because you already know a lot about them. You can focus marketing efforts on an interest they have already established. For example, you can pick out all your frequent flyers who travel to Europe and offer them a special low fare to Germany. This will get a much better response than mailing to some other mailing list. It may cost you money to offer the bonus awards, but the payoff will be more purchases by your frequent users. The cost of bonuses is generally less than the cost of marketing to nonfrequent users in hopes of getting them to buy more. The success and continued growth of these types of programs are proof-positive of how effective marketing to this type of customer has become.

How to Improve an Offer

To give you some practice evaluating offers, we have listed seven problematic offers below with suggestions on how to make them better.

Problem offer: Have a sales representative contact me. This is the worst offer made today. How many people want a salesperson calling them? From our experience, salespeople will only contact about 12 percent of the names you give them. Fortunately, most people who indicate that they want a salesperson to call are often satisfied with the materials you send them in advance of the salesperson setting up an appointment.

Better offer: Please evaluate my current situation. This offer will lead you to the same results as having a sales rep call. The key difference is that prospects answer key questions about their qualifications and needs first, either via a response mailer or via a phone call to you. Now, your sales reps can focus only on the qualified prospects—and make contact with all the information they will need to make the sale.

Problem offer: Send more information: More information only gives prospects more data to make their own decisions without you being able to "sell" them on the reasons to buy. When you send information and expect it to make a sale, you are betting on prospects reading and understanding the information. It is possible they may overlook the benefits that would convince them to buy, because you don't know what information will help the process. This offer can clog your selling program with lists of literature collectors without moving you closer to sales.

Better offer: *Show me how your product can work for me; my needs are...* You still send information with this offer. But the prospect first fills out a questionnaire, so that you can send more targeted information. The more dialogue you create between yourself and your prospect, the higher the probability of making a sale.

Problem offer: *Renew now and save 40 percent on the cover price.* At first glance, this looks like a very good offer for your current subscribers. The problem arises when you're offering new subscribers *50 percent off* plus a free gift at the same time. If the difference between offers is too great, subscribers will take advantage of new subscriber offers. In addition, you may get a lot of first time subscribers who have only signed up for the great gift with no plan to renew after the first year. This increases the costs of sustaining your subscription base, because you will have to go after new subscribers to fill their space. Finding new subscribers always costs more and is more difficult than renewing current subscribers, who already read and like your magazine.

Better offer: *As a valued subscriber, we would like you to have this free portable telephone for renewing your subscription for five years.* Use the same free gift you are using for new subscribers to convert one-year subscribers to multiple-year subscribers. This reduces your renewal costs for five years and makes your current subscribers less likely to use new-subscriber offers.

Problem offer: *Respond today and receive a real leather-like vinyl wallet.* The problem here is the gift. Remember what we said about free gifts; if you are using a premium-supported offer, you should actually sell the premium more strongly than you sell the principal product. You need to position the gift as positively as you can without being dishonest. In this case, "leather-like" is certainly suspect in the minds of most consumers and their skepticism is only borne out with the word "vinyl." The premium won't be a big puller.

Better offer: *Respond today and receive a personal money-storage unit with special store-everything compartments.* This is the same vinyl wallet, but it sounds a little more glamorous. While dressing up the wording on an offer may get you a better response, be careful you don't dress it up too much. You don't want the respondent's expectations to be so high that he or she is bitterly disappointed when the free gift arrives.

Problem offer: *Buy before month-end and we will donate a portion of the proceeds to charity.* This approach is a good start, but it is too vague. Be specific so people can understand exactly what you are going to do if they take the action you are asking for.

Better offer: *Buy before month-end and we will send three needy kids to summer camp.* By making a specific statement about what you will do, you don't have to count on the target to interpret what you mean—perhaps incorrectly. Tell them what to do and what will happen as a result of their actions.

5

Define Your Prospective Customers

Before you can begin creating any desktop marketing programs, you need to define who your target customers are and get lists of those targets. This step is extremely crucial to the success of any program. It doesn't matter how good your product or service is—if you don't send your offer to appropriate targets, there's no hope that they will accept it.

This chapter will help you think about how to define your best prospects, whether your prospects are businesses or consumers. After reading this chapter, you should be able to come up with a list of criteria you can use to make up a list of prospects. In many cases, you can use some of the new technology and your Macintosh to select the best list for your needs. If you can't satisfy your list needs with the electronic possibilities, Chapter 6 explains how to maneuver the list-rental business to get a list as close to your definition as possible.

Defining Your Customer

To develop a definition of your potential customer, begin by describing your best customers. People who match the description of your top customers are also likely to have a need for your product or service and will hopefully buy as much as your biggest customers do now.

To come up with a description, ask yourself questions about your customers. For example, if you sell to other businesses, ask yourself questions like:

- What type of businesses are my customers in?
- How many people do they employ?
- Where are the companies located?
- Who in the company usually makes the purchase?
- What type of equipment does the company use?
- What are their annual revenues?
- What associations do they belong to?

If your customers are individual consumers, you can ask yourself another series of questions:

- Where do they live?
- Are they male or female?
- How old are they?

- How much do they earn?

- What hobbies do they have?

- What type of lifestyle do they have?

- Do they have children?

- Do they own their homes?

If you're starting a new business or line of work, you may have to use your imagination to picture your best customer. Be as concrete as possible spelling out what you know about the customer. Although you may not be able to use all the information when you go to look for customers, the more you know the easier it will be for you to find sources for names.

Once you've defined your best prospects, you need to start looking for lists of prospects. You'll use these lists as the basis of your direct mail or telemarketing campaigns. Until recently, everyone was forced to use their own customer lists or rent lists from outside services. With the arrival of new technology, you can do prospect definition and list creation right on your desktop. One of the most powerful new lead-generation tools is MarketPlace Business by MarketPlace Information Corporation.

In order to get the most out of MarketPlace, you should have a good understanding of exactly how it works and what it includes. Even if you don't plan to use MarketPlace Business, you may find it useful to read the following explanation, as it explains in detail the process of selecting a targeted list.

MarketPlace Business

MarketPlace consists of names, addresses, and marketing information on over 7 million businesses across the United States and the software you need to target your market, choose your best prospects, and actually create prospecting or mailing lists. The product works on a Macintosh with a hard disk and 4 MB of RAM. MarketPlace Information Corporation recommends using a Mac/SE or a more powerful system with 8 MB of RAM to get quicker response, but any Macintosh will work. Because the MarketPlace products are delivered via CD-ROM, you will also need a 100 percent Apple-compatible CD drive.

CD-ROMs are like audio CDs, except they deliver huge amounts of information in a compact manner. In fact, the amount of information on one CD-ROM is equivalent to approximately 200,000 typewritten pages. When you place the MarketPlace CD-ROM in your CD drive, you can use it just as you use any software on a hard disk.

There are three basic steps to using MarketPlace:

1) Define list.

2) Examine list.

3) Use list.

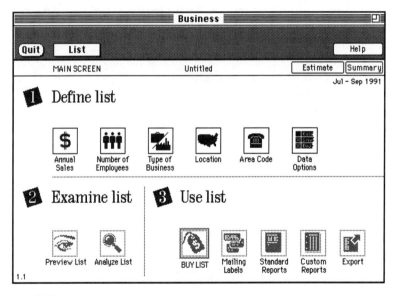

Figure 5.1: The numbered steps on the main screen of MarketPlace help you determine the order you should follow.

1) *Define list:* The definition section of MarketPlace consists of a collection of selection criteria you use to describe exactly the type of records you want in your list. When defining a list, you can use one or more of the possible selection options (Location, Type of Business, etc.) and choose the parameters you want. At any point in your list definition, you can click the Estimate button to get an

estimate of how big your list would be with the current list definition. You can also click the Summary button to get a quick summary of all the selection criteria.

2) *Examine list:* The two options under Examine List are Preview the
list or Analyze the list. Selection of either of these options actually
pulls together the list you've defined. When you build the list,
MarketPlace refers to your list definition and goes to the CD to
locate all the records that match the definition. Depending on
your computer, the amount of RAM, the specifics of your list definition, and the size of your list, building a list can take a fair
amount of time. If you choose Preview, you can scan all the
records in the list. If you choose Analyze, you will get analysis
reports. (Analysis is described in detail in Chapter 7.)

To Improve List Building Performance

If you have 8 MB of RAM, set your RAM cache to 3072 K. If you
have 5 MB, set the cache to 1024 K. If you have 4 MB, set the
cache to 256 K.

If you're not ready to use the list at this point, you can save it. If
you want to compare several lists before using them, you can save
them all under different names. MarketPlace won't save all the
names and addresses onto your hard disk, but it will put pointers
as to where to find each record on the CD. When you open the
file again, MarketPlace will be able to quickly pull up the same
information.

TIP

Pointers are electronic addresses to a specific part of a disk or file.

---

3. *Use list:* You can analyze and preview all the records on the CD-
ROM as much as you want. When you actually want to use a list
(printing it out or transferring it to your hard disk), the records
are passed through a software meter. This meter operates very
much like a postage meter—you pay to fill it up and empty it
with use. When you buy MarketPlace, the meter initially has

3,000 units. You can refill the meter at any point by buying meter refills from MarketPlace Information Corp.

TIP

You refill the software meter by entering a special code.

To pass the list through the meter, you click an icon labeled Buy List. You have the option of buying just the name and address for one meter unit, the name and phone number for two meter units, or the name with additional descriptive information for one meter unit. If you want *all* the information for a record, it will cost you four meter units. Once a list is "bought," you can use it as many times as you want in as many ways as you want. MarketPlace allows you to print out the records as mailing labels, standard reports, or custom reports. You can also save the complete list to your hard disk if you want to use the information with another software package.

Information in MarketPlace Business

MarketPlace Business consists of the names, addresses, telephone numbers, and marketing information for over 7 million business establishments across the United States. The data comes from Dun's Marketing Services, a company of The Dun & Bradstreet Corporation, the industry leader of business-to-business marketing information. Dun's Marketing Services gathers information from extensive phone interviews, mail verification, and other sources.

All the business information is delivered on one CD-ROM, which can be updated quarterly for an additional annual subscription fee. Each establishment record in the database consists of the following information:

Business name

Address

Phone number

County

Metro area

Annual sales

Number of employees

4-digit SIC code (Standard Industrial Classification: The government's system of business classification which classifies every business within a three-level hierarchy based on their primary service or business.)

Rank within SIC

Executive name

Executive title

D-U-N-S number

What's an Establishment?

MarketPlace treats every branch office or subsidiary of a company as a separate establishment. Because most separate locations do act independently for many purchase decisions, it makes sense to treat them as separate entities. Often, a branch office will buy supplies and equipment locally, paying little attention to what the head office does.

For the purpose of specifying a specific collection of businesses, you can select names with five different criteria:

Annual sales

Number of employees

Type of business

Location

Area Code

To help you understand why you might choose any one of these criteria, let's take a look at each selection criterion individually.

Annual Sales

This selection criterion is fairly easy to understand. The managerial control and analysis of American business is measured in dollars as a common denominator. We usually equate annual sales with success; the higher the sales, the more successful the company. These sales figures are tied to gross sales, not the profits the companies make on these sales.

You should think carefully before deciding what range of sales you want your prospects to have. Annual Sales in MarketPlace is divided into 11 ranges, from below $200,000 to over 1 billion. The information is displayed as a horizontal bar graph, and you select a sales range by clicking on the appropriate bar (Figure 5.2). The selection graph shows roughly how many establishments fall into each sales category, so that you can get a quick overview of the potential size of each sales range.

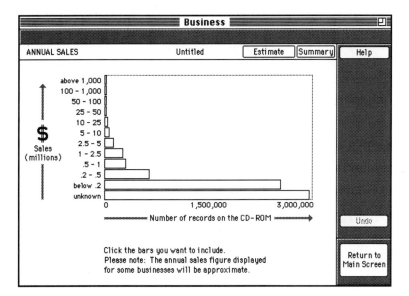

Figure 5.2: Because most companies are privately owned, Dun's can't always specify annual sales accurately.

TIP

To select a range of bars, hold down the shift key, click the bottom bar of the range, and then the top bar.

You'll find the sales ranges are not 100 percent accurate. The information is often estimated because private companies will not release their sales figures. The estimations are based partly on company knowledge and on industry facts and figures. Although it is unlikely that you will find a company whose sales estimates are wildly inaccurate, it isn't unusual to find the estimations for a company to be somewhat off.

When planning who your targets are, it's easy to say you will only go after the companies with the biggest sales, but this can be a mistake. Nearly everyone wants to go after the big fish, so you will have a lot more competition. Unless you're a big operation, you may have a harder time convincing a large corporation to take you on as a supplier. You're more likely to run across corporate purchasing guidelines that don't take into account local businesses. It may also be much more difficult to figure out just who you need to talk to.

Jean Hanley offers a bookkeeping service. Initially, she did mailings and telemarketing to the largest companies in her city, in hopes of landing a big fish. When her results were dismal, she thought out her strategy again. She realized once businesses make over half a million dollars a year, they have their own accounting and financial staffs. By changing her list criteria to revenues under $500,000 a year, she began to get an excellent response rate.

On the other hand, if you do succeed in landing a big account, it can often boost your business up another notch toward success. Because purchasing in big companies is ruled by inertia, once you're in, you're probably in for awhile. Although you shouldn't focus all of your attention on the biggest corporations, it makes sense to make a concerted effort with a few promising accounts.

When choosing sales ranges, it can also be a mistake to cross off all of the smallest companies. First of all, if you look at the sales breakdown graph, you'll see that the vast majority of companies make less than $500,000 a year. Companies that are just starting out often have need of a wide range of products and services. Small companies also look for timesaving purchases, because time is usually their most valuable commodity. It makes sense to get in on the ground floor of a growing concern, in hopes it remains loyal to you as it grows.

"Good" annual sales can vary tremendously from one type of industry to another. What are great annual sales for a publishing company could be very low for a manufacturing company. To get a sense of the financial structure of different industries, you should go to the library and look it up in a publication called the RMA (Robert Morris Associates). This book lists the financial structure of various industries, dividing each industry into small, medium, and large companies, depending on their sales volume. For example, $1.5 million sales for a publishing company may make it a large company, but for a manufacturing company, that would mean a medium-sized company.

Keep in mind the difference between Annual Sales and Number of Employees. Just because a company has high sales does not mean that it has a large number of employees, and vice versa. If your products or service depends on the presence of many employees to be successful, you shouldn't use the Annual Sales criterion to define company size. For example, a company selling time clocks should make sure that there are many employees before making any effort to sell to a company.

Number of Employees

If you sell products related to the number of employees in a company, you should use this criterion to define your list. Health insurance, pension planning, office equipment, and memberships are all examples of products and services tied more to the number of employees than to annual sales, because the amount you sell is inextricably linked to the number of employees.

The Number of Employee selection criterion is also organized in ranges, from one employee to over 10,000 employees (Figure 5.3). Since over 95 percent of the businesses in the United States have fewer than 100 employees, it is not surprising to find a huge quantity of companies in the range from 1 to 24 employees. You select any range by clicking on the appropriate bar.

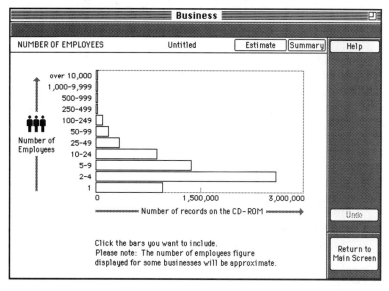

Figure 5.3: Use the criterion of the Number of Employees as another method to define your prospects by size.

If you use the Number of Employees selection criterion, you may be able to create an offer based on assumptions about how the basic structure of a company changes with size. Companies with fewer than 25 employees tend to have an owner who is responsible for all major purchasing decisions. Although other staff members may have a role, it's the president who has the final vote. Therefore, it's reasonable to market directly to the head executive, because the head executive will ultimately decide on purchasing matters.

Above 25 employees, you begin to find layers of management. Because MarketPlace only supplies you with the name of a head executive at any establishment, you may have to do more work to find your appropriate prospect. To find who you should target within the company, you can call to find who purchases your type of product. If telephoning is too expensive, you can plan on using a more generic address format, such as "Head Purchasing Agent," "Marketing Director," "Office Supply Buyer." In establishments above 100 employees, generic labeling may be wasted, because no one in the mail room is likely to make an effort to help you out. With the largest companies, you should take the time and effort to find out who you need to contact; hopefully, any sales you make will more than make up for this additional time and money spent. If you export your list to a database management package, you can enter the other names as you learn them.

Let's look at an example. David Gaston sells fax machines. When he first began doing mailings, he chose his lists only on the basis of type of business. But he soon discovered he got very good responses from the small companies but virtually none from the bigger companies. His mail into big companies was addressed to the head person, not the person who made the fax-purchasing decisions. He began creating two different lists. The first list still consisted of specific business types, but he added the specification that they have fewer than 25 employees. For that list, David used the executive name that came with a MarketPlace list. The second list consisted of the same type of businesses, but they all had more than 25 employees. For this list, he used the title, "Purchasing Agent." Suddenly, he began to get some response from big companies.

You may find that branch offices of large companies are excellent targets, because they are often a mix between small businesses and large offices. Branch offices are generally small, so that there aren't many levels to go through or many rules and regulations. But, as distant relations of a large parent corporation, they often have greater financial resources than single location businesses of the same size. Branches are often more willing to invest in advanced technologies and to try new deals, because their parent companies are already advanced technologically.

Type of Business

Type of Business in MarketPlace is classified according to the Standard Industrial Classification (SIC) system. The basic structure of the hierarchy can be seen in Figure 5.4.

The 11 primary classifications are labeled by one of the letters, A–K. In Figure 5.4, you can see *Division G—Retail Trade* in more detail. In this case, there are eight subcategories in Retail Trade. Each subcategory is labeled with a two-digit number known as the two-digit SIC code. If you go further into category *56) Apparel and Accessory Stores*, you get seven further subcategories, each labeled with a four-digit SIC code.

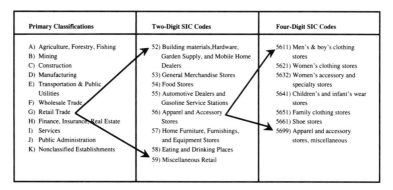

Primary Classifications	Two-Digit SIC Codes	Four-Digit SIC Codes

A) Agriculture, Forestry, Fishing
B) Mining
C) Construction
D) Manufacturing
E) Transportation & Public
    Utilities
F) Wholesale Trade
G) Retail Trade
H) Finance, Insurance, Real Estate
I) Services
J) Public Administration
K) Nonclassified Establishments
	52) Building materials,Hardware,
	    Garden Supply, and Mobile Home
	    Dealers
	53) General Merchandise Stores
	54) Food Stores
	55) Automotive Dealers and
	    Gasoline Service Stations
	56) Apparel and Accessory
	    Stores
	57) Home Furniture, Furnishings,
	    and Equipment Stores
	58) Eating and Drinking Places
	59) Miscellaneous Retail
		5611) Men's & boy's clothing
		    stores
		5621) Women's clothing stores
		5632) Women's accessory and
		    specialty stores
		5641) Children's and infant's wear
		    stores
		5651) Family clothing stores
		5661) Shoe stores
		5699) Apparel and accessory
		    stores, miscellaneous

Figure 5.4: Women's clothing stores (5621) are a subset of Apparel and Accessory Stores (56), which in turn are a subset of Retail Trade (G).

To use the Type of Business selection criterion in MarketPlace, highlight a category and click Open to view its subcategories. Whenever you highlight a category, MarketPlace gives a detailed definition of the category in the right-hand window (Figure 5.5). Sometimes, this may be the only way to figure out what is included in a category, because the government classification schemes can be a little difficult to understand. If you want to include a specific category in your list definition, click Include and a black box will appear next to the item, indicating that it has been selected.

TIP

Double-clicking a category name will also open it to the next level.

If you're unsure where in the SIC hierarchy to find the type of business you want, use the Find feature (Figure 5.6). The Find feature is extremely useful because the categorization scheme the government came up with is often difficult to fathom. Fuel oil dealers are under Miscellaneous Retail; computer software stores are under Home Furniture, Furnishing, and Equipment Stores; heavy construction equipment rental is under Business Services. To use the Find feature, click Find on the Type of Business screen.

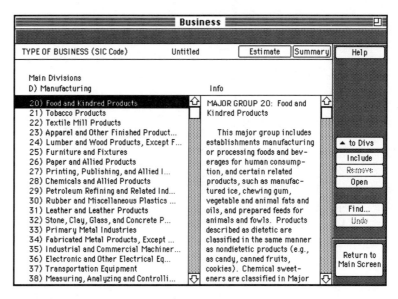

Figure 5.5: You can learn more about the contents of the Food and Kindred Products category by reading the right-hand window.

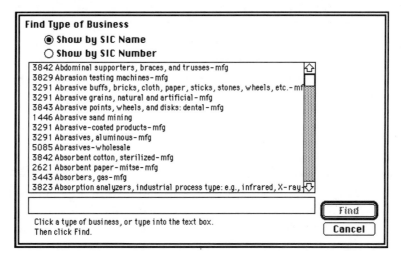

Figure 5.6: When you have no idea what SIC code holds a particular type of business, use the Find feature.

The Find box contains a list of hundreds of business types listed either alphabetically or by four-digit SIC code. Enter the type of business you're looking for and the list moves to match what you type. If you don't find what you want with the first attempt, try alternative words just as you do when using the Yellow Pages. For example, both the Yellow Pages and MarketPlace's Find feature list almost everything to do with cars under *Automobile*, not *Car*.

Unfortunately, SIC codes won't satisfy every classification need you have. Sometimes the government has grouped several apparently different types of businesses into one category. If you're interested in just one of the disparate groups, you'll be frustrated by your attempts. For example, Flying Instruction falls under *8299) Schools & educational services, not elsewhere classified,* which also includes music schools, dance schools, standardized exam preparations, and more.

SIC Code Enhancements

Dun & Bradstreet has developed its own enhancement to the SIC code. They've added an additional four digits to allow them to further classify disparate businesses. Within MarketPlace, you cannot select a business according to this eight-digit SIC code, but you can get the information about a specific business when you buy the list. If you absolutely must classify your list by a certain eight-digit SIC code, you should rent your list directly from Dun's Marketing Service.

In addition, because SIC codes classify companies by their primary business, companies that sell multiple products can only be listed in one category, which means you may miss some potential targets. However, Dun's attempts to categorize the different branches of a large company according to the specialties of that branch. For example, different branches of Procter & Gamble are categorized under Soaps & detergents, Sanitary paper products, Drugs & toiletries wholesale, and more. Finally, although the SIC hierarchy is government-based, the actual categorization of a business is done by the staff of Dun's. They can make mistakes in putting companies into a category.

You may find when you examine your current customer list that you have a broad business base, with no particular focus. Even if that's the case, it can make sense to divide your list into different business segments. You can then focus your desktop marketing programs to the needs of particular industries. For example, you can create one marketing program explaining how your service is perfect for accountants and another selling the exact same service but emphasizing its benefits for lawyers.

If you do select different types of businesses for your desktop marketing program, consider selecting each business type in a separate list. This will allow you to test the success or failure of your offer with each type of business so that you can focus on the most successful type of business in the future. (More on testing later in the book.)

Location

Most likely you market to a specific part of the country. Either you're the head of a small business located in one area, or you are in a regional branch of a large business. The fact that MarketPlace Business covers the entire United States should not discourage you from using it. With MarketPlace, you have total control over the area you target, down to the five-digit ZIP code.

MarketPlace uses maps and lists to help you make geographical selections. To begin your selection, MarketPlace gives you a map of the United States (Figure 5.7). To select a specific state as a part of your list definition, click Include. A black selection box appears next to the state name to show it's been included. You can look in detail at any state by highlighting the state name and clicking Open.

TIP

Double-click the state name to see the state detail.

Selecting More Than One State

If you're selecting multiple locations, it's a nuisance to bounce back and forth between the location name and the Include button. Just hold down the Option key and click all the locations you want to include.

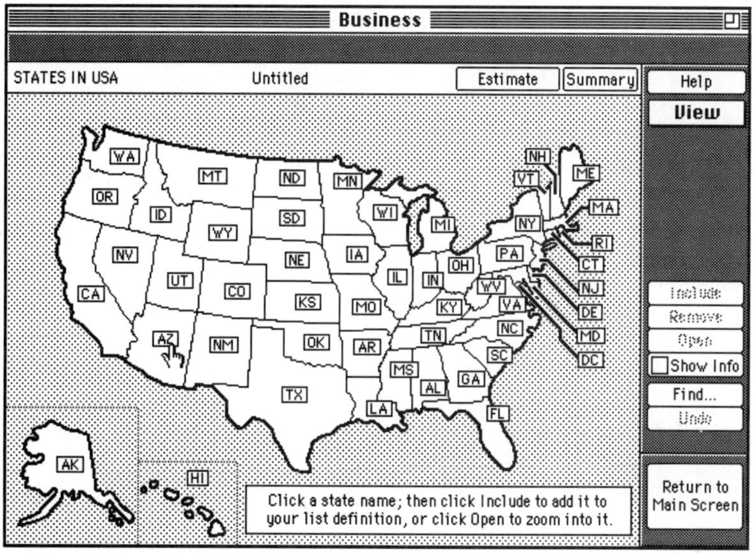

Figure 5.7: You can focus on any state or collection of states by clicking the appropriate state name.

By default, MarketPlace displays a state divided by three-digit ZIP codes or SCF (sectional center facility). Because many people use MarketPlace for direct mail, it focuses on mailing boundaries such as SCF. However, you can easily change the view to geographical boundaries you feel more comfortable with. By clicking on the View menu, you can select to view each state map by SCFs, counties, metro areas, or five-digit ZIP codes (Figures 5.8 and 5.9). You can also choose to see the geographical selections either as a map or as an alphabetical listing.

T I P

Five-digit ZIPs and nationwide metro areas can only be displayed as a list.

A metro area includes the actual city it is named after, as well as the surrounding suburban areas. In the metro map of Arizona (Figure 5.10), the metro area of Phoenix includes the communities of Mesa, Chandler, Apache Junction, Scottsdale, and more. You will find metro areas extremely useful when you're targeting cities, because cities tend to overflow their official boundaries.

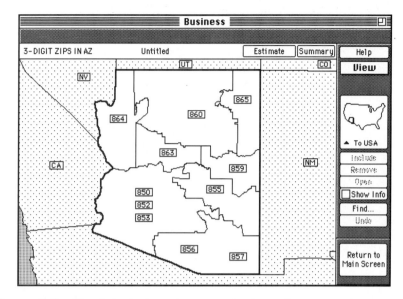

Figure 5.8: The default view of a state is by three-digit ZIP codes—also known as SCFs.

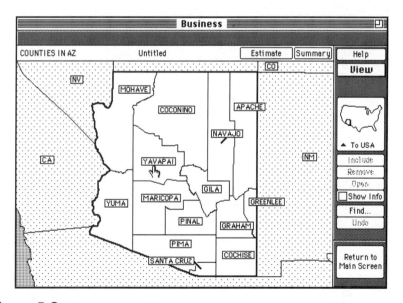

Figure 5.9: You can switch the view to county boundaries if you're more comfortable marketing by county.

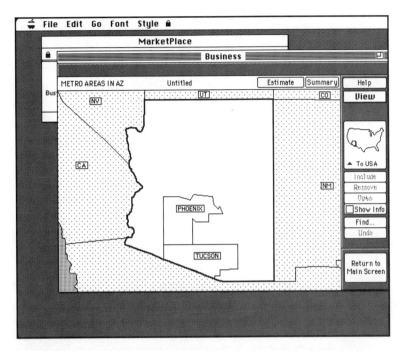

Figure 5.10: There aren't many metro areas in Arizona to display.

Because MarketPlace lets you select an area as small as one five-digit ZIP code, it should be easy to duplicate the sales territories in your company, whether your territories are based on states, counties, or ZIP codes. Even within major cities, you can use ZIP codes to break the city down into different districts. Because of this, you can base your analysis and list building on your territories, not someone else's predefined geography.

> **Timesaving Tip:** Once you have defined a standard sales territory, save the List Definition. When you need to use the same territory again, you can retrieve the old definition and add any additional selection criteria.

MarketPlace's Location function can also help you learn more about areas you're less familiar with. If you click the Show Info box, you can investigate any area you click. A box appears telling where that area is and how many businesses are in it. Use Show Info to give you a quick overview of an area before you select it for your list.

If you're picking areas in a part of the country you aren't familiar with or are looking for a specific location, you can use the Find feature to speed up your search. Like the Find feature for Type of Business, it will take you exactly where you want to go.

Once you're in the Find dialog box, click a radio button to indicate whether you want to search by metro area, county, 3-digit ZIP by Name, 3-digit ZIP by Number, 5-digit ZIP by Name, or 5-digit ZIP by Number. You then type in what you're looking for, and it will show you your entry on a master list (Figure 5.11). If it's the location you want, click Find again, and you'll be taken directly to the area on the map. Searching by 5-digit ZIP by Name can be particularly helpful when you know the name of a town you want but have no idea where in a state it is located. In fact, you can search for a town or ZIP within a particular state or throughout the entire country. Surprisingly, there is little performance difference whether you search statewide or nationwide.

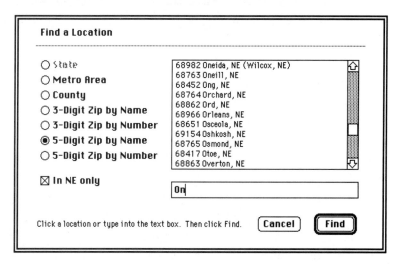

Figure 5.11: You can find almost any town in Nebraska using the Find feature.

> ## How ZIP Codes Work
>
> ZIP codes are not contiguous. Do not pick a collection of ZIP codes in numerical sequence under the assumption that they're next to each other. If you're not certain where a ZIP code is, it is usually safer to check on a map.

Area Codes

Although the Area Codes selection capability may seem to duplicate Location, it can be a powerful tool if you're planning a telemarketing campaign. The Area Code feature divides the United States into the eight Bell Telephone territories. You can select any Bell region by double-clicking on the box.

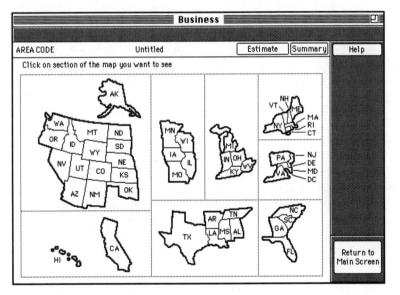

Figure 5.12: The Area Code map is an alternative method to select different areas of the country.

Area codes are placed on the maps in rough proximity to the area they represent. If you're making a large volume of calls, grouping the lists together by area code can make it easier for the telemarketers. You may even consider hiring telemarketing companies in different parts of your overall telemarketing region to decrease your toll charges. Dividing the list by area code can be particularly useful if you'll be telemarketing to areas in different time zones. You can sort your contact sheets so that telemarketers will call the easternmost areas first and finish with the areas in the West, giving your telemarketers the best opportunity for success.

Makeeta Talu sells many of her services through telesales. Each of her telesales representatives is assigned to three or four area codes for their territory. By selecting by area code, instead of counties or ZIP codes, Makeeta can give her reps only the names in their territories and avoid battles on who gets the commissions.

Data Options

The Data Options selection gives you a variety of choices to fine-tune any list you've already created to fit your requirements. The different data options fall into two basic categories: those that let you pick records that have changed since the last quarterly CD-ROM, and those that contain specific information (Figure 5.13).

Changed Data

The ability to choose records that have changed since the last CD-ROM is particularly useful for updating and maintaining any lists you've already created and saved. When you get a new CD-ROM, you can use the same list definition as your saved list but add the option asking for new or modified records. You can then buy only the few records that have changed and use them to update your regular list.

When using these options, don't assume a business is a new business just because it appears on the CD-ROM for the first time. Dun's Marketing Services, the data vendor, may simply have missed it earlier. You don't want to make the mistake of welcoming the company to the area or congratulating it on its opening, unless you are certain the company is actually new.

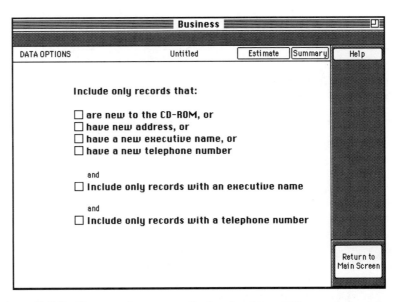

Figure 5.13: You can fine-tune a list by checking different data options.

Complete Records

Finally, if the name of the executive or a telephone number is vital to you, you can specify that you want only records in which they are present. If you're doing telemarketing, it makes a lot of sense to specify the presence of telephone numbers, because calls to directory assistance can get very expensive. If you exceed your minimum allotted calls per month, directory assistance can cost $.34 per call or more.

Phone numbers are present in 95 percent or more of the records in the database. This isn't surprising when you consider that Dun & Bradstreet does a lot of its data verification via the telephone. However, executive names may be missing on more of the records on your list, depending on the location, type of business, etc.

Examples of Creating Lists with MarketPlace

 n most cases, you will need to use more than one selection criteria to define your best list. The following three examples show how three different people use the selection criteria in MarketPlace to create a list that is perfect for each of their needs.

Where Should We Expand?

Daniel Savage is the sales director for Bake Tools, Inc., a company that makes ovens and other kitchen tools for large-scale bakeries. Until now, the company has been based in the Pacific Northwest, but Daniel would like to expand into Northern California. Before deciding whether to hire a sales rep for the territory, Daniel would like to explore the potential of the market by doing some telemarketing. If the business looks promising, he'll hire a sales rep to cover the new territory.

First, Daniel turns to MarketPlace to create his prospect list. He begins by defining the Type of Business he's looking for, because that's one selection criterion he feels certain of. He clicks Type of Business on the Main Screen and clicks Find. He types *Bakery* and gets a long list of possible bakery businesses. The first six are:

> 5963 Bakery goods, purchases: house-to-house-retail
>
> 3556 Bakery machinery-mfg
>
> 5461 Bakery products produced primarily for sale on the premise-retail
>
> 2052 Bakery products, dry; e.g., biscuits, crackers, pretzels-mfg
>
> 2051 Bread, cake, and related products
>
> 5142 Bakery products, frozen-wholesale

The fifth entry—*2051) Bread, cake, and related products*—looks about right, so Daniel clicks Find to locate this entry in the SIC hierarchy. After reading the description of the category, Daniel decides to make category 2051 his first selection by clicking Include (Figure 5.14). The 2051 category description also encourages him to go to category *5461) Bakery products produced primarily for direct sale on the premise.* Since 5461 covers all the stand-alone bakeries, Daniel also includes it. With his business types defined, he clicks Return to Main Screen.

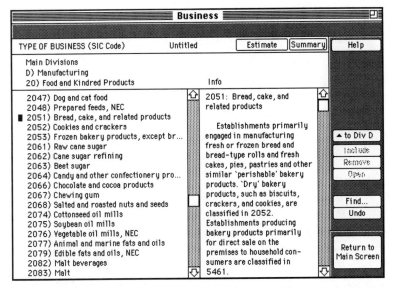

Figure 5.14: Daniel uses the Find feature and the SIC code definitions to help him find all bakery-related businesses.

Next, Daniel would like to specify the territory he wants to telemarket in, so he goes into Area Code and double-clicks California. He isn't exactly sure where he should draw the boundaries between northern and southern California, but he knows he wants San Francisco, area code 415. He holds the Option key and clicks on 707, 916, 415, 209, and 408 to include all of those areas in his list definition (Figure 5.15). To get a sense of how many companies he's selected so far, Daniel clicks the Estimate button and learns he has selected about 1,500 records.

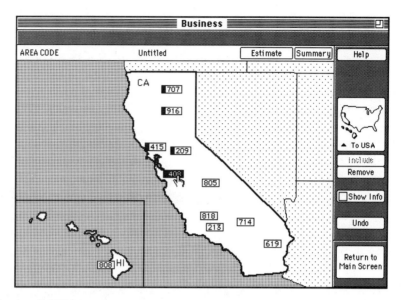

Figure 5.15: Daniel selects all the Area Codes in northern California to test his potential market.

To narrow his selection some more, Daniel decides to add a sales criterion as well. He clicks Return to Main Screen and clicks Annual Sales. He chooses bakeries with sales over $500,000 by clicking the bars from .5–1 to >1,000. He again clicks Estimate and learns he has decreased his count considerably, to only 110 records. To make a larger list, he adds the .2–.5 range to his criteria for an estimated 240 records.

Daniel returns to the Main Screen and chooses Preview list to actually build the list. He can then buy the list and assign the different names to his telemarketers to begin testing the waters.

Where the Pilots Are

J.K. Pierce is a self-employed pilot who wants to relocate from Texas to the Southeast. Although he usually uses MarketPlace to find new clients, in this case he hopes to use MarketPlace to help him find a position. He feels the service should have at least 10 employees, because that number of employees implies success and the potential need for more employees.

J.K. starts by clicking Location. Using the United States map, he clicks each of the states he's interested in—Florida, Georgia, North Carolina, South Carolina, Alabama, and Tennessee—and clicks Include after each state. As he progresses, a black box appears next to each state title, indicating that it's been selected.

After picking his preferred locations, J.K. makes his business selection. He clicks Type of Business and looks at the major categories. Since he has no idea where he would find air courier services, he clicks Find. When he types in *air courier*, he gets *3444 Air cowls, scoops, or airports....* That's not what he wanted, so he tries again with *courier*. This time, he hits the jackpot with *4513 Courier services, air*—just what he's looking for. He clicks Find to take him directly to the listing in the SIC hierarchy, and he clicks Include. At this point, he clicks Estimate and learns that his list definition to this point will probably give him about 190 records all located in the six southern states, a reasonable number to target.

After returning to the Main screen, J.K. clicks Preview to build an actual list. He takes a look at some of the companies by clicking on the company name so that company information appears in the right-hand window (Figure 5.16).

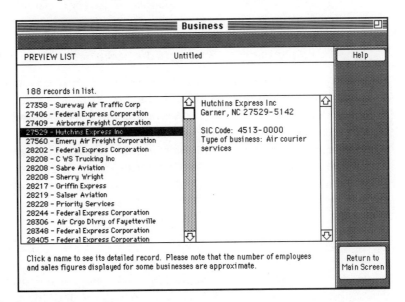

Figure 5.16: When you Preview a list, you can get a sense of the contents of the list before you buy it.

Because he will have to buy the names before he can get the addresses to send his resume to, J.K. decides to buy the list—but one state at a time. He rebuilds his list six times, defining his location as a different state. After saving them all, he passes the Florida list through his meter to buy the list.

He's certain one of these air courier services will be eager to hire a talented pilot like him. And, if not, he can go back and try the lists from the other states.

Where Should We Have a Meeting?

Kate Day is the meeting planner for a rural college in New England. She must convince companies and associations from all over New England to choose her college as the location for their off-site meetings. After reviewing previous attendees and their comments, Kate realizes the college's rural location makes it particularly attractive to businesses located in cities.

To compile a list to target, Kate turns to MarketPlace. She starts by limiting her list to the largest companies, since very few small companies schedule off-site meetings far from their offices. Because meetings have more to do with number of employees than sales, Kate clicks the Number of Employees icon. She clicks the bars from 100–249 to over 10,000.

After returning to the Main Screen, she chooses Location and arrives at the United States map. Although she covers all of New England, she decides companies in Maine, Vermont, and northern New Hampshire are so close to rural areas that her college's rural location would have little attraction. As a result, she begins by double-clicking on NH (New Hampshire). Once at the New Hampshire map, she clicks the View menu to switch to Metro Areas in NH. The map now displays the two metro areas, Manchester-Nashua and Portsmouth-Dover, both of which are located in southern New Hampshire. She clicks on each of them and clicks Include.

Without leaving the New Hampshire map, Kate double-clicks the box labeled MA to quickly move into Massachusetts without going back to the United States map. She chooses to include all of the metro areas in Massachusetts, except Pittsfield, since Pittsfield is located in the rural

Berkshire's area (Figure 5.17). Kate double-clicks into Connecticut to include Hartford and finishes by choosing the Providence-Pawtucket metro area in Rhode Island.

TIP

You can move from state to state in map view by double-clicking the state names.

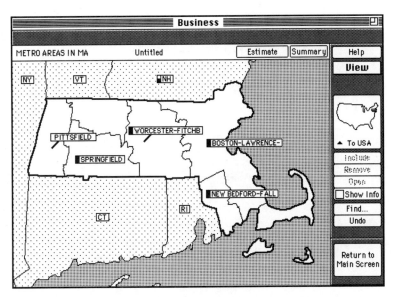

Figure 5.17: Kate can select metro areas across many states at one time.

At this point, Kate has no idea how many prospects she may have selected, and she's a little worried that she has selected too many. Doing an estimate, she finds there are approximately 6,400 records available to match her criteria. Although this knowledge will be useful for planning, it is more than she can handle with sales calls. Kate goes back and removes all the metro areas except for two in Massachusetts, Boston-Lawrence-Salem-Lowell-Brockton and Worcester-Fitchburg-Leominster. With these two metro areas, Kate's list is now an estimated 3,500 establishments.

Kate returns to the Main Screen and clicks Preview to get MarketPlace to create her list of prospects. The actual list size proves to be 3,856—more prospects than she can handle at once. To get just a piece of the list, Kate clicks the List menu on the Main Screen and selects Sample List, which will allow her to take a random sample of the list. She decides to take 150 records initially (Figure 5.18). Kate clicks Save Sample and Remainder, so that she will have both a small beginning list of 150 records and a big source list of 3,706 records to go back to later.

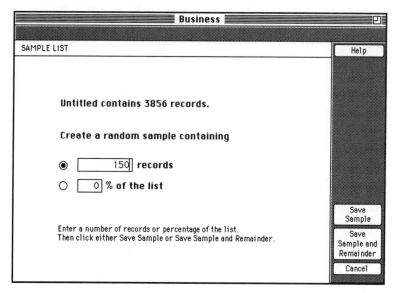

Figure 5.18: If you can't handle an entire list all at once, or you want to test a list, use the Sample List feature.

Defining Household Prospects

Although there are no other CD-ROM products like MarketPlace Business to use to create lists of consumers, you can rent lists to locate the type of customer perfect for your business. There are 80 million to 100 million households across the United States that you might be interested in marketing to.

Define Your Prospective Customers

Marketers use various general categories to select a list of consumers:

- Gender

- Income

- Age

- Location

- Lifestyle

- Marital status

- Mail order purchase history

What Is a Household?

Many of the lists that are rented are based on households rather than individuals. It's useful to understand what is usually meant by the term *household*. Generally, a household exists if there is a man and a woman with the same last name at the same address. If a married couple has two different last names, they will be treated as two separate "households," not one. (This explains why couples with different names get a lot of duplicate mailings.)

To help you understand why you might use a particular selection criterion, we'll go through each one individually.

Gender

Usually, sex classification is calculated by comparing an individual's name to a large database of male or female names. For example, the name *Susan* is in the female category and the name *John* is in the male category. If a name is ambiguous, such as *Chris* or *Pat*, the person's gender will be classified as unknown. If the person's name isn't in the name database—usually, when the name is unusual—it is also classified as unknown.

105

The sex of a respondent can make a big difference in any desktop marketing effort to a household. Some items clearly should be addressed either to a man or a woman. If you sell discount pantyhose, you don't want to waste your efforts on men. On other items or services, your decision of gender may not be as clear-cut. In spite of traditional expectations, the woman manages the finances in the majority of the households in the United States. Therefore, when in doubt, it makes sense to target the woman of the household.

If possible, you may consider addressing the letter to both members of a household who otherwise match your list definition, since it's more likely the most interested person will take charge of reviewing the offer. For example, if you're running an environmental organization asking for charitable donations, the more environmentally conscious person in a couple is likely to read your offer.

Income

When just starting with desktop marketing, almost everyone thinks they should use income as a category to define their target market, and they assume it's best to go after the wealthiest households. Unfortunately for all of us, there are very few wealthy households in the United States. If you go after the wealthier individuals, you'll have a tremendous amount of competition, because everyone else thinks the wealthy make a great target, too.

TIP

Most mailing lists estimate an income range based on various facts known about the consumer.

In reality, there are not a lot of products or services that require a person to have a lot of money. If you are selling a true luxury service, such as a Mercedes Benz or round-the-world luxury cruises, then you should go for high-income levels. But, many products can be successfully targeted to middle-income ranges. Depending on their stage in life, households are interested in a multitude of products and services. If you can convince them they have a need, people will set aside money to buy your products.

Don't disregard the lower-income ranges either. If you're offering spectacular savings or heavy discounts, you may find a strong response in the lower income ranges. Your pitch to lower income levels will probably be most successful if you focus on concrete benefits to the person's life. For example, households making from $15,000 to $20,000 a year may be willing to spend $100 to purchase educational materials to help their children succeed in school but wouldn't be willing to spend $100 for a sweater. In some cases, incomes may be low but spending high. Young, single people will have more disposable income than a family and may be more willing to spend it on less essential items. Income levels of senior citizens are often deceiving, since they are usually living off their assets, rather than an income.

Age

Age ranges can be an extremely powerful way to segment a market. Although it isn't always true, people at certain ages tend to experience similar life events. If you can pick the right age ranges, you can increase your chances of making sales.

For example, if you are selling a diaper service, you might focus on age ranges from 21 to 40. Although there are people who have children at ages younger than 20 or older than 40, the likelihood goes down dramatically. If you market a diaper service to the other age ranges, a lot of the recipients will shake their heads in confusion. Similarly, if you send information on retirement villages to households with age ranges from 21 to 35, you're likely to get the same type of bemusement.

Location

When you're familiar with the area you're marketing in, you may already subconsciously use location to do a lot of list definition. You automatically know the areas where "the rich people live" or "senior citizens retire." When you're renting a list, you simply put this subconscious decision to a more concrete definition. For example, you can simply choose the appropriate location to fit your current knowledge of market dispersal.

If your direct marketing is tied to generating foot traffic for a retail store, you should target only those households within a reasonable distance. Remember that people may commute to your area, so think about including the suburbs where the commuters live. When you are using desktop marketing to enhance advertising efforts, choose the subscription areas of the newspapers or magazines in which you are running your ads.

Lifestyles

Several of the more sophisticated list rental companies develop a type of *lifestyle* rating for the households on their lists. Lifestyle marketing is frequently done in the country's largest packaged-goods corporations and advertising agencies. PRIZM is one of the better-known methods of categorizing households. One company, Equifax, uses a system it calls MicroVision to divide consumers.

With MicroVision, the country is divided into one of the smallest geographic levels possible, ZIP+4. There are over 28 million ZIP+4s in the United States, with each ZIP+4 representing one side of a block. The small size of the ZIP+4 region allows extremely careful targeting. MicroVision describes each ZIP+4, modeling more than 100 variables, including credit-related data and comprehensive demographic information, to create 48 unique market segments that share common interests, purchasing patterns and financial behavior. Basically, lifestyle divisions are based on the concept that "Where you live describes who you are."

Picking by lifestyle is helpful when you want to find a particular type of household at a specific point in its life. It's often the best way to pick out families or young singles. With lifestyles you can target more exactly, even within a single 5-digit ZIP code. As with all of the selection criteria, you should expect some mismatching when you use lifestyles to make list selections. Look at MicroVision for example. Because ZIP+4 areas are quite small, there is usually a tremendous amount of similarity between neighbors. But, there are also likely to be exceptions—those people who are different from the majority of their neighbors.

> **A Typical Lifestyle Description**
>
> *Large Families, Medium Education, Medium-High Income, Technical/ Sales, Precision/Crafts, Two Workers*
>
> This segment is characterized by large, young families in urban areas. They are predominantly white, with a medium education, and medium-high incomes. The majority of occupations are in technical, sales, and administrative support areas, and a significant number are employed in precision/crafts. It is common to have both spouses work outside the home. This segment has the third highest percentage of homeowners, and more than half of these homes were built between 1960 and 1974. (MicroVision Name: Family Ties—Segment 11, Group 2.)

Marital Status

Making list choices can be tricky, especially since it means you have to think a little stereotypically. Single people could be more likely candidates for take-out food, entertainment, and, of course, dating services. Remember that single does not necessarily mean young or without obligations. There is a large population of divorced parents with children and widows or widowers in their later years. Don't make the mistake of sending 70-year-olds invitations to the opening of a new dance club, unless it's a ballroom dance club. By using marital status in combination with lifestyle information and age, you can make a more accurately targeted list.

Mail-Order Purchase History

A lot of the lists you can rent let you make selections based on the purchase histories of the people on their list. This can be very useful, particularly when you want to sell a product or service that's similar to the product sold by the list renter.

For example, you may want to sell skiing and snowmobile accessories. If you can find someone to rent you a list of people who bought ski tickets, you're probably better off than you would be with a list of garden club members. That's not to say the garden club list might not work; it's just not as likely to be an effective list.

Examples of Defining Consumer Lists

A gain, it is not as simple as selecting just one criterion to get the perfect list. Usually, you have to mix and match several criteria until you get just the list you want. The following three examples show you how different types of companies might define a list using a wide variety of selection criteria.

Hometown Bank

Jack Wang is the marketing manager for Hometown Bank, a local bank in Charlotte, North Carolina. After doing some analysis, he believes there is real money-making potential in attracting older households to Hometown. Older households tend to have more expendable capital, many assets, and a strong ethic to save. Therefore, he develops a specialty account for people over 50 that will give them convenience, good savings, and little risk. In addition to marketing the new account to his current customers, Jack would like to broaden the bank's base and find new customers. First, Jack narrows his list down by location. Knowing that people don't like to travel more than 15 minutes to their bank, he makes a list of all the 5-digit ZIP codes within a 15-minute radius of Hometown's two branch offices. After choosing a location, Jack decides on an age range of anyone above 55.

Next, Jack decides to put some income parameters on his list. Income with older households can be misleading. Their income may not be very high, but expenses are usually much lower. Also, income selections often don't take into account any of the savings the older household may have. Therefore, Jack is conservative and decides to pick anyone who earns more than $25,000.

Now that he's defined his most important list variables, Jack is ready to find a list that conforms to his needs.

Made for You

Lori Gal runs a custom clothing design company, Made for You, in Seattle, Washington. Until now, she has depended primarily on word-of-mouth to expand her business, but now she would like to grow even faster. To do this, she intends to do a mailing to women in the Washington areas, offering her services She hopes to appeal to their desires to be both stylish and individualistic.

Her first and most obvious list criterion is gender. Since her market is 95 percent female, she needs to find a list that allows her to select women exclusively. Next, she begins to think about the locations she wants to mail to. She's found that women living in cities tend to be more fashion-conscious. Therefore, it makes sense to try to keep her list selections to the metropolitan areas of the Pacific Northwest—primarily Seattle and Portland. Finally, she thinks of the type of product buyer she wants to find. The best type of list would allow her to select people who have purchased women's apparel in the past. Even better, it might let her choose people who have spent over a hundred dollars on clothes. Because Lori's clothes aren't cheap, she'd rather not waste her time with women who would never spend more than $100 on an item of clothing.

Now Lori begins her search for a list to match her ideal customer imaginings.

Heat Your Home More Cheaply

Kathleen Ahern runs an insulation business in Butte, Montana, and she wants to offer homeowners a free estimate of how much they could save by insulating their homes. Because her contractors can only travel a limited distance to do a job, Kathleen will first need to limit her offer by location. Butte is located in the 597 SCF area. After looking at the map, she decides the boundaries of the SCF are reasonable boundaries for her contractors. As a result, she knows she'll need a list that lets her select by SCF.

As Kathleen thinks about it, she realizes it would be nice if she could be sure that she's reaching homeowners instead of renters. It might be difficult to find a list of actual homeowners, but she might be able to increase the likelihood with another selection. One option she comes up with is eliminating anyone who lives in a multiple-family dwelling from her list. Many list rental companies can remove any addresses that refer to apartment numbers from their lists. People who live in a single-family home are more likely to be homeowners.

List Selection Options

A lot of list companies give you some advanced options when you're selecting a list. Several of these list options are also available in MarketPlace. We'll explain how they work in MarketPlace so that you can get an idea how you could use them in any list rental situation.

Sample List

There are many cases when you may not want to use an entire list you have created, but you want to use just a portion of it. The MarketPlace Sample List feature allows you to take a random sample of any list you have created. To set up the sampling, you click the List menu on the Main Screen and select Sample List. You then can type in exactly how many records you want, or what percent of the list you want to use. After creating the sample, you can choose to save just the sample or both the sample and remainder.

If you are doing market research, it is very common to do sampling to predict how the larger universe might behave. Since it's cost-prohibitive to survey everyone in that universe, you select a smaller, random sample and project the results to the larger survey. In the case of market research, you would only save and buy the sample, because you will never need to use the rest of the universe.

You may also do sampling when you want to test a new offer or a new type of list. You may come up with a list of 150,000 households, but you want to try doing a mailing to 3,000 of them first. If the results are good, you can roll out the mailing to the remaining 147,000 households. If the results are bad, you haven't wasted a lot of money mailing to 150,000 people. Because you may want to mail to the unsampled people on the list, you should always save the sample and the remainder. Initially, you only need to pass the sample through the MarketPlace meter. You will only need to pay for the remaining 147,000 names, once you know that the direct mail campaign will be a success.

Finally, you may want to do sampling when you have only limited resources to do fulfillment or follow-up. If you are a small business, you want to make sure you can respond quickly to every potential customer. Therefore, you may want to stagger your mailings, doing only 100–200 a week. You can easily do this by sampling some 100 records at a time, saving the remainder each time. You can continue this until the list sample is entirely depleted.

Merge List

MarketPlace gives you the ability to combine different MarketPlace lists to give you any type of hybrid list you want. To get to the merge feature, click the List menu and select Merge Lists. Once you have the Merge List screen, click the Open button to enter the name of each list you want to merge. You open one list on the right and one list on the left. Once you select a list, MarketPlace displays a brief description about the list.

You have five choices of how the lists may be merged. The five options are displayed as Venn diagrams, with the left circle representing the left-hand list and the right circle representing the right-hand list (Figure 5.19). When you select any of the five options and click Merge, the lists will be merged. You can merge lists whether they've been bought or not. List rental companies or lettershops can usually do merging of this sort with different lists. You should therefore understand the different merge options.

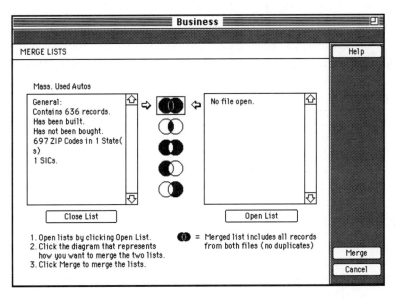

Figure 5.19: The MarketPlace Merge feature lets you combine two lists any way you want.

Option one—The first choice shows all of the circles filled in. If you make this selection, you get all the names from both lists without any duplicate names. This could be useful if you define two different markets for your product or service, but the two markets may overlap.

For example, Bob Walsh thinks he can sell his product to any business with fewer than 50 employees within his metro area. He also thinks that realtors throughout the state might be interested. If he just created a list for each of those criteria and mailed to the names on the two lists, there would probably be duplication. It is very likely there are realtors in his metro area with fewer than 50 employees. He can avoid the mail duplication problem by merging the lists, using option one.

Option two—The second choice shows only the intersection of the two circles filled in. When you do this type of merge, you get only the names that fall on both lists. This capability could help you in many examples. Marta Fuentes sells a high-tech product. She thinks her best prospects will be households that are likely to have CD players *and* a computer. To get a list like this, she defines one list of people who have bought CD players and another list for people who have bought computers. When she does this type of merge, she'll have a list of those who have bought both.

Option three—The third choice has the two circles filled in, except for the intersection of the two. You will get all the names on *both* lists, unless they are on both lists. If Marta's mailing is a big success, she may decide to expand the marketing program to include the rest of both the lists. To do this, she would use the original CD player list and the original computer list and select everyone who isn't on both. She can now send out a mailing without duplicating the mailing to those who were on both lists.

Option four—The fourth choice gives you all the names from the left-hand list, except for those names that are also on the right-hand list. This is the option described earlier for creating a list of single people. This option can also be perfect when you've already bought a list and mailed using it. You then come up with another list you would like to mail to, but some of the names may be the same.

For example, let's say Bob Walsh had already done a mailing to the small businesses in his metro area. After he got the results, he finds that realtors are big responders. At this point, he decides to roll out his offer to realtors across the state. To make sure that he doesn't mail to people he has already mailed to, Bob opens the new list of realtors across the state on the left-hand side. He then opens his previously bought list on the right-hand side. By choosing the fourth merge option, he will get a list of realtors of all sizes across the state, except that it will be only realtors with more than 50 employees in the metro area.

Option five—The last choice is exactly opposite from the fourth option; it gives you all the names from the right-hand list, except for those names that are also on the left-hand list.

6

Get the Names You Want

If your list needs can't be satisfied with a CD-ROM-based list, you'll have to explore the list rental business. Companies of all kind rent the names on their lists for other companies to use in direct marketing. Before you actually rent a list, you may find it helpful to have a good idea how the list rental business works.

Industry Structure

There are three principle businesses involved in the list rental industry:

■ List owner

■ List manager

■ List broker

All of them have different responsibilities and different loyalties. You should understand which you are dealing with when you choose to rent lists.

List Owner

The list owner has created the list either through direct-response offers or the compilation of other information. It's the owner that has decided to put a list on the market for rental, generally to create additional revenue from his/her customer base. As with any company that offers a product, the list owner is very enthusiastic about how responsive or effective the list will be for your direct marketing efforts.

As in any good business, the owner wants to maximize revenue on the rental of the list. The owner is looking for "stock turn," multiple use of the names on the list. Because rental will be greater if exposure is greater, the list owner usually turns the management of the rental business over to a reseller. The owner will usually distribute the list for 20 to 40 percent of the price to be charged the renter.

List Manager

The list manager represents the list owner and tries to increase rentals of the list. Managers market the list to the broker network, using advertising, trade shows, direct mail, catalogs, and any other methods that will get brokers to recommend the list to their clients. The managers are responsible for creating the data card for each list, that is, the basic specification sheet describing the list.

The manager is paid a commission on sales. Usually, the manager has a responsibility, if not a direct agreement, to rent a minimum number of names from the list in order to maintain a relationship with the list owner. Although list managers can sell directly to the renter, they usually are also willing to share a commission with a list broker to increase potential list distribution.

List Broker

The list broker acts as an intermediary between list owners or managers and the list renters. You're most likely to work with a list broker if you want to rent a list. A broker may specialize in a special kind of list rental, but most brokers will claim to have knowledge of thousands of lists and hundreds of markets. To ensure the most useful guidance, ask the broker questions about your industry to make sure that he or she knows it well enough to understand your needs.

Remember, the broker represents the list owner and will be getting paid a commission worth 10 to 20 percent of the list rental. Therefore, it's common for list brokers to be motivated by the following desires:

1) To recommend lists that pay the highest commission

2) To recommend lists that are the most expensive

3) To recommend lists that have big potential in the event that the test mailing is successful

4) To recommend lists that pay commissions on the special selection charges. Some lists only pay commissions on basic rental price, not selection charges.

5) To not work too hard for small orders. Like any other sales person, a broker can't spend a lot of time servicing a company that will generate a small list order.

Renter's Rights

Because the focus for the owners and brokers of the list industry is to sell a large volume of names, it's important for you to be prepared and aware. You do have rights as the renter of a list, and you should be ready to exercise those rights any time you rent a list.

1) You have the right to know the true source of a list and how subsets are defined.

   ■ Some owners rent the names of people who simply inquired about their products or services. You have the right to know whether the names you're renting actually bought products or were only inquirers. (An inquiry file may work better for you than a buyer file, but you should understand where the names originated.)

   ■ In order to increase the size of the file so that there are more names to rent, some owners offer sweepstakes to get more names. You have the right to know if sweepstake respondents are included in the overall list count.

   ■ Some owners accumulate several smaller purchases by a customer in order to categorize a customer as a higher dollar-spender than the individual purchases would have warranted. You should ask how spending categorization is determined.

2) You have a right to have selection terms, such as *hot line*, defined by the owner:

   ■ Some owners categorize names as being recently active even if the only modification is an address update. *Recently active* should mean that the person or company has purchased or inquired within X number of months.

   ■ Some owners use a name for six months before they include the name in their rental database. Therefore, a name they define as new is really six months old.

   ■ Some owners use vague descriptions of the source of the name and include questionable names.

3) You have the right to know what overlay information has been applied to a list in order to gain demographic or business data, rather than information the owner has accumulated through other sources.

Database Overlays

Overlay information is usually standard information that companies like to have associated with their lists. Some of the largest database creators will sometimes rent their database overlays to another database provider. The most mundane example of a database overlay is the National Change of Address (NCOA) service operated by the United States Postal Service. The Postal Service creates a massive database of all the changes of address reported by all the individual post offices. A company can then use the NCOA overlay to compare the old addresses to any address it currently has in its database.

There are typical overlays for both business lists and consumer lists. A common business overlay might be the addition of SIC codes. A list owner would rent an overlay that can assign SIC codes to known businesses on his list. Lifestyle codes are frequently added as overlays to consumer lists, since the codes are generally based on ZIP codes or location.

4) You have the right to talk to anyone in the distribution process to gain the information you need to make a decision—the owner, the manager, or the broker.

5) You have the right not to get a *loaded* list (a high performing subsection of the list) for a test and the general list for future use. If the broker calls the test list a random selection, it should be exactly that.

6) You have a right to know how the company takes a small sample (5,000 or so names) for a test mailing. In order to cut down on their processing charges, some companies have 5,000 name tapes already prepared and will ship those tapes to anyone who rents within a given time frame. This will give you distorted results, since several other businesses will be mailing the same names at the same time.

7) You have the right to review the list you rent. Even if the owner insists on only shipping the list to a third party, such as a lettershop, you have a right to receive a random printout of the file for visual inspection. You should allow yourself time for this step; most lists arrive on computer tape just in time for merge-purge or at the lettershop just in time for addressing. This eliminates any time for proper review.

8) You have the right to know the concentration of names per establishment on a business list. You shouldn't have to accept an over-concentration of names per location, since this will reduce the effectiveness of your mailing.

Types of Lists

 ith this understanding of the list industry, you'll be better prepared when you go out to rent a list. There are six different types of lists you can borrow. Each type has its advantages and disadvantages, as reviewed below.

Response Lists

Response lists contain names of people or companies that have made purchases through the mail or over the phone. If you are in the mail order business, a response list can be good to rent, particularly when the products are similar to your own.

Advantages

■ Since the names got on the list because the people responded to a direct marketing effort, the list members have demonstrated an affinity to buy over the phone or through the mail.

■ They have paid for products or services.

- If they're still on the list, the list owner still considers them active.

- The list often has phone numbers on file, because people who are ordering via direct mail or telemarketing are usually asked their phone numbers in case something goes wrong with the order.

- You can get a sense of the interests of the list members by knowing what they've bought.

Disadvantages

- The list distribution tends to be geographically sparse.

- You can usually only segment the list according to buying behavior and geography.

- The data standards are set by the list owner.

- The names and addresses may not be available for your use on your personal computer.

Subscription Lists

Subscription lists come in two forms: paid and controlled. Most consumer magazines and subscription clubs (such as record clubs), are paid subscriptions. In business, there are many magazines that are available without charge to managers or technical specialists. These magazines are called controlled publications. To qualify to receive the publication, the subscribers need to complete a questionnaire with a great deal of information about their companies and their jobs.

You generally select a subscription list when you think people who are interested in the magazine's editorial product would also be interested in your product or service.

Paid Subscription Advantages

- The subscribers have a known editorial interest.

- They have spent money to get the magazine.

- You can usually get the list in whatever format you want: labels, diskette, or tape.

- People who already subscribe to one or more publications are more inclined to buy other subscriptions by mail or phone.

Paid Subscription Disadvantages

- The owner usually doesn't have any demographic information about the subscriber.

- The list doesn't have phone numbers on file.

- You cannot segment the list by anything other than geographic options.

- The data records are maintained in a record format most convenient to the publisher.

- Subscribers don't behave as other direct response buyers do, even though they subscribed to the publication by mail or phone.

Controlled Subscription Advantages

- The readers have a known interest; the more specific the editorial content of the magazine, the higher their affinity to the subject.

- Because each subscriber had to fill out a detailed questionnaire to receive the publication, a lot is known about the subscriber.

- The questionnaire data can be used to segment the list by many different criteria.

- The subscribers have been acquired through mail solicitation.

- You can usually get the list in a variety of formats: labels, diskette, or tape.

Controlled Subscription Disadvantages

- The data is geographically sparse.

■ Renting the list is usually expensive because of the selectivity of the lists.

■ Controlled subscribers don't behave as direct response buyers do, even though they subscribed to the publication by mail or phone.

Membership Lists

Membership lists are simply lists of people who belong to some organization. You should consider these lists if you think people who are interested in your products or services are also likely to belong to these organizations.

Membership List Advantages

■ The strongest advantage is that the members have an affinity for the organization they belong to. If you can tie your offer to the organization, you will improve your sales.

■ Most membership organizations charge some type of dues. This means higher quality prospects, since they have already proven willing to spend money.

■ Phone numbers may be available for your marketing program.

Membership List Disadvantages

■ Since organizations like to have many members, the lists may be out-of-date in order to keep the organization count high.

■ Even though many membership organizations use mail and phone for membership maintenance, members are not necessarily mail responsive.

■ Usually, little data is known about the members.

■ Membership in national organizations is usually sparse locally. Local organizations will have more members geographically but rarely enough to meet your needs.

- Membership organizations will charge top rates for their lists.

- Availability may be a problem. Rules seldom apply across an entire organization so you may be able to use a list in one town but not in the next, because of different rules.

- Many organizations are so protective of their lists that they will only supply labels, and the labels must be sent to a mailing house.

Compiled Lists

A compiled list is created for the purpose of list rental. It consists of people who fit certain categories, such as those who live in certain areas or are members of a certain profession. Compilers take a wide variety of information and compile it into one, large list. Some of the sources list compilers use are: phone books (white and yellow pages), city directories, car registrations, trade association memberships, warranty card registrations, census data, reader service-card product inquiries. It can be difficult to know what the source of compilation is for some lists, because techniques are kept confidential in order to keep ahead of competitors.

Compiled List Advantages

- Compilers segment their lists according to the different categories they obtain when compiling the information, so that they sell the ability to select on many variables.

- Compiled lists are dense geographically. If you are marketing to a certain area, a compiled list is a good choice.

- Household compiled lists usually contain both names and phone numbers, so that you can use either direct mail or phone-based marketing.

- Compilers will supply their lists in almost any format.

Compiled List Disadvantages

■ Compiled lists have more of a problem keeping current, because they're based on published sources that aren't necessarily kept current. You can have information that is 15 to 18 months old, if you use a compiled list just before it's updated.

■ Pricing can get quite high for using different selection criteria, since most lists charge a fee for each list definition you make.

Commercial Databases

This is the trend in the list industry. Commercial databases contain a combination of some or all of the above types of lists. The database is a compilation of response, subscription, membership, and compiled names. They then use information overlays from sources such as the government to enhance the information in the file.

Commercial List Advantages

■ The lists are geographically dense in any trade area.

■ Because the lists combine so much information, you have a number of selection options to choose from when you define a list.

■ Phone numbers are often available for these lists.

■ Commercial database companies will provide you the lists on any type of format, from labels to diskette.

Commercial Database Disadvantages

■ Not all the names in the database are response-oriented.

■ Like compiled files, the database owners are challenged by the size of the information-gathering task and the need to be current. The information on these files ages rapidly.

House Files

You probably have a list of customers, contacts, and prospects. The best part of this type of list is that you own it and the worst part is—you own it. Most companies have difficulties maintaining their own files as well as they would like for marketing purposes. However, you'll find that no matter what shape your list is in, your house file (no older than three years) will always perform better than an external list.

Getting a Rental List

Now that you know about the different types of rental lists, how do you go about renting names from them? When you think the best possible list is the list of a local store or a statewide organization, go directly to the source and ask to rent its names. Even stores or organizations which have never rented their customer lists before may be interested if you approach them. After all, it can be an excellent source of revenue with minimal costs to themselves.

However, if you have no specific list in mind and you're new to the direct marketing business, you're probably better off going to a reputable list broker to start with. Because a list broker makes money off of a wide variety of lists, he is rarely wedded to renting a specific list.

If you get a good list broker, he should listen to your needs and then take some time to investigate the possibilities. He might come up with a unique concept of how to locate prospects for your business. The broker should get back to you within a few days with suggestions on lists you can try.

If you prefer to do list searching yourself, you should get your hands on the *The Direct Mail List Rates and Data*. This hefty book is a monthly publication produced by SRDS (Standard Rate and Data Service), and it lists virtually every nationally available list and list brokerage service. The lists are categorized so that you can find the type of lists you're interested in quite easily.

For example, if you're selling a new type of drill for dentists, look under *79 Dental.* A sampling of the lists you might find include:

- ADA American Dental Association Dentists & Students, a list of 175,00 members of the ADA.

- Australian Dentists, a list of 4,800 dentists listed by A.H. Direct Marketing, Inc.

- A list of 104,000 subscribers to *Dental Economics.*

- Recipients of the *Dental Products Report.*

- A list of 797 manufacturers that make dental supplies and equipment compiled by Business Mailers Inc.

Each monthly publication is about two inches thick, so that you're very likely to find something that seems promising. Look in your library to see if they have a copy, or ask a friend who does advertising if there's an old one lying around the office. (The entries change very little each month, so that it doesn't usually hurt to use an old one.) If you can't locate a copy anywhere, you can contact SRDS directly at:

Standard Rate & Data Service
3004 Glenview Road
Wilmette, IL 60091
(708) 256-6067

With SRDS you can track down the lists that look most promising and directly call the company listed. Be aware that the company listed is often a list broker or list manager, not the actual list owner.

How Lists Are Defined and Priced

Rental lists usually have a set price for names. The standard industry pricing format is price per thousand names, written as $X/M—with *M* meaning thousand. You must pay that price for every thousand names you rent.

In addition, most lists charge extra for additional *selects*. You must pay an additional price per thousand for the selection criteria you use to define the list. Most companies let you select by location with no additional charge, but will charge you for more specific selections, such as company size or gender. They may also charge for including additional information, such as a telephone number. It's very important for you to keep these extra charges in mind, because they can greatly affect the ultimate cost of your rental list.

For example, a company called SmartNames, Inc. has a compiled list of a hundred million consumers. Its basic rental rate varies from $19/M to $8/M, depending on the quantity of names you order. SmartNames lets you define your list by a great many selection criteria, but the costs can quickly add up.

Basic list	$19/M
Specific occupation	3/M
Married	4/M
Specific states	5/M
Prizm lifestyle	10/M
Total cost	$31/M

That's quite an increase! The list rental companies add these extra charges because it takes them more data processing time and effort for every selection criterion you select. Be sure that you're aware of how these extra selections will affect your bottom line.

Minimum Orders

Most list renters require a minimum order size before they'll rent you a list. This is because it costs them a certain amount of money every time they set up the database to generate the list, and they must be certain they can still make a profit.

Some list companies define this minimum by number of names ordered and others base it on dollars. For business lists, the minimum order is generally 5,000 names; for consumer lists, it's generally 10,000 names. If the minimum is based on the fee, check to see whether the selects charges are counted toward the minimum; some companies only count the basic rate.

Limits to Renting a List

Virtually all list rental organizations require that you send them a sample of what you plan to mail or the script of what you're planning to telemarket *before* they'll agree to rent you a list. For the most part, this is a precaution to ensure that you aren't trying to sell anything illegal or pornographic to their list members. Many private list owners also want to make sure that you aren't selling anything competitive with their products or services. Don't be surprised if your chief competitor seems unwilling to rent you its list.

Don't think that the rental company won't notice a switch in your direct marketing packet after they've given you approval and sent you the list. Almost all list renters *seed* their rental lists with "false" names. These are generally real people, but they don't necessarily fit your list description. Instead, they monitor what you mail and how often you mail to them. They monitor the number of times you mail to them because when you agree to rent a list, you usually agree to rent it *one-time only.* If someone on the list responds and sends you back his/her name, that person now "belongs" to you and your customer list. But, if someone doesn't respond to your mailing, you can't mail to that name again without paying the rental fee again.

Alternative List Access

S ome of the larger commercial databases give you an alternative method to select the names you want for your list. They allow you to use a modem and software they supply you to dial their mainframe computer and access the database directly. One of Dun & Bradstreet's subsidiaries has a service like this, as do some other leading database owners.

A powerful benefit of this process is that you can do the list manipulation yourself *and* you receive the names in an electronic form which you can then manipulate on your personal computer. In addition, since you generally pay for each name you transfer (or download) to your computer, you aren't limited by list minimums. This type of list access is quite similar to using MarketPlace, which lets you access the list directly on your computer.

Use of these services can be expensive though. Usually there is a connect charge, meaning the company charges you for every minute you remain connected to its mainframe. If you're not very efficient using its software or you're not sure exactly what you're looking for, these charges can add up quickly. In addition, the companies tend to charge a premium price for each name you transfer. This is understandable since you can access the name immediately and you have control over using the name more than once.

Unfortunately, almost all of the direct access databases are oriented toward the PC, not the Macintosh. If you want to access and download names through these services, you'll need to use a PC. However, most of the lists are delivered in a generic computer-text format that can easily be transferred to the Macintosh with a little effort. If you're thinking of subscribing to one of these direct connection services, you should discuss the Macintosh compatibility issue in detail before you subscribe.

7

Market Analysis

In Chapters 5 and 6, we explained how you can use MarketPlace and other rental lists to find your prospective customers. But you perhaps feel the need to spend some time getting a better grasp on the markets you're trying to penetrate before you generate a list. Although you may have an intuitive feel for a market, you may be surprised to see the results of some actual numerical research.

It's not unusual for smaller businesses to do very little market analysis or research. Probably you know that it's a good idea, but you're swamped by the day-to-day aspects of running the business and making sales. Generally, it's difficult to get the market information, and even when you do, it's in a form difficult to use.

By combining data with some of the available analytical tools, you can begin to do extremely thorough and effective analysis. A lot of this chapter focuses on how you can use MarketPlace Business to analyze a market or list. You should be able to apply the same concepts and methodology to a lot of other lists, including rental lists. However, you must be prepared to pay for the analysis, since rental companies must take the time and manpower to do the analysis for you.

Use MarketPlace Business to Analyze a Market

MarketPlace Business does more than simply create lists that you can buy and mail to. Because you have all the data on your desktop and are able to access it as much as you want, MarketPlace can serve as a powerful analytical tool. The product even comes with its own simple, but powerful, analytical tools.

Counts

The simplest way to get a handle on different markets is to get a count of how many people are available in those markets. One tried and true way to get the information is to use the resources of your local library. If you're marketing to households, you can make use of U.S. census information to get the raw numbers of different populations. Many business publications list estimates of all types of businesses.

You can also use list brokers or MarketPlace to learn the size of a market. To do this, define the market and learn how many records fit the criteria. You may be surprised to find that a market you thought was immense is actually quite small, or vice versa. Counts are good as a quick reality check on any market.

With a list broker, you usually have to wait a day or two after you give the definition before the broker will call you with the counts. If you have MarketPlace, you can get market counts as many times as you want, without ever buying a list.

TIP

A list broker shouldn't charge you to give counts.

For example, Melvyn Bregman runs a successful discount office furniture store in Berkeley, California. Business has been fantastic, and Mel is considering opening another store in the area. However, he'd like a quick idea of the best place to locate his store before he begins extensive site selection research.

Mel turns to MarketPlace Business for a quick look. He knows from experience that his best customers are service businesses with 5 to 500 employees—big enough to need furniture but not so big that they're getting pretentious about the office decor. His intuition is that the Stockton, Sacramento, or San Jose metro area would be best for a new store.

First, Mel double-clicks on the Number of Employees icon and selects the range between 5 and 499. He then double-clicks the Type of Business icon and selects the main divisions of Finance, Insurance, Real Estate and Services. Finally, he double-clicks the Location icon and selects the map of California. He changes the view to metro area and selects Sacramento. With his list criteria defined, Mel gets an estimate of the list size. In moments, he learns there are approximately 599 prospective businesses in Sacramento.

With the numbers for Sacramento calculated, it is a simple matter to go back into Location to redefine the selected metro area. Mel quickly creates a list and gets counts for Stockton and San Jose. He also gets counts for the total number of businesses for each town, so that he can get a better sense of the breakdown of ideal prospect businesses to the total population. The estimated numbers tell it all:

CHAPTER SEVEN

	Prospects	Total	Percent
Sacramento	5,900	38,000	16%
Stockton	1,400	10,000	14%
San Jose	6,700	42,000	16%

According to the estimated numbers, it looks as though San Jose might be the best opportunity. Not only does it have the highest number of prospective businesses, but the concentration of prospective businesses to total businesses is quite high.

Counts can be a good quick-and-dirty analytical tool, but you can go a lot further with your analysis. MarketPlace includes a feature called Analysis which is designed to help you gain in-depth understanding of your lists. It can do two types of analysis: standard analysis and custom analysis.

Standard Analysis

MarketPlace's standard analysis gives you summary information on any list you create. For each list, it calculates the following information:

Business

- Total number of businesses
- Total annual sales
- Average sales per business
- Average number of employees per business
- Total number of four-digit SIC codes
- Total number of five-digit ZIP codes
- Total number of single-location businesses
- Total number that are headquarters
- Total number that are subsidiary headquarters
- Total number that are branches

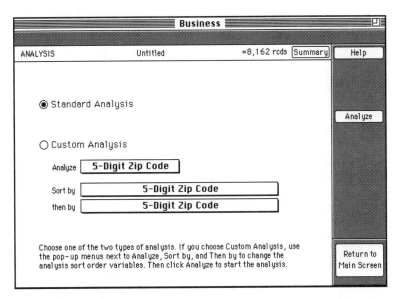

Figure 7.1: Once you build a list in MarketPlace, you can select one of the two analysis features: standard or custom.

Standard analysis gives you a quick way to find out more about a list you have created. In Mel's case, he may discover that although there are more prospects in one town, the average revenues are higher in another. The higher average revenues may mean bigger and more expensive purchases, which could offset any difference in the number of actual prospects.

To do the analysis, Mel retrieves each list he just built. Instead of clicking Preview, he clicks Analysis. He clicks the radio button next to Standard Analysis and then clicks Analyze. After some processing, a window appears with the completed analysis. For example, the standard analysis for San Jose can be seen in Figure 7.2.

With standard analysis, you can find the quick answers you need for presentations or reports. You may find you're taken more seriously if you can describe a new territory or market as having 5,000 businesses with total sales revenue of $475,000, rather than "having a lot of potential." The use of concrete numbers adds confidence and credibility to the marketing decisions you make.

You can also use standard analysis to do competitive research. Use it to find out how many businesses like yours are located in a given area.

Standard analysis will give you both their total revenues and their average revenues, giving you a sense of the level of competition you face.

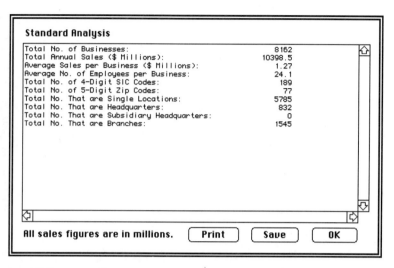

Figure 7.2: Standard analysis gives an in-depth summary of the records from the San Jose metro area list.

A standard analysis report can give you a quick overview of the diversity of a region. This can be particularly helpful if you are investigating an entirely new part of the country. An area with businesses across very few SIC codes may not be sufficiently diversified to survive hard economic times—or the region may be the newest economic star, if the primary businesses are in large demand.

Custom Analysis

Custom analysis goes deeper into the nature of a market by breaking a list into subgroups and calculating information for each subgroup. You choose which types of subgroups will best guide your marketing decisions. When you *analyze* by some criterion, MarketPlace calculates basic information for each division within that subgroup. For example, when you analyze by 5-digit ZIP codes, MarketPlace will make summary calculations for every 5-digit ZIP in your current list. The results are displayed in a series of rows and columns, very much like a spreadsheet.

TIP

Both analysis features can take a lot of time to calculate, depending on the size of your list.

You can analyze any list by the following subgroups:

Business

- 5-digit ZIP codes
- 3-digit ZIP codes
- County
- State
- Area codes
- SIC divisions
- 2-digit SIC
- 4-digit SIC
- 8-digit SIC
- Annual sales
- Number of employees

Summary information for each division in the subgroup is given on: city and state, number of businesses, total sales, total employees, average sales, and average number of employees.

To more easily evaluate a custom analysis, you can rearrange the results by a multitude of criteria. When MarketPlace displays the analysis results, it will rank the subgroups based on the criteria you chose. MarketPlace lets you sort your results by:

- Number of businesses
- Total sales
- Total number of employees
- Average sales per business

- Average number of employees per business
- 5-digit ZIP codes

Let's go back to the example of Mel Bregman. Based on his initial analysis, the San Jose area is looking particularly promising. However, the San Jose metro area is a big space. He'd like to get a better idea of the most promising locations for his stores—at least, as far as prospects go. With a better sense of the concentration of prospects, he'll feel more prepared when he begins site searching, lease negotiations, and so on.

To get a better sense of the area, Mel opens the San Jose prospect list and clicks Analysis again. This time he picks the radio button next to Custom Analysis. Since he wants to pick the best location, he decides to analyze the list by 5-digit ZIP codes. Because he's found that the number of employees in the area companies is crucial to making furniture sales, he decides first to sort the list analysis by number of employees. If a 5-digit ZIP area is tied for number of employees, he selects that the second sorting should be based on total sales.

After performing the analysis, it's apparent that an area in Santa Clara (95054) and in San Jose (95112) are almost tied for the largest number of employees. However, when he looks at the total sales for the two areas, Mel finds that the businesses in Santa Clara have almost *three* times the sales of the San Jose area (Figure 7.3). The analysis report is full of helpful information that Mel can use to further narrow his search for a new location.

Other Analytical Tools

You can use the analysis features in MarketPlace as a starting point for more extensive analysis with other Macintosh analytical software. You may want to do further analysis, combining data from MarketPlace with other market information you have or you may want to view MarketPlace data in a different manner. Because you can save all MarketPlace data in a tab-delimited ASCII format, it's easy to use it with other Macintosh software. For example, combining total market data from MarketPlace with your own customer data can give you a lot of information about your market penetration. You'll be able to see what percent of the total market you've managed to sell to.

```
┌─────────────────────────────────────────────────────────────────────┐
│  Custom Analysis                                                      │
│  ┌──────────────────────────────────────────────────────────────┐   │
│  │ 5-Dig Zip Name                    No. Bus Tot Sales Tot Emps Avg S│△ │
│  │ 95054     Santa Clara, CA             326   977.1    10856      │  │
│  │ 95112     San Jose, CA                432   313.0    10327      │  │
│  │ 94086     Sunnyvale, CA               338   572.5     9039      │  │
│  │ 95110     San Jose, CA                265   404.8     7694      │  │
│  │ 95008     Campbell, CA                443   311.2     7569      │  │
│  │ 95050     Santa Clara, CA             261   250.7     7029      │  │
│  │ 95113     San Jose, CA                253   493.5     6918      │  │
│  │ 95128     San Jose, CA                322   352.3     6895      │  │
│  │ 94301     Palo Alto, CA               311   354.4     6543      │  │
│  │ 95131     San Jose, CA                200   436.0     6532      │  │
│  │ 94043     Mountain View, CA           221  1049.9     6321      │  │
│  │ 95014     Cupertino, CA               287   317.0     6195      │  │
│  │ 95035     Milpitas, CA                215   318.8     5430      │  │
│  │ 94304     Palo Alto, CA               133   231.5     5366      │  │
│  │ 95126     San Jose, CA                272   444.8     4994      │  │
│  │ 94305     Palo Alto, CA                76    39.8     4949      │  │
│  │ 94306     Palo Alto, CA               238   162.7     4847      │  │
│  │ 95125     San Jose, CA                258   425.2     4642      │  │
│  │ 94087     Sunnyvale, CA               195    36.2     4224      │▽ │
│  └──────────────────────────────────────────────────────────────┘   │
│  All sales figures are in millions.   [ Print ]  [ Save ]   [  OK  ] │
└─────────────────────────────────────────────────────────────────────┘
```

Figure 7.3: The custom analysis shows that Santa Clara and San Jose have the largest number of employees but that sales are much lower in San Jose.

To make it easy to build on MarketPlace data, you can save the information you get from a MarketPlace analysis or from a MarketPlace list as a text file. You can then import the text file into virtually any other Macintosh software package to do more research.

Spreadsheets

Spreadsheets, such as Microsoft Excel or Lotus 1-2-3, can add a lot of power to your analysis. You can use a spreadsheet to do additional sorting of your data, to add additional information, or to compare results with customer information you already have. With a spreadsheet, you can quickly calculate percentages, totals, or any other number. You can also use the spreadsheet to customize an analytical report to a different type of layout.

Virtually all Macintosh spreadsheet products allow you to open MarketPlace text files as a spreadsheet. To do so, use the spreadsheet's

File Open command and select the text file you created in Market-Place. For some products, such as 1-2-3, you must indicate that you're looking for an ASCII text file, or it won't list the MarketPlace file in the file list. Once you select the ASCII file, the software brings it into the spreadsheet and places all the data into the proper rows and columns.

In addition to numerical analysis and number crunching, you can use a spreadsheet to generate graphs of the resulting data. While some people understand rows and columns of information, many will grasp your point more easily if you demonstrate it visually. Most spreadsheets can create a multitude of graph types, including line, bar, pie, and area charts. Depending on the spreadsheet you use, you can make the charts 3-D, change labels, add colors, and move around the information.

Mapping Software

Mapping software, such as GeoQuery or MapInfo allows you to analyze your data in a geographical context. You may find that ZIP codes and county names are meaningless to you. Because the data is all described in words, it's difficult to imagine what geographical impact this information might have. For example, what ZIP codes are next to 92174? How big is Dallas county? Are these places near each other? Mapping software helps you answer these types of questions.

Once you import the data, the mapping software puts the data on a map. For example, let's say that you have a list of all the semiconductor manufacturers in the United States. You can import the data into the mapping software, and it will generate a map of the United States with all of the semiconductor manufacturers pinpointed.

Mapping software imports data with some form of geographic content. Most of the packages priced below $1,000 calculate location based on five-digit ZIP code, although you can buy more expensive packages that will calculate location down to the street level. Data can generally be imported from the leading spreadsheet and database packages, as well as from text files. It's common for mapping software to come with one or two basic maps (usually a map of the United States). If you need more detailed maps, such as county maps, you can buy them from the software manufacturer.

CHAPTER SEVEN

Visualizing your own data or prospect data in terms of a map can be effective in several ways. You can use a map to help plan sales territories. Many packages allow you to create your own boundaries, so that you can examine how many prospects are available within any given territorial breakdown. You can use mapping software to help you plan a new distribution center. With the software, you can easily measure distances between your possible distribution centers locations and your retailers. By mapping your customer data, you can plan sales trips by seeing which companies are near each other.

Perhaps most powerfully, mapping software lets you see exactly where you have the greatest concentration of prospects and print out the results. There is nothing to compare with going to your boss with a recommendation for a new market, accompanied by a map showing exactly where all of the prospects are.

To see how all these analytical tools can work together, let's take a close look at the steps one sales director took to analyze her market.

Shannon Analyzes Her Market

Shannon Quinlan is the Director of Sales for the pipette division of Med-Lab Tools, the manufacturer of specialized laboratory tools. Her pipette division focuses on physical research facilities and pharmaceutical companies in the Midwest. Senior management is interested in growing Med-Lab Tools considerably in the next five years. They've asked Shannon to analyze the potential for growth in the pipette division and recommend a sales strategy to achieve the growth.

Shannon first decides to take a look at their current business, to learn the potential for growth in their present territories. She goes to MarketPlace Business to study the market. First she double-clicks on Location. She holds down the Option key and clicks on all the midwestern states Med-Lab Tools currently covers (WI, MN, IL, IN, IA, MO). With her territory defined, she clicks Return to Main Screen and goes into Type of Business. She double-clicks *D) Manufacturing* and scrolls to *28) Chemicals and Allied Products*. Shannon double-clicks again to open the category to the 4-digit SIC level. She includes both *2833-Medicinals and botanicals* and *2834-Pharmaceutical preparations.*

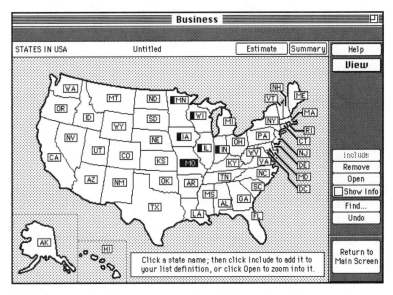

Figure 7.4: Shannon picks the states in her sales territory.

Because her other two business categories are in another section of the SIC code, Shannon uses the Find feature as a shortcut and types in *Physical research*. With *Physical research, commercial* highlighted, she clicks Find and finds herself in another part of the Type of Business hierarchy, at *8731) Commercial physical research*. She includes that category, as well as *8732) Noncommercial physical research*.

With her basic territory defined, Shannon clicks Analysis. Because she hasn't actually created this list yet, she clicks Build to tell MarketPlace to process the creation of the list. Once the list is created, she clicks the radio button next to Custom Analysis and chooses Annual Sales so she can look at the results by Sales grouping. She then clicks Analyze. The analysis takes some time, because each custom analysis has to be drawn from over 7 million records on the MarketPlace CD-ROM.

Ultimately, a screen pops up with analysis results similar to those in the accompanying table.

Custom Analysis

Sales Range	No. Bus	Tot Sales	Tot Emps	Avg Sales	Avg Emps
	905	0.0	67000	0.0	74.0
below .2	782	7.7	5334	0.0	6.8
.2 – .5	157	49.9	950	0.3	6.1
.5 – 1	81	69.4	1254	0.9	15.5
1 – 2.5	71	126.7	1583	1.8	22.3
2.5 – 5	31	119.8	1301	3.9	42.0
5 – 10	20	153.0	2035	7.7	101.8
10 – 25	21	356.4	1946	17.0	92.7
25 – 50	7	236.0	1597	33.7	228.1
50 – 100	7	455.2	1624	65.0	232.0
100 – 1,000	7	3159.7	2600	451.4	371.4
> 1,000	8	30508.0	25660	3813.5	3207.5

Already Shannon has a lot of information. First of all, for the majority of the businesses, the total sales are unknown. However, for those that are known, more than half sell less than $200,000 worth of goods per year. Although there aren't very many of them, the companies with the largest sales have captured a huge share of the overall sales in the category. Obviously, Med-Lab won't be able to grow without the aid of the largest companies.

Shannon now wants to compare this overall market information with the information she has on Med-Lab's customers. Because she can't manipulate her own data within MarketPlace, she chooses Save on the Analyze screen, names the file *Pipette Territory by Sales Revenue*, and saves it to her hard disk.

Shannon then opens this file into Microsoft Excel, a spreadsheet software package. She first erases the columns labeled *Total Employees, Average Sales*, and *Average Employees*. She then adds five columns between *Number of Businesses* and *Total Sales*, labeling them *Current Customers, Market Share, Percent of Customers, Pipette Sales*, and *Percent of Sales*. To the right of *Total Sales*, she adds a column *% of Total Sales*.

She then reviews her database of customers and approximates how many fall into each revenue category and how much money they bring in for her division. After entering the data and writing a few formulas, her spreadsheet appears (see accompanying table).

Pipette Division Analysis

Sales Range	# Bus	Current Customer	Market Share	% of Customer	Pipette Sales	% of Sales	Tot Sales	% of Sales
unknown	905							
below .2	782	150	19.2%	38.8%	10.1	2.0%	727.0	1.4%
.2 – .5	157	45	28.7%	11.6%	1.1	0.2%	49.9	2.3%
.5 – 1	81	72	88.9%	18.6%	1.8	0.4%	69.4	2.6%
1 – 2.5	71	45	63.4%	11.6%	3.7	0.7%	126.7	2.9%
2.5 – 5	31	26	83.9%	6.7%	3.2	0.6%	119.8	2.7%
5 – 10	20	16	80.0%	4.1%	3.4	0.7%	153.0	2.2%
10 – 25	21	10	47.6%	2.6%	12.3	2.4%	356.4	3.5%
25 – 50	7	4	57.1%	1.0%	10.3	2.0%	236.0	4.4%
50 – 100	7	7	100%	1.8%	25.0	5.0%	455.2	5.5%
100 – 1,000	7	5	71.4%	1.3%	122.00	24.2%	3159.7	3.9%
above 1,000	8	5	62.5%	1.3 %	312.00	61.8%	30508	1.0%
	2097	387	18.4%	100.0%	504.93	100.0%	35,961.1	1.4%

Based on the market share data, it looks as though Med-Lab has a strong penetration of many of the largest labs in its territory. Shannon also sees a strange drop with companies in the $10 million to $50 million sales break. Because these companies could be worth a lot of money, she would like to market to them aggressively. Shannon uses the spreadsheet to create a few graphs to help her visualize the situation and for inclusion in her final report.

To increase growth in their current territory, Shannon plans to recommend two steps. The first is to increase personal sales calls to the largest facilities, with a special emphasis on the companies they have been missing in the $10 million to $50 million area. The second is to eliminate all sales calls to the smaller players and replace them with a combined direct marketing and telemarketing campaign. Although the sales potential of these smaller companies is too small to warrant costly direct sales calls, Shannon sees a lot of sales potential, if Med-Lab can create an almost automated system of servicing these smaller accounts. Telemarketing could also be a good method of training new sales reps, to allow them to become familiar with Med-Lab products before sending them out into the world.

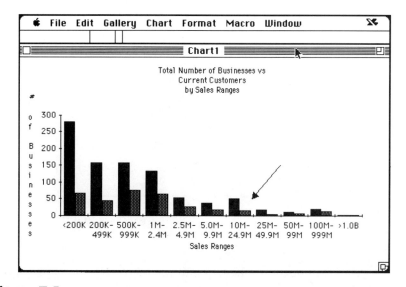

Figure 7.5: This bar chart was made in Microsoft Excel combining MarketPlace data with Med-Lab customer data.

However, if Med-Lab really wants to reach its growth goals, Shannon realizes the pipette division is going to have to move beyond its current territories. To evaluate where to go, Shannon combines MarketPlace data with mapping software.

First, she uses MarketPlace to create a list of prospects in neighboring states (MO, KY, OH, PA, MD, DE, WV, VA, ND, SD, NE). To use most mapping software, Shannon would now have to buy the list of names and export it as a text file. However, Shannon has GeoQuery, a mapping program with direct links to MarketPlace. When she asks GeoQuery to bring in data from MarketPlace, it can access the CD-ROM directly, even building a list that hasn't been built yet. This direct connection can be extremely powerful, because Shannon has the ability to create and map multiple lists in an iterative analytical process—without ever having to buy a list.

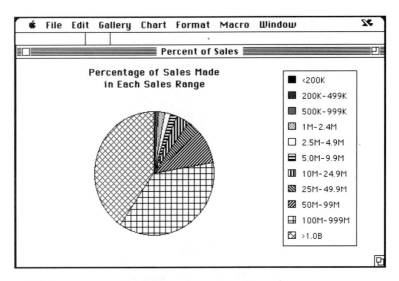

Figure 7.6: Microsoft Excel can also create helpful pie charts analyzing a market.

By loading all of the data into the map, Shannon gets a dramatic overview of her expansion possibilities. She has GeoQuery shade the states according to the number of prospects in each state (Figure 7.7). By viewing the shaded states, it's apparent that the biggest potential lies to the east—in Ohio, Pennsylvania, Virginia, and Maryland.

With her decision made to go east, Shannon decides to start planning sales territories. She creates a MarketPlace list for the eastern states that includes only those target businesses with sales over $5 million, the type of companies the reps will focus on. She again brings the data into GeoQuery, but this time she displays the data as pinpoints. She enlarges the eastern states, so that she can look at them more carefully (Figure 7.8)

With the distribution of prospects spread out in front of her, she begins to plan the optimal placement of one or more sales reps. Using GeoQuery's drawing tools, she creates differently shaped territories, then has GeoQuery generate reports of what is in her newly drawn territory (Figure 7.9). Before long, she creates two sales territories and selects where each rep should be located for optimal sales performance.

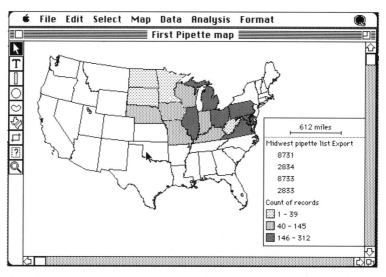

Figure 7.7: GeoQuery lets you map data from MarketPlace without buying the list, making it a powerful analytical tool.

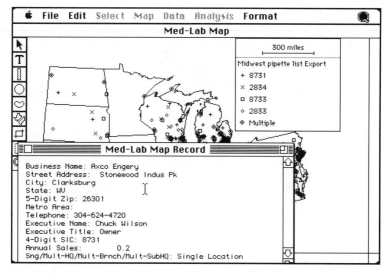

Figure 7.8: Every pinpoint on this GeoQuery may indicate another target business.

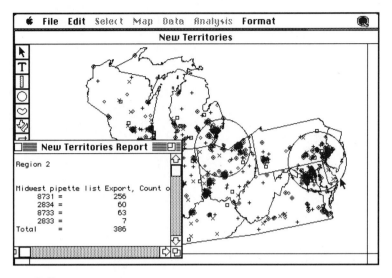

Figure 7.9: GeoQuery lets Shannon break down Region 2 according to the number of businesses in each 4-digit SIC code.

With these three Macintosh analytical tools and her own know-how, Shannon is now ready to create a powerful recommendation for the executives of Med-Lab, a report that will include hard data, charts, and maps to reinforce her recommendation. You should now have some idea of how you can use the same type of tools to analyze your markets more thoroughly.

8

Develop a Direct Mail Package

You've learned how to analyze your market, create a compelling offer, and pick the best potential customers. Of course, none of these will help increase sales or your market share if you don't deliver your offer to those prospects. In this chapter and Chapter 9, we show you how you can use desktop marketing to deliver your message via mail or telephone.

The tools of desktop marketing enable you to create and send effective direct mail pieces to your prospects and customers. The direct mail format allows you to select from a wide variety of creative options, and Macintosh software can help you to create these options.

When planning your direct mail package, think of direct mail as a paper sales contact—the letter is the conversation that extolls product benefits to the reader; the brochure is the demonstration that explains your product to the reader; and the reply form is the closing document that asks for the order or response. The biggest difference between direct mail and a salesperson is that it's a lot easier for a reader to put down or throw away your direct mail piece than it is to get rid of a salesperson with a mission. Therefore, the different elements of your direct mail package must work harder to keep the reader's attention.

Elements of Direct Mail Package

There are four elements to almost every direct mail package:

- Envelope
- Letter
- Brochure
- Reply Device

Some packages will expand on one element or another, and occasionally an element may be eliminated altogether. However, if you concentrate on these four elements, you will be far ahead. Later in the chapter, we go into detail about creating each of these elements.

Envelope

The envelope is the first thing your prospect sees. When you design your envelope, you're planning the first impression your company or offer will give the target. If that impression is bad, your mailing will end up in the trash before you can even begin your pitch.

Fortunately, you have human curiosity on your side. Most people will examine an envelope to discover who it's from and to guess what it's about. The trick is to create an envelope that invites the reader to open it, not trash it. If you're mailing to corporate offices, you may have the additional challenge of making it through the mail room and secretaries. It is their job to keep managers from receiving "frivolous" mailings. Often, they open envelopes and paper-clip the envelopes to the letter. For this reason, keep in mind that your business prospects may not review your envelope.

There are three envelope variables you can make use of with your direct mail effort:

- Text on the envelope (including the return address)
- The mailing address (addressing method)
- Postage

Letter

The letter is the sales pitch. Your success will be the result of a relevant, personal message delivered to individuals. The copy should be written with the target in mind. It should focus on the benefits of your product or service and what it can do for the reader, not on the wonders of your product or company.

Brochure

The brochure, or other enclosures, are like the sales support tools a salesperson uses. The brochure is not expected to be a personal piece like the letter. It is a company-to-individual piece that is usually mass-produced. Although it's not a personal piece, you should take care that the brochure supports the message of your letter. The brochure is also the demonstration portion of your mailing. Through the use of photographs, illustrations, testimonials and case histories, you allow the prospect to sample your product or service.

A brochure is not always required or advisable. For example, a brochure giving an overview of the product or service may provide insufficient information to make a sale, but enough information for readers to determine that the product or service isn't for them. Whether or not your mailing requires a brochure is directly related to the objective you've set for the program. If the objective is the direct sale of a product, the mailing should probably include a brochure explaining the details of the product or service. If you're trying to generate leads or store traffic, a brochure may be excessive.

Reply Device

The reply device is the most critical element of the direct mail package—it's where you ask for action. The result of this action will determine whether your direct mail effort is a success or not.

You should begin your creative process by focusing on the response device. By creating the response device, you finalize in your mind the ultimate action you want the prospect to take as a result of your direct mail. With the response device designed, you can create the letter and brochure around the action you want the reader to take. This sounds simple enough, but it's rarely done by newcomers to direct mail. More often than not, they spend weeks on the letter copy and put together a response device as an afterthought.

Types of Direct Mail Packages

The biggest challenge in direct mail is breaking through the clutter of mail that your prospect receives every day. You need some breakthrough creativity to stand out from the clutter. In some cases, breakthrough creativity may mean just getting your mailing read. This can be a real challenge in markets where there are a few buyers and many sellers. For example, hundreds, or even thousands, of companies want to reach the MIS managers of Fortune 1000 companies or the "rich" people who are fewer than one percent of the population. Imagine how much mail crosses their desks every day.

The following sections list a variety of direct mail package formats from which you can choose. Of course, you're not limited to these formats, but you'll probably find it useful to build from tried and true methods before you branch out to your own creative style.

Business Letters

Business letters are generally used for direct communication to business people and people at home. The business letter comes in a closed-faced, number 10 envelope addressed from one individual to another. It has no promotional copy on the outer envelope, and it shouldn't have address labels. In many cases, the letter is personalized. The letter inside is signed by the individual sending the letter. A brochure may or may not accompany the letter. There is a low-key response device.

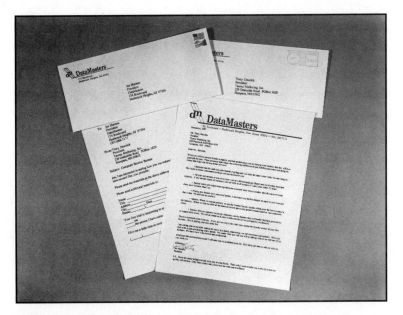

Figure 8.1: Although it doesn't look very remarkable, this type of business letter can often get through to business people more easily.

Letter Packages

A letter package is a direct mail promotion that uses the same size envelope used for business letters. It can range from an invitation-size envelope to a number 10, regular business-size envelope. The envelope often has a window. Letter packages generally carry personalization on only one piece of the package; the outer envelope for nonwindow envelopes, or the letter or response device for window envelopes. A typical letter package mailing includes:

- The letter, which is generically addressed to "Dear Executive" or "Dear Neighbor"

- A brochure

- Response device

- Business reply envelope—if the response device isn't a business reply card

The window letter package often proves to be more cost efficient than the business letter format, because it costs less to put together. The cost savings come from putting the name and address on only one element of the direct mail package. This in turn leads to easier addressing and time savings, because you don't need to match different components of the mailing package.

Using a window envelope can be the most efficient method of creating a letter package. By positioning the name and address on the inside material in such a way that it also shows through the window, you can create the image of personalization in several places for the cost of doing it only once. Because the window envelope makes it clear that your mailing isn't a personal letter, you can use teaser copy on the outer envelope to help involve the reader with the package and encourage them to open the envelope.

When a window envelope is used, the address label is often put on the response device to make it easier for a prospect to respond. With the address label already on the response device, the prospect doesn't have to write down as much. Because you have placed the label on the response device, it can also help you capture accurate coding information about any prospect who responds.

Figures 8.2 and 8.3 show you how different two letter packages can be.

Figure 8.2: This businesslike letter package was designed using Microsoft Works and QuarkXPress.

Oversize Packages

Any mailing package that's larger than a number 10 business envelope is considered an oversized mailing by the Postal Service. The most important value of the oversize package is its size. A lot of people will pay more attention to and handle oversized packages more carefully just because they're bigger. You're taking subtle advantage of the notion that bigger is better. Oversize mailings are becoming much less common because of all the new postal regulations and the inability of automated machines to handle different size envelopes. Some of the oversize packages that are still being used are mock-ups of overnight mail envelopes, to imply urgency.

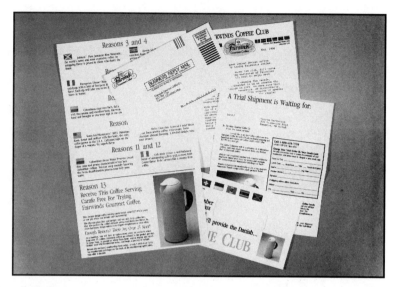

Figure 8.3: This household-oriented appeal is much more graphically oriented, although it too was designed using Microsoft Works and QuarkXPress.

You would be wise to bring a mock-up of your oversized package to the Post Office before you actually produce it. There are rules governing the dimensions of larger packages to be sure that they can fit postal machines and thus reduce handling costs. It's possible you may be able to save yourself an additional handling fee just by changing one feature of your design. In fact, if you follow the rules, you can often send an oversized package via third-class mail at the same price as a letter. Unfortunately, you will always have to pay extra for a bigger package going via first-class mail.

Dimensional Mailing

Dimensional mailings are large in a three-dimensional sense. A box, tube, or even an envelope containing something thick is considered a dimensional mailing. These packages or thick letters tend to come up on top of everyone's mail pile. The use of a dimensional mailing can be effective in breaking through to a prospect you have been trying to reach. Because everyone likes to get packages, prospects tend to be a bit more curious about the contents. The mailing can be directly related to your offer or just a different approach to get the prospect's attention.

Figure 8.4: Planned Parenthood hopes to get the attention of recipients by using this large-sized envelope.

One company sent a six-gallon can of popcorn labeled with a fake OSHA placard to presidents of industrial companies in the metal grinding industry. The purpose of the mailing was to generate leads for a $40,000 filtration system. Sales were made to 14 percent of those who received the popcorn. The sales reps found the prospects remembered the package up to a year after receiving it—now that's a breakthrough mailing!

Figure 8.5: It's understandable why this mailing was paid attention to by its recipients.

Although dimensional mailings have the highest rate of being opened and reviewed, a dimensional mailing doesn't ensure sales to pay for the mailing. Once prospects review the materials, it's your offer that will convince them to act.

Self-Mailers

It's possible to forgo the outer envelope entirely by using a self-mailer. With a self-mailer, you print all the elements of your promotion on one sheet of paper and fold it to a size that can be mailed. Self-mailers are generally inexpensive to produce; they get your target audience involved without opening an envelope; and they allow you to state your offer quickly.

Response Devices with Self-Mailers

When you use a self-mailer, the response device must be part of the single sheet of paper. Generally, the response device is a business reply card printed on the back part of the mailer. The edges of the business reply card are perforated so that the recipient can easily detach the card and mail it.

Because the reply device is part of the self-mailer, you're often limited to printing it on paper stock that's .007 inches thick, since Postal Service regulations require any mailed item to be at least that thickness. Unfortunately, this stock can be expensive and somewhat unwieldy for printing and folding. As an alternative, you can use paper that is .0035 inches thick and require the respondent to fold the reply device in half to achieve the .007 inch requirement. If you go with folding the response device, include a glue strip so that the respondent doesn't staple it closed. Because staples get caught in the Post Office machines, the Post Office may ask you to pay extra return postage if respondents use staples.

Most self-mailers are designed so that the response device doesn't carry the original address label. Figure 8.6, designed with QuarkXPress, shows this approach. There's an alternative format that includes personal addressing and coding both on the face of the mailer and on the response device. This method is preferable, because it makes it easier for you to capture all of the coding information. Figure 8.7 is an example of this format. If you must get address information in the label format, you must use the one-label format. However, if you can arrange to get the names electronically and your printer can handle it, you can use the two-label technique.

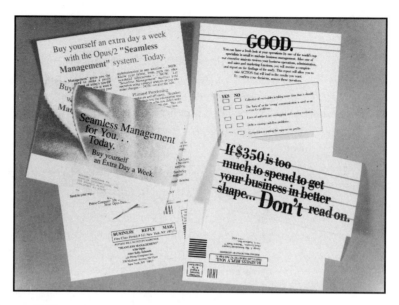

Figure 8.6: Anyone receiving this self-mailer must fill out all the information on the reply card, since the address label isn't on it.

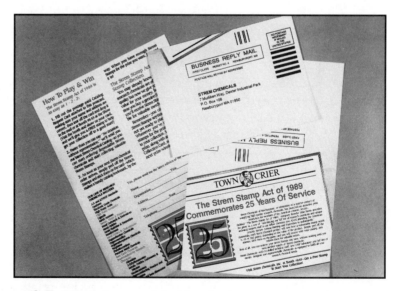

Figure 8.7: Using the same label for the initial address and the response card is less common.

Lettergrams

The historically familiar yellow format of the Western Union telegram has high deliverability and readership, because telegrams originally were used only for urgent and important messages. This format has been copied, expanded, and used by many mailers in order to capitalize on the high rate of opening and reading mailings that come in this format.

Copy for lettergrams is usually written abruptly to simulate the terse format of most telegrams. The lettergram should contain only a letter—no insert—to maintain consistency with the telegram format. You can design and print your own lettergram forms using desktop publishing software or you can buy preprinted forms in many office supply stores.

Although they may seem a bit corny, lettergrams can work very successfully, even with high-ticket items. In the early 1980s, a destination resort decided to sell half of its units as co-ops. The resort mailed 45,000 lettergrams a week, 40 weeks a year, for three years. Within three years, they had sold all the co-op units. The resort tested the mailings against five or six other formats over the course of the three years, but nothing ever pulled better than the lettergram.

Catalogs

The catalog is one of the most widely used direct mail selling vehicles. There are approximately 6,000 consumer catalogs in the United States and an unknown number of business catalogs selling equipment parts, valves, paper, etc. Unlike solo direct mail, a catalog is a device that offers a potential buyer the choice of more than one product or service in the same promotion. Think of a catalog as a shopping vehicle, while direct mail is a targeted sales call (Figure 8.8).

A catalog doesn't have to be an expensive, four-color magazine such as the ones offered by L.L. Bean or Spiegel. For example, card decks are a less expensive form of catalog marketing. With a card deck, offerings from many different companies are printed on 3 x 5 cards, gathered together in an envelope or cellophane wrapper, and mailed to a specific list. The card deck is extremely easy to respond to, because each card also serves as its own business reply card. Generally, card decks are organized by organizations that rent lists, such as magazines or trade associations.

Figure 8.8: Catalogs come in all shapes and sizes.

How to Create a Direct Mail Package from Your Desktop

The varieties of direct mail are immense, from a simple postcard to a full-color catalog. Deciding what type of a direct mail package to choose begins with the market information you have obtained and the objectives you want to achieve. By now, you should have a mental image of whom you want as customers. You have defined and selected your target list with thought to their personalities and buying motivation. Their personality styles and buying motivation should guide the development of your direct mail format, copy, and graphics.

Except for the outer envelope and any reply envelope, each element of the direct mail package should be able to stand alone if separated from the package. Each element should contain your product benefits, your offer, and a way to respond to you by mail and/or phone. A mailing may be disassembled in the prospect's office or on the kitchen counter. Because the prospect may save only a portion of the mailing, let each piece sell for you.

Create an Envelope

It takes a reader five seconds to decide whether or not to open a direct mail package. The envelope must present the appropriate image to convince your prospect to open it. The type of design you use depends greatly on whether you're mailing to a business or a household. As you think about the design, imagine what your prospects are doing as they examine your mailing.

- People in households are standing in the kitchen, reviewing your mailing within five minutes of coming home from work.

- Small business owners look at your mailing as they go through the mail looking for checks or purchase orders.

- Corporate employees review your mailing while sitting at their desks.

Teaser copy or teaser graphics can be used on the outer envelope to get the reader to open the envelope. When developing the teaser, think of the motivators you're using in the offer. Such words as *Free gift inside*, *Limited Time Offer*, and *Super Savings*, may be clichés but they have the right spirit. Copy that attracts the curiosity of your prospect will do an excellent job of getting him to open the envelope.

If you're trying to make your piece look like a personal letter or a business letter, do *not* use teaser copy or graphics. Teaser copy can be particularly harmful in a business setting where mailroom clerks have been advised to throw away all direct mail pieces.

Addressing the Envelope with the Macintosh

Although it may seem like a small part of a mailing, addressing the envelopes will probably be one of your greatest trials of desktop marketing. If you've ever tried to properly align labels or feed envelopes into your printer, you know how tedious and difficult it can be.

One of the first decisions about addressing the envelope is whether you should use mailing labels or print the address directly on the envelope. The decision depends on to whom you're mailing, whether you're doing the addressing yourself, and from where you're getting the names.

With a business letter mailing, it's better not to use an address label on the envelope. Address labels are generally a different color from the envelope. More often than not, they're affixed to the envelope a little askew. These small incongruities point to the fact that this letter has not received the type of attention most business letters get. If you must use labels for your mailing, don't try to mimic a business letter; spend your money and efforts on other elements of the mailings.

Label Aid

Avery/Dennison sells clear labels you can use with a laser printer. With clear labels, the color of the envelope shows through the label, so that it looks almost as if you've typed the name and address directly on the envelope. These labels could be an alternative if you like the look of a business letter but must use labels.

If you're using MarketPlace to generate your mailing list, you can produce mailing labels or print on envelopes directly from the software. To do so, you first must buy your list, indicating you want you use it. Once you have bought the list, the Mailing Labels option will be activated. Click on the Mailing Labels icon to begin the process.

With the Format menu, you have a choice of 64 different mailing label formats and sizes, including brand name Avery labels, index cards, and envelopes (Figure 8.9). As with any other Macintosh software, you can also choose the font type and font size you want on the labels. Be careful when choosing fonts and sizes that you choose a size that will fit on your selected label.

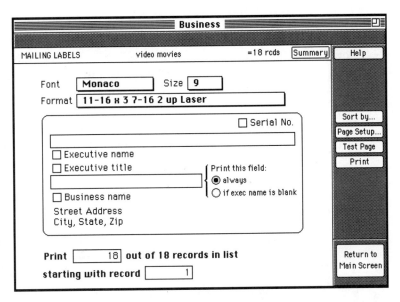

Figure 8.9: The MarketPlace Mailing Labels section gives you a lot of control over the appearance of your mailing label.

MarketPlace Business allows you to place a serial number in the upper right-hand corner of the label, if you want to have a unique number on each label. There is a space at the top of the label to type in a universal entry or a special code for each specific list.

When you get to the actual address portion of the label, you can choose whether you want to use the executive's name or prefer to use a standardized title such as *Marketing Director* or *Head Purchasing Agent.* You'll get the best results with a standardized label if you're as specific as possible with the title, even if it means putting something as obvious as, *Person Who Selects Long Distance Services.* MarketPlace also gives you the ability to enter a generic title *only* if the executive name is missing from the record. For example, you can have MarketPlace put *Chief Executive* if the actual name is missing. Considering that anywhere from 10 to 50 percent of the records will lack an executive name, it's always a good idea to specify an alternative title.

Before you begin to print labels using MarketPlace, be sure to use the Test Page feature. This allows you to put your envelopes or labels in the printer to make sure your selected layout will fit properly and is aligned properly. If you discover a problem after your actual list starts printing, you must start all over again, wasting a lot of labels and envelopes.

If you want to have more control over the creation of your labels and envelopes than MarketPlace allows, or you're doing a mailing with your own customer database, there are specialty label generation products you can buy. MacEnvelope Plus by Synex and Mac LabelPro by Avery/Dennison allow you a tremendous amount of flexibility in the entire design of a label or envelope. If you plan to use teaser copy or graphics, you should seriously consider using either of these products, because they allow you to copy your graphics right to the envelope or label. You can use label software in combination with your own customer database or any other electronic list, if the names are in tab-delimited text format. This format can be easily imported by either label-generation product.

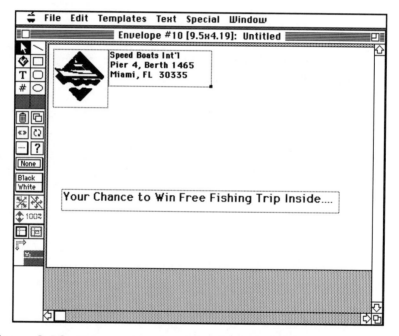

Figure 8.10: You can get quite elaborate with MacEnvelope Plus, generating teaser copy at the same time as the address.

> ## Laser Printing Envelopes
>
> If you're going to address a lot of envelopes using a laser printer, consider buying envelopes made especially for laser printers. Ordinary envelopes have an excessive amount of glue, which can gum up the works of a laser printer.

Postage

A key part of the envelope is the type of postage you use. Postage choices impact several areas: mailing costs, mailing time, and package impression. There are three methods of applying postage to a mailing:

- *Preprinted:* The type of postage is printed on the mailing piece as part of the printing process.

- *Metered:* The postage meter applies a postage imprint directly to the piece or to a meter strip to put on the piece.

- *Stamped:* Actual stamps are affixed to the mailing.

Preprinted postage is fine for promotional mail but will kill you if you're trying to make your piece look like a business or personal letter. When was the last time anyone you know sent you something with pre-printed postage?

If you're simulating a business letter, use metered postage; most businesses use postage meters in their day-to-day operations. On the other hand, stamps can be an attention-getting device on a business mailing, since people see them so rarely in business. It gives the impression of much greater personal involvement.

For household mailings, metered postage supports an official-looking promotional format. If you're trying to mimic a personal letter, use stamps.

There are two basic postage rates for direct mail:

- *First class:* The cost is fixed for the first ounce and the package is restricted in size to no larger than 6 1/8 by 11 1/2 inches and no smaller than 3 1/2 by 5 inches. Additional weight costs extra per ounce up to a maximum of 12 ounces.

- *Third class or bulk:* The cost is fixed for the first 3.3667 ounces with no size constraints. Additional weight costs extra per ounce up to 16 ounces maximum. A minimum number of pieces is required for a third class mailing.

Each of these two classes of postage also has reduced rates for presorting your mail by ZIP, tying the mail in ZIP bundles, and preparing bag bundles. Check with your local post office for the ways you can reduce your mailing costs.

Postage can be a major expense for direct mail efforts, and first-class costs almost twice as much as third-class. If you're mailing small quantities at a time, you can only mail via first-class. To mail third-class, you need at least 200 pieces, a permit from your post office, and a completed postal form.

The speed with which you want your pieces delivered may also affect your decision to use first- or third-class postage. First-class mail is normally delivered within three to five days. Third-class mail can take as long as 15 workdays to be delivered nationwide.

Speed of delivery can also be affected by whether or not you take advantage of some of the Postal Service's new technologies. ZIP+4 was initially developed to help the Postal Service speed delivery. Many list rental companies have assigned ZIP+4 codes to their addresses or will do it for you at a minimal cost. If you can use a ZIP+4, it's definitely worth your while—if only for faster delivery.

If you use MacEnvelope Plus to create your envelopes, you can take advantage of several of its features to speed up mail delivery. To ensure that your addresses can be read by the Postal Service's optical character readers (OCR), MacEnvelope Plus will print labels in OCR-readable format. In addition, MacEnvelope Plus can automatically generate and place a bar code on all your pieces based on the ZIP code. This bar code enables the Postal Service machines to quickly sort the mail to its proper destination. And, if you're using third-class postage, there's an additional discount if you prebarcode all of your envelopes.

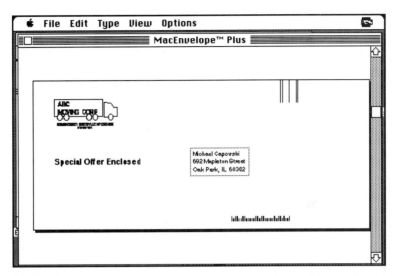

Figure 8.11: MacEnvelope generated the barcode on this envelope by analyzing the address ZIP code.

Besides price and speed, the other difference between first-class and third-class is what happens to mail that is undeliverable. With first-class, mail will be forwarded for 12 months if the former addressees have left a forwarding address. After 12 months, the mail will be returned to you with an address correction attached. This can be particularly helpful in maintaining your in-house lists. Getting returns from MarketPlace lists or rented lists may not help you maintain a database, but it does give you a sense of the true size of your mailing. Ordinarily, third-class mail is thrown away if the person is no longer at the address. For an additional fee, you can request that all undeliverable mail be returned to you with the address correction.

Create Your Letter

A successful letter is one that has a relevant, personal message for the individual receiving it. You have 10 seconds to get their attention and create involvement.

In his book, *Successful Direct Marketing Methods* (3d ed., Lincolnwood, Ill.: Crain), Bob Stone summarizes several key points to the direct mail letter:

Promise a benefit in your headline or first paragraph—your most important benefit. You simply can't go wrong by leading off with the most important benefit to the reader. Some writers believe in the slow buildup. But most experienced writers I know favor making the important point first.

Immediately enlarge on your most important benefit. This step is crucial. Many writers come up with a great lead, then fail to follow through. Or they catch attention with their heading, but then take two or three paragraphs to warm up to their subject. The reader's attention is gone! Try hard to elaborate on your most important benefit right away, and you'll build up interest fast.

Tell the reader specifically what he or she is going to get. It's amazing how many letters lack details on such basic product features as size, color, weight, and sales terms. Perhaps the writer is so close to his proposition he assumes the reader knows all about it. A dangerous assumption! And when you tell the reader what he or she's going to get, don't overlook the intangibles that go along with your product or service. For example, he's getting a smart appearance in addition to a pair of slacks, knowledge in addition to a 340-page book.

Tell the reader what she might lose if she doesn't act. As noted, people respond affirmatively either to gain something they do not possess or to avoid losing something they already have. Here's a good spot in your letter to overcome human inertia—imply what may be lost if action is postponed. People don't like to be left out. A skillful writer can use this human trait as a powerful influence in his or her message.

Rephrase your prominent benefits in your closing offer. As a good salesperson does, sum up the benefits to the prospect in your closing offer. This is the proper prelude to asking for action. This is where you can intensify the prospect's desire to have the product. The stronger the benefits you can persuade the reader to recall, the easier it will be for him or her to justify an affirmative decision.

When you're writing your letter, use the language and style of your prospects. Write as if you are having a one-to-one conversation with the reader and keep your words simple and your sentences short. Try to avoid the jargon of your industry, since no one knows it but other people in the industry.

Once they begin writing the letter, many desktop marketers want to know how long it should be. In the direct mail business, there's a constant battle between those who advocate long letters and those who think short is better. The answer is—make your letter long enough to deliver your offer, but not so long that it becomes boring. As a further guide, take a clue from your target customers. If their jobs entail a lot of reading, they may be attuned to long letters. On the other hand, people who are on the go may prefer short messages. To determine whether a short or long letter is better for your targets, try both in test mailings and see which is more successful.

P.S.—What Your Letter Needs

Consider adding a postscript at the end of your letter. The P.S. is often the most read section of a letter. Studies have shown that a prospect looks at the letterhead to see who the message is coming from, the salutation to see if he is the right person for the message, the signature to see if it's from someone he wants to listen to, and the P.S. right below the signature. If the postscript doesn't grab the reader with the biggest benefits he will receive, or tease him into reading the rest of the letter, the whole direct mail package is headed for the trash.

Make a Macintosh Letter

You can use any Macintosh word processing software package to create your letter. Once you type the letter on the computer, you can change and modify the copy as many times as necessary. In addition, you can make modifications to the letter to fit different lists. For example, if you're doing a mailing to doctors and lawyers, you can first write a letter that focuses on benefits to doctors. Then, take the same letter and modify it to focus on benefits to lawyers.

You may face one temptation when you use a Macintosh word processor for your direct mail letter. The Macintosh makes it very simple to use multiple fonts, different font sizes, boldface, italics, and other such graphic enhancements to the text. Although it *is* a good idea to use bold, italics, or underlining to focus the reader's eye—too many text enhancements turn a letter into a brochure. When you use boldface or italics, enhance key words, not entire sections. If you underline an entire paragraph, it becomes visual mush and readers won't focus on it. As a rule of thumb—if you have more than four uses of boldface, italics, or underlining on one page, you've overdone it.

Once you finish composing the letter, there's a simple test you can do to check its selling effectiveness. Use global search and replace to substitute your competitor's name and product wherever your name and product currently appear. If your letter could sell your competitor's product just as well as it sells yours, you haven't differentiated yourself. Make sure your sales pitch works only for you.

To Personalize or Not to Personalize?

Once you've composed the perfect direct mail letter, you're still left with one major decision—do you want to personalize it with the prospect's name and address. Putting a prospect's name on the letter immediately attracts the eye. It serves as an element of recognition that increases involvement. Direct mail can be personalized more than any other marketing medium, but personalization is not always possible or advisable.

If you are using your own mailing list or have received a mailing list in an electronic format, it's relatively easy to personalize any letter you create with almost any word processing software. First, the list of names and addresses should be in a tab-delimited text file. Next, start up your word processing software and open the newly composed direct mail letter. Position the insertion point the first place where you want the personalized information to be placed in the letter. Next, call up the merge feature in the word processor to indicate what information about the prospect should be positioned where the cursor is. Most merge features let you indicate which document holds the name and address information and then select the name of the type of information you want—last name, state, and so on.

What's a Tab-Delimited Text File?

Virtually all personal computers and word processing software is capable of understanding ASCII text or text files. An ASCII text file consists only of the electronic symbols for characters, including the electronic symbols for spaces and tabs. If you receive a text file, there will be no formatting, different fonts, or special spacing, since all of these are controlled by the individual word processor.

A tab-delimited text file is usually a database, such as a database of names and addresses. The name and address information for each person is in a separate row. Each piece of information is in a column, such as a first name column, a ZIP code column, and so on. In order for the word processor to understand where one piece of information ends and another begins, there must be a tab symbol between the entries. A typical tab-delimited text file might look something like this:

F_Name	L_Name	Street	City	State	ZIP
Michelle	Grady	807 Shoreline Rd	Chicago	IL	60610
Jennifer	Ganshirt	456 Mission Viejo Rd.	Belen	NM	87002
Cathy	Morelock	36 Eatonia St	Allston	MA	02134
Mark	Hansen	P.O. Box 1354	Minneapolis	MN	55354

With the simplest form of personalization, you merge the name, address, and salutation portion of the letter (Figure 8.12). It's also possible to sprinkle the person's name or any other piece of information throughout the letter. If you're unsure exactly how long the inserted information might be, position the merge indicator at the end of a line so that a particularly long piece of merged information won't print over any other words in the letter.

There is a danger in using personalization. You know no list is going to be 100 percent accurate. With almost any list you use, anywhere from 5 percent to 20 percent of your list may be out-of-date by the time you use the list. These inaccuracies can be particularly blaring if you use personalization techniques. Many people will overlook inaccuracies in the address on the envelope but may feel you are sloppy if the inaccuracies are also in the letter. Of course, the vast majority of your letters *will* be correct, so you have to weigh the potential negative reaction.

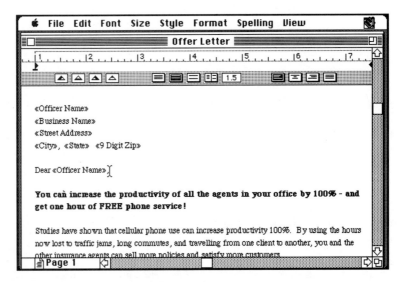

Figure 8.12: This letter merges address information with the basic text of the letter.

You should be more careful of using personalization with mailings to business. Since personnel turn over so quickly in companies, you're more likely to make an addressing mistake. This is less of a problem if you are going after small businesses. When you mail to a large company, you may be better off using a title such as *Person Responsible for Office Supplies.* However, you should definitely use personalization as much as possible when mailing to a home address.

Personalization Printing Techniques

There are two techniques used to print personalized letters:

- Full print
- Match print

With full print, you print the entire copy of the letter with each new address you're sending to. You can use either an ImageWriter or a LaserWriter, although you'll find the LaserWriter generates higher quality results. With match print, a commercial printer or copy shop preprints the body copy of the letter and then you overprint the address and salutation on the preprinted letters. This method can save a lot of time if you're using an ImageWriter, because there are fewer lines to print. There's no time savings with match printing if you use a laser printer, because laser printers take the same amount of time to print every page of text, no matter how much text is on the page.

If you use the match-print process, make sure the commercial printer uses the same font styles and sizes for the letter copy as you'll be using for the names and addresses. If you plan to type the addresses with an ImageWriter, have the printer use dark grey ink instead of black ink when printing the body copy. The ribbons in ImageWriters fade very quickly from black to grey, so using dark grey ink will insure a better match. Also, always order more preprinted letters than you need, so that you have plenty available as you work out the proper printer alignment for adding the personalization.

Whether you use full print or match print, you can still speed up your efforts by preprinting several elements. If your letter has a second page without personalization, you can print all of those ahead of time. For a one-page letter, you can also prepare letterhead with the appropriate signature already printed. Make sure you know how long your letter will be before you print up thousands of signature sheets; you don't want to find out you don't have enough room for the letter copy *and* the signature. Print the signature in basic process blue ink, for the least expensive, good-looking results.

Create a Brochure

The brochure you develop should support the message of the letter. Don't introduce new points that aren't already in the letter or you may end up confusing your prospect.

Because the brochure is the demonstration part of your package, it's the place for graphics. The brochure should look clean and easy to understand. Again, try not to overdo it with fonts and type sizes. Limit the type to one or two fonts, or you'll drive the reader crazy. Also, remember the value of white space. You don't have to fill every inch of your brochure. If you leave plenty of white space around the text and graphics, you give a more professional appearance.

If you can afford it, you should certainly use color in your brochure. It doesn't have to be a four-color brochure; two colors can be very effective and powerful. Color adds emotion to any pitch, even if it's for very seemingly mundane products. For years and years, catalogs for industrial manufacturers of products such as hand-carts and casters used only black-and-white catalogs to sell the products. However, in the mid-1980s, they all went to four-color. Why? The first company that switched to color increased sales 25 percent.

There is an exception to the use of color. If you're using a hard-luck pitch, you may want to do your entire package in black and white. A philanthropic organization discussing hard times and its desperate need for money may make the greatest impact with a very simple, plain mailing.

The size of the brochure doesn't really matter. You should view the size decision as another creative decision. If you want a reader's undivided attention, you can create broadsides like the ones Time-Life Books uses. When you unfold one of their brochures, it captures your undivided attention. By dominating the space around the recipient, you can dominate his/her attention. You can also gain reader involvement by adding interesting folds, flaps, or bends.

Make a Macintosh Brochure

The creation and layout of a brochure is easy with any of the desktop publishing software packages for the Macintosh. Desktop publishing packages allow you to combine text and graphics easily on one or more pages. If you plan to do complex brochures or you have some design background, you should consider using top desktop publishing packages, such as Aldus PageMaker or QuarkXPress. Otherwise, consider simpler packages such as Aldus Personal Press or Letraset's Ready, Set, Go!

Figure 8.13: You can layout a complete brochure using desktop publishing software like QuarkXPress.

Laying out a brochure yourself is trickier than just typing out the text. Desktop publishing software lets you create multiple columns and handle exactly how the text should flow. You can control a lot more elements than you can with a standard word processor, such as the spacing between words, exact margin sizing, and spacing. Perhaps most importantly, desktop publishing lets you combine text and all forms of graphics in your brochure.

This factor is crucial, because you depend on your brochure to show what your product looks like. You can use either photographs or illustrations. Generally, you should use photos if you have a fairly straightforward product or if you want to emphasize the appearance of the product (clothes, artwork, and so on). Use illustrations if you have a complex product or if you need to illustrate the processes your product or service follow.

The difficulty of actually putting graphical images into your brochure depends on what type of images you're using. Desktop publishing software can import illustrations you've created in draw or paint software programs. There are also dozens of Clip Art packages with large collections of illustrations and graphics already created by artists and designers. You can copy any illustrations you need from a clip-art collection and paste them into your brochure.

If you're using photos and plan to produce the brochure yourself, you have to put the photos through a scanner to create an electronic image. With the proper paint software, you can then edit the photo just as you would any illustration. If you don't want to invest in a scanner for your company, you can probably find a desktop publishing firm or graphics company nearby that will scan photos for a small fee. The more advanced desktop publishing software lets you create extremely sophisticated catalogs combining photos, graphics, and text (Figure 8.14).

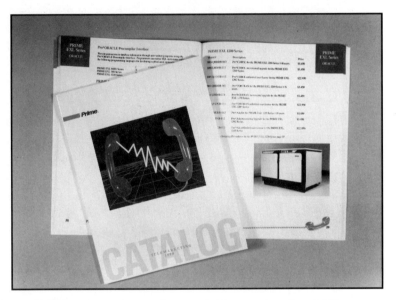

Figure 8.14: This entire catalog was laid out using QuarkXPress.

If your mailing isn't too large, you can print all the brochures and fold them yourself. Otherwise, use a printout of your brochure design as the mechanical for professional printers. The printers use the mechanical to create plates for their printing presses. If you want the brochure to be in color, work with the printer to learn how to mark up the mechanical to indicate where the color should go.

Scanners

A scanner is a peripheral for the Macintosh or some other computer. You use it to convert a graphical image into an electronic format. The scanner passes light over the image and evaluates light and dark areas of the image. It then converts the light and dark areas into a collection of electronic information.

The quality of the electronic image will vary tremendously depending on the scanner you use and the type of software the scanner uses to interpret the image. In general, the greater the resolution (dots per inch) and the greater the grey-scale capabilities, the better the image.

TIP

If you're not printing the brochure yourself, indicate where in the brochure the photos should go and give them to the printer.

Even if you don't feel comfortable designing and creating brochures on your own, you can experiment with a number of ideas on the Macintosh and then pass them on to a graphics designer. You will find designers come up with much better results if you give them good direction—which can be easier to give if you try to do it yourself first.

Create a Response Device

The response device should be easy to understand, and direct about the action you want the prospect to take. Ask for the action and nothing else. If you introduce new concepts or new choices at this point, you give the prospect something to object to or to get confused by. The response device isn't the proper place to give new information; that leaves your prospects with unanswered questions.

Many people skip the letter and brochure and go directly to the response device. They treat the response device as a summary of your offering—what you're selling, how much it costs, and what they need to do to get it. Since the response device may be your only point of contact with your prospect, he or she should be able to understand what you're offering by reading the response device alone.

Avoid Commitment

The response device shouldn't look like a legal document. Anything that looks like a legally binding commitment will diminish your returns dramatically. If your offer requires some legal commitment, save the legalities for the follow-up to the initial response. By then, the respondent has already made some commitment to your offer and is less likely to be scared away.

Every response device must have a space for a customer's name and return address. Some of the direct mail package alternatives make this section very easy for the respondent by placing the mailing label on the response device. This ensures that you get correct information and any coding information you may have placed on the label. In addition to the name and address area, you should have one section where the respondent has to make a mark showing interest in your offer. This often consists of one or more check boxes next to something like *Please send me...* or *Yes, I want to support...*. It helps to have the user take some action (Figure 8.15).

If your offer is tied to ordering a product or service, be sure you have an area for the respondent to indicate how he or she plans to pay for the product or service. This may include some of the following options: C.O.D, money order, check enclosed, bill me later, or credit card. In general, you should not ask for excessive information from your respondents. Most people know that you only need their names, addresses, and money to send them a product, brochure, or whatever else they're asking for. If you ask for a lot of additional information (usually to enhance your own customer list), you'll begin to decrease your response rate. You can usually get away with a few related-looking questions—but don't push it. Chances are, a lot of respondents will simply skip those questions.

The response vehicle should display your phone number prominently—this helps improve response rates. Rather than fill out a form, many prospects will call you instead. The prospect's impulse to call the phone number on the response device quickly creates a personal relationship between you and the prospect and improves your chances of making a sale. However, don't depend entirely on telephone responses. Although 80 percent of prospects will call if given the opportunity, there's still a small but important percentage that prefers correspondence.

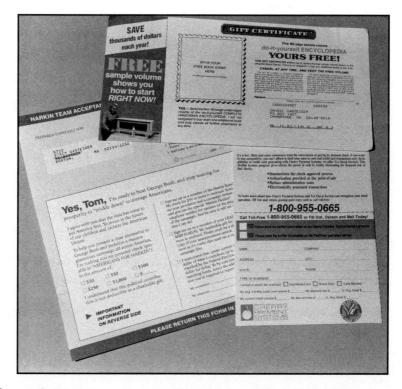

Figure 8.15: These response devices use a variety of techniques, including stickers, check boxes, and using the initial label.

Types of Response Devices

You have three options for getting a response device back to you: a business reply envelope, a business reply card, and the respondent's own postage.

The most common response method is the prepaid business reply envelope (BRE). To use either of the business reply formats, you must first apply to the post office for a reply mail number. The post office will give you the required layout for any BRE. You've probably seen the variations many times—the bars to the left of the postage and the bar codes at the bottom of the envelope. The size and spacing of those bars are crucial, because they are read by the automating machines at the post office. Since the BRE is more of an administrative piece, it's not worth the time or creative efforts to try to make it any fancier. Black printing on a white envelope is fine for an effective BRE.

Paying for Business Reply

When you apply for a business reply number, the postal service requires that you give them an initial deposit. The size of the deposit depends on the volume of mail you're expecting. Once the business reply envelopes begin coming in, the postal service subtracts the cost of each piece of mail that comes in from your initial deposit. The post office will then bill you for new deposits as the first one runs out.

An alternative to the BRE is the Business Reply Card (BRC), which is very much like a postcard. The response information is printed on one side of the card and the business reply information is printed on the other. BRCs can be effective if you need very little information, and you want to make it extremely easy to reply.

Some people feel uncomfortable responding with BRCs, however, because the information they give you is exposed for anyone to see. In particular, people are unwilling to give you their credit card numbers when they know it will be exposed for any postal employee to read. Obviously, you also can't expect anyone to send you a check if there is nothing for the respondent to put the check into. Also keep in mind that you must print your BRC on paper stock .007 inches thick or more to keep within Postal Service regulations, and that this can increase your printing costs.

The third and final reply option is to ask respondents to supply their own postage. You can either include a self-addressed envelope with no postage or no envelope at all. This method is certain to decrease your response rate, but any responses you *do* get will be more highly qualified. If a prospect takes the time and money to respond, you know that prospect has a definite interest in your product or service.

If you're mailing to businesses, you may want to avoid using either BREs or BRCs. They're a dead giveaway that the piece is direct mail and can make it harder to get the piece across the secretary's desk. For businesses, you may just want to include a self-addressed envelope. Prepaying postage doesn't seem as critical in the business world, where prospects have access to mailrooms and postage meters. It can obviously save you a lot of money if you don't have to pay postage both ways.

However, if you're mailing to households, try not to skimp on the return postage. Finding envelopes and stamps is a much greater chore in households, and by not supplying them, you'll greatly reduce your response rate. In addition, prospects are more likely to resent using their money to tell you they'd like to buy from you.

Carrying Out Your Direct Mail Program

O nce you plan your direct mail program, you have to carry it out. You must look at all of the elements and consider who will do what, how long it will take, and how much it will cost. In general, the brochure will take the longest amount of time for any direct mail program. If you're using a four-color brochure, it will take you from two to three weeks to create the brochure and another two to three weeks to print it. You should be able to do all the other elements within that six-week timeline.

It is possible to create and produce every portion of your direct mail effort using your Apple Macintosh, a laser printer, and assorted software packages. However, depending on the size of your mailing and your expertise, you may want to farm out portions of the job to outside companies.

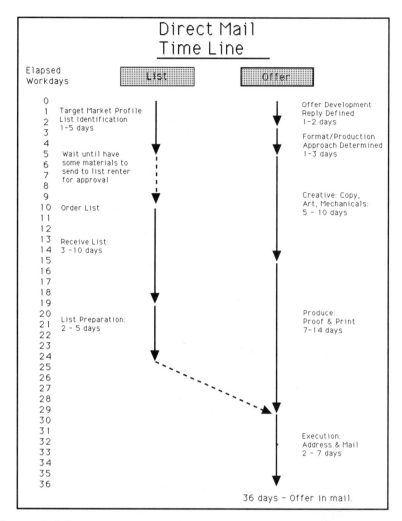

Figure 8.16: Your time line for the creation of a direct mail package will depend on the complexity of the package and the vendors you use.

Graphic Artists

You can hire a graphic artist to help you create the brochure, the envelope, or any other part of the mailing. The artist's knowledge of layout and design will often give you a more polished piece than you could create on your own. Many designers have their own desktop publishing businesses and do all their work on a Macintosh. If necessary, you can even get the final design delivered to you in electronic format, so that you can modify it or produce it directly from your Macintosh. Graphic artists charge either by the hour or by the project. You should allow for two to three weeks for the design and production of a four-color brochure.

Copywriters

Copywriters are professional writers who can help you to write a brochure or letter. Writing for direct mail campaigns is a skill different from other writing. You can either hire a copywriter to start the writing from scratch or to polish and edit something you've already written. If you decide to hire a copywriter to start from scratch, you should hire him or her to write the letter, brochure, and response device to insure a consistent message. If you decide to go to an outside writer, look for someone with direct mail experience and knowledge of your industry. Like graphic artists, copywriters charge by the hour or by the project.

Commercial Printers

A commercial printer can be anything from the copy center on the corner to a large-scale, four-color printer. If your brochure is black and white, the local copy shop can probably do an excellent job printing it. If you plan to use four colors, particularly if you have photographs and illustrations, you should probably turn to a professional four-color printing company.

You can also use the copy centers or printers to print any non-personalized letters. Just give them your stationery and a clean printout of the letter, and they will copy the letters onto your stationery, even adding an appropriate blue signature at the bottom.

Depending on the quantities you need and the complexity of the print job, printing can take anywhere from 24 hours to three weeks. As soon as you know you'll need printing services, it's wise to call the printer to get yourself into the printing queue.

Envelope Printers

Envelope printing is a specialized skill. Because of the complexity of creating envelopes, envelope printers will take the longest to produce your order. If your direct mail package calls for custom-made envelopes, it will take from seven to nine weeks for them to be produced.

Mail House/Lettershop

A mail house or lettershop can put together all the pieces of your direct mail package and drop it in the mail. Many of these firms have machines that fold letters and stuff envelopes automatically—a big relief when you're doing a large mailing. If you plan to use a lettershop, contact them before you actually create the mailing materials to ensure that their machines can handle what you're creating. Otherwise, you may end up with an extra fee, because they'll have to manually insert everything in the envelope. The extra fee may only be a few cents per piece, but it adds up with a large mailing.

Lettershops can also label envelopes for you. If you're using a product like MarketPlace, you should discuss a way for them to create labels directly from the electronic versions of the list. Then you can export a MarketPlace list and deliver it to your lettershop on a floppy disk. If you're renting a list, list owners will generally send you either Cheshire labels or pressure-sensitive labels; if it doesn't matter to you which is used, discuss the least expensive option with the lettershop (usually the Cheshire labels).

Lettershops are also extremely useful when you're doing a mailing to several different lists at once. You want to make sure that you're not wasting your money with duplicate mailings to the same names. To ensure nonduplication, many lettershops can do a merge/purge of all the lists. To do so, the lettershop must receive the lists on electronic tape that it can load onto its mainframe or minicomputer. They then compare the names on all the lists and eliminate any apparent duplicates as they create one cohesive list for the mailing. The lettershop then generates labels or can print the address information directly onto your mailing pieces.

TIP

Many list owners will send electronic tapes only to bonded lettershops to ensure that no one will steal their names.

Lettershops tend to be extremely aware of postal regulations and will bundle your mail in the most cost-effective manner. If you are doing small mailings, most lettershops will allow you to use their bulk mail permit, saving your company the cost of applying for such a permit.

Generally, a lettershop can turn your mailing around anywhere from two days to a week, depending on the complexity of the insertions, labeling, and mailing. Billing is usually on a per piece basis, although most have a minimum cost of about $200–$250. If you're doing a small mailing, you should keep that in mind when you're deciding whether to do the envelope stuffing and labeling yourself.

Final Planning

Now that you understand what's involved in direct mail, you can plan your first direct mail effort. Use Worksheet 5 in Appendix A to help work out the costs of any package you are considering creating. This worksheet will help you quickly see if your creativity is outrunning your budget.

Don't panic if your first effort at direct mail isn't successful. It takes a little time to get direct mail right. A key advantage of direct mail is that you will get feedback, so that you'll have a better idea of what you should change for next time. Every mailing you do can lead to a more successful effort the next time.

9

Develop a Telemarketing Plan

The telephone can be an extremely effective part of any desktop marketing plan. It gives you instant two-way communication with your prospect or customer and facilitates your efforts to make a sale. As the cost of a sales call has increased, more and more companies have turned to the telephone to fill the sales gap in a more cost-effective manner. You can use the telephone to set up appointments, follow up on customers, or actually sell your product or service.

In this chapter, we describe how you can use the telephone for either telesales or telemarketing. Because telesales is not really direct marketing, we focus on the different ways you can use telemarketing—inbound, outbound, or with direct mail. Finally, we explain how you can plan a telemarketing campaign to fit your needs.

Marketing Uses of the Telephone

There are two principal ways you can use the telephone in marketing:

■ Telesales

■ Telemarketing

Telesales uses the telephone to replace a face-to-face sales contact. Many companies have actually divided their sales force, with one portion out in the field and the other portion in the office on the telephone. You can use telephone salespeople for a wide range of goals:

■ To sell into geographically distant areas

■ To service your B-level customers who generate a fair amount of sales but not enough to justify having a field sales rep assigned to them

■ To sell follow-up services or products to your current customers.

You can use the telesales portion of your sales force to help train new salespeople. It is a *safe* area where reps can learn a lot about your products or services before being on their own in the field. However, you may find some people will excel on the telephone and others will only excel in the field. There are certain abilities that seem difficult to translate from one selling arena to another.

Telesales is a flexible medium; the salesperson may have a goal in mind but can vary selling strategies for every customer. Although telesales can be an extremely effective way of making sales, it is not truly direct marketing. Telesales is difficult to measure and replicate because every salesperson does it differently. Measurability and control are crucial for any direct marketing program. Once you hand over prospects or customers to a salesperson, either a field sales rep or a telesales rep, you lose control.

The other form of telephone selling—telemarketing—alleviates this loss of control.

Telemarketing

Telemarketing is best described as direct mail by phone. It is:

- Controllable, measurable, and not dependent on the individual for its success
- It can be used to support direct mail or as a stand-alone campaign
- It is a planned series of contacts, using a constant message, seeking to produce a lead or an order
- It builds and maintains a database and is completely measurable in its cost and results

The first sentence in the definition instantly differentiates telemarketing from telesales. With telemarketing, you should get the same results no matter who is on the telephone. The consistent message ensures that it's the offer and the message that are making the sales, not the charisma of the individual phone communicator.

There are two forms of telemarketing, inbound and outbound.

Inbound Telemarketing

Inbound telemarketing is the easier of the two methods to arrange and set up. You can instantly have inbound telemarketing by sending out direct mail with an option to let prospects phone you to fulfill your offer. As soon as you have prospects or customers calling you and you're dealing with them in a systematic fashion, you're using inbound telemarketing.

The most important step in inbound telemarketing is the simplest, but one that is sometimes overlooked—let your staff know to expect the calls. Nothing upsets a staff more than having someone call about an offer they know nothing about. (Not to mention how your prospects will react when they call your company and no one seems to know what's going on.) Don't just tell the people you've assigned to handle the calls. Be sure the switchboard operators and secretaries are aware as well. Also make sure you've delegated enough people to take the calls.

Planning staffing for inbound calls can be tricky. Not only do you need enough people to handle the calls, you need enough phone lines for prospects to get through. If you do a small mailing or ad, this may not be an issue, but a good offer you send out to a lot of prospects can generate a lot of calls. Try to make sure that there are enough phone lines to handle all the calls: research has shown that a large percentage of prospects won't call back if they receive a busy signal on the first call.

If you're expecting a lot of calls and don't plan to make a habit of it, you may consider using an outside telemarketing service. The outside service can usually dedicate one or more 800 numbers for use by your company, as well as assign trained telemarketers to answer the calls. By using an outside service, you can alleviate the disruption inbound calls can put on regular office routine.

Fortunately, you can predict when you'll get the bulk of your calls. If you're mailing to households, you should get most of your calls within five days to two weeks after you drop your mailing. If you're mailing to businesses, inbound calls will be stretched out more, since business people are more likely to be away or too busy to deal with your offer immediately. If you don't want to use an outside service and you don't have the staff or phone lines to handle a large number of calls in a one to two week period, consider staggering your mailing, so that the calls are spread out over a longer period.

How to Handle Inbound Calls

Whether you use internal resources or go to an outside service, you should develop a consistent manner of dealing with inbound phone calls. Write a simple script that your telemarketers can use on every call. The first part of the script should ask for the name, address, and phone number of every caller. Since they already have some interest in your product, inbound callers are generally happy to give out this information. Individual consumers may be more hesitant to give you their names and phone numbers. If it seems to bother the caller a lot, instruct your telemarketers not to press too hard; you don't want legitimate prospects hanging up just because they aren't immediately willing to give their names.

In addition to capturing the name and address, your telemarketers should find out where the caller heard of your offer. It's important to gather this information so that you can analyze which markets are most responsive to your offer. For example, you may find that people from one list respond twice as often as people from another list. If you have coded all your mailings or advertisements, ask the caller to refer to the code printed on the mailing or ad. However, a good proportion of your callers will not know how they heard of you or your offer.

The advantage of gathering all the information up front is obvious. It allows you to enhance your database, even if you don't make a sale. You can compare the list of responders to the initial mailing list to learn more about people who are interested in your offer.

Here's a sample script your telemarketers can use to facilitate the collection of this information:

> Hello, this is Helpful Corporation; this is_____(fill in blank) speaking.
>
> What's your name please?_____
>
> And what's your address? _____
>
> And is there a phone number where you can be reached during the day?_____
>
> And where did you hear about Helpful Corporation?_____
>
> Do you have that in front of you now? (If yes) Could you please read me the three-digit number in the upper right-hand corner? _____
>
> Now what can I do for you today?

Of course, this script works best if you're using a dedicated phone number for your desktop marketing responders. If you had to use your main phone line in your direct mail piece, you should have the persons answering the phone hold off gathering the name and code information until you're sure the caller is responding to your direct mail offer.

Once the telemarketer has gotten the basic information from the respondent, he or she should follow a basic script to answer questions, gather information, or sell product. If the respondents are actually buying product, it's a good idea to have a checklist of information the telemarketer must request, such as size, color, quantity, billing information, and so on. By having a systematic way to deal with the inbound callers, you keep the results replicable and have true desktop marketing.

Telemarketing Preparation on the Macintosh

On the simplest level, you can create a telemarketing script with your word processing software. If the script has blank spaces for information to be filled out, make sure you print or duplicate enough copies of the script to equal your expected number of calls. The telemarketer can enter all the necessary information on the script, and you can actually use the filled-out script as the basis of your fulfillment process.

Depending on the number of Macintoshes your business has and whether you have dedicated people on the phone, you may choose to put the script directly onto the computer in the form of a database system. As each new call comes through, the telemarketer brings up a blank, electronic form. The telemarketer then types in the appropriate information as it is given. As each script is completed, it is added to a database of all the respondent information collected so far.

This form of tracking can be incredibly powerful. You can use this computerized database to handle a lot of the desktop marketing paperwork. For example, at the end of each day you can print out a list of orders with delivery information—you can even set up the database to generate the appropriate shipping labels. At the same time, you have an up-to-the-minute record of the results of your desktop marketing campaign. With all the data in electronic form, you can easily generate reports evaluating different offers or lists or areas of the country. (Read more on using computerized database management systems in Chapter 11.)

Inbound telemarketing can be a quick way for you to get results and measure the success of your desktop marketing efforts. However, inbound telemarketing is entirely reactive. Outbound telemarketing allows *you* to take the initiative.

Outbound Telemarketing

With outbound telemarketing, you call your prospect or customer directly. As with direct mail, you bring your offer to the prospect's location. But, unlike direct mail, the telephone is difficult to ignore. In general, the advantages of doing outbound telemarketing are:

■ Interactivity—the efficiency of the two-way communication of a phone call cannot be equalled by any other form of desktop marketing

■ Higher response rates

■ Increased measurability of responses

■ Immediate feedback on your offer

■ More information for your database

In addition, if used in conjunction with direct mail, telemarketing can improve your response rate anywhere from 15 percent to 30 percent.

With outbound telemarketing, the entire conversation between your telemarketers and your prospects is planned in advance. Outbound telemarketing doesn't give the telemarketer the flexibility to modify the offer or to sell different products; everything is scripted and controlled. Although a telemarketer should be trained to handle the most common objections, the telemarketer shouldn't be expected to have vast product knowledge or be able to carry on long sales pitches with your customers or prospects. In most cases, telemarketing should only be done for commodity products, especially when you're selling to households. There's no simple way to explain a product or service over the telephone when the listener has no visual knowledge of what you're talking about.

Telemarketing is a very tedious and boring job. A telemarketer dials the phone twenty to thirty times an hour and only gets through to a small percentage of those calls. Then, when a telemarketer does get through, he's likely to hear the word *No* more times than he's ever heard it in his life.

If you're going to do outbound telemarketing, you shouldn't use your current staff to make the calls unless it's a very short-term project. If your staff didn't originally sign on for this type of job, they'll very quickly come to resent you and your telemarketing efforts. And you'll be forced to spend a tremendous amount of time monitoring their efforts. If you must use your own staff, try to limit their telemarketing time to two or three hours a week—two or three hours that are explicitly set aside to make those calls. This is probably the only way to make sure the work gets done and avoid employee revolt.

On the other hand, outside telemarketing firms specialize in doing the very calling that will probably drive your staff crazy. A telemarketing firm will charge you anywhere from $30 to $60 an hour to do the calling for you. When you interview a telemarketing firm, one of the things you should inquire about is the background of the actual telemarketers. Try to find a firm where they have some familiarity with your type of business, so that the telemarketers will have less trouble understanding what you're trying to accomplish.

Planning an Outbound Telemarketing Campaign

 ou should put together a telemarketing campaign with as much care as you would give to a direct mail campaign. You must think through what you plan to offer, who you plan to call, and what the telemarketers will say once they make the calls.

Who to Call

Your first big decision is who should you call. As in all desktop marketing endeavors, the list you choose will be crucial to your success. Perhaps even more than when you're doing direct mail, it's a good idea to segment your prospects as homogeneously as possible. Not only will this help you learn how different markets react to your offer, it will help your telemarketers become familiar with the similarities within each group.

Kris Woods uses outbound telemarketing to convince retail stores to carry his line of storage containers. Instead of grouping all his targets into one list, he divides the list by type of store. That way, his telemarketers can call a series of department stores and then a series of grocery stores. Because similar stores are more likely to react in similar ways, Kris' telemarketers quickly learn to emphasize the most important benefits to that *type* of store. It also helps the telemarketers to become quickly familiar with the standard objections for each store type.

If you are marketing to households, be sensitive about people's concerns with being called at home. Although a lot of people resent being called at home to sell, this method can be very effective. If you're just starting out with telemarketing, you might consider beginning your efforts by calling your current customers.

Because you already have a relationship with your customers, they're less likely to be upset by a call. When a connection already exists, many people feel you're somewhat justified in calling. Think of items or services you sell that would be of particular interest to current customers—refills, products related to items they've already bought, or new versions of your product. When selecting your list, try to categorize the people you'll be calling. You can pick out the biggest buyers, the most consistent buyers, those within a 10-mile radius of your store, those who haven't bought for a while, or any other category you want.

You'll find that renting lists with telephone numbers is more difficult and more expensive than renting a list for mailing. Several direct mail companies have never captured the telephone numbers of the people on their lists, because all of their sales are done through the mail. For example, although magazine subscription lists are usually very accurate, they almost never have phone number information.

CHAPTER NINE

Use MarketPlace Lists for Telemarketing

If you're marketing to businesses, you can use MarketPlace Business to generate a list of prospects with phone numbers. Because phone numbers are generally considered more valuable than an address, it will cost you two units from the meter to buy a record with a phone number as opposed to the one unit for a record with an address.

To facilitate using its records for telemarketing, MarketPlace Business includes an Area Code selection criteria, so that you can build a list knowing all calls will be within certain calling areas. To save you from buying records that may not have phone numbers, you can also use Data Options to build lists that only include records with phone numbers. In general, you'll find that 95 percent or better of the records do contain telephone numbers.

Even if they do have the phone number, many list owners will not rent them out. This is particularly true of owners of household lists. Because many people don't like to be called at home, they are afraid that you may annoy or antagonize some of their best customers. Since they have no control of the behavior of your telemarketers, they would prefer not to rent you the phone numbers at all.

If a list owner is willing to rent you phone numbers, the numbers usually come at a premium. The addition of phone numbers can run anywhere from $5 to $15 a thousand—yet another reason companies focus on telemarketing to their own customer list.

Whatever list you decide to use, you should give some thought to preparing it in the best possible format for telemarketing. Most people find the easiest way to distribute prospect information is to prepare a single sheet of paper with all the necessary information about each prospect. This might include contact name, address, phone number, and other pertinent information, such as size of business. By putting each prospect on his or her own sheet of paper, you can easily transfer prospects between different telemarketers if calling rates vary, and you also give the telemarketer plenty of room for taking notes on the call.

TIP

If it's easiest to produce names and phone numbers on labels, use pressure-sensitive ones and stick them on the top of each page.

You can generally access more information about a prospect than just name and phone number, particularly if you're calling your own customer list. However, you may not want to expose your telemarketers to too much detailed information about each prospect. The information may predispose the telemarketer to alter the telemarketing script to *fit* the prospect. Or, if a telemarketer finds one type of prospect a better respondent than another type, he may focus all his efforts on easier prospects. This focus could skew your overall results and affect the measurability of the telemarketing results.

For example, one of Kris' telemarketers may find that she has better luck convincing stores with fewer than 25 employees to carry Kris' storage containers. To improve her individual results, she may pull out all records with fewer employees and call only those. This would skew the response rate and make it difficult to predict results in the future. Her *discovery* may also be a fluke that wouldn't pan out if she continued calling a broader variety of stores.

The Calling Process

Contacting prospects via telephone can be a frustrating business. Each telemarketer should be able to make between 10 and 30 dialings per hour. At any given time, you will find that 5 percent to 15 percent of businesses cannot be contacted, due to changed locations, disconnected phones, or going out of business. You can expect an actual contact rate of about 30 percent to 40 percent when calling businesses. This means that you will go through four to twelve records per hour. If you have 100 companies to call, this activity will take between 8 and 25 hours to complete.

The percentage rate for calling homes is similar, although it depends a lot on the type of household you're calling. Your efforts will take longer however, because your calling hours are much shorter. Unless you're calling the retired market, you should make your calls between 5:00 and 9:00 p.m. when the family is centered in the kitchen where most homes have their primary phone.

Typical calling patterns can be seen below:

Calls to make	100
Numbers that are reachable	90
Dialings per hour	15
Contact rate (percent available)	40 percent
Prospects contacted per hour	6
Time required to complete calls	15 hours

If you're telemarketing to a company, you've only begun the battle when you reach the prospect company. Next, your telemarketers have to locate the appropriate person to talk to. If you're selling to small businesses, the telemarketers should talk to the owner or manager. If the company is larger, the telemarketers may have to do some good guessing to locate the correct person. They can use the same techniques on the phone as you would use in direct mail, asking for "the advertising manager" or "the purchasing director." Of course, because the telemarketers often don't have the actual name of the person they're trying to reach, they may alert switchboard operators and secretaries to the fact that they're selling something. In cases like this, many support staffs have been directed not to connect the calls.

Even when the telemarketer does determine who he or she needs to speak with, the prospect may be in a meeting, out of the office, or busy. If your prospect is not available, the telemarketer should leave a message with his name and your company name, stating he'll call back. Your telemarketer shouldn't elaborate on why he's contacting the prospect or he may not be allowed through the next time.

Reaching the proper person in a household is generally easier, because there is often only one or two decision makers in any given household. Be sure that the telemarketers get an adult on the phone and that they make their pitch only to adults. In many states, it's illegal to try to sell to children, not to mention that fact that parents will resent your effort to do so. Since they'll probably be paying for the product or service, you don't want to antagonize them.

It's important that you set a limit on how many times a telemarketer will call a number before giving up. Otherwise the telemarketers will spend a lot of time calling with no connects. In business-to-business telemarketing, the limit is usually eight calls for an unknown prospect. Of course, if it's a guaranteed sale or a good customer, you may just keep calling until you actually get through. If you are doing telemarketing to your household customers, you should limit your calls to three or four attempts.

Calling Records

In order to evaluate the results and costs of your telemarketing, telemarketers should keep track of every call they make and the results of each call. The easiest way to track results is with a calling record, which you can easily prepare with your word processor.

With a calling record, each prospect has its own sheet of paper. In the upper right-hand corner, the record lists the name, address, and phone information. If you have information about the prospects you're calling in database management software, you can merge the information about each prospect with the calling record. To do this, use the same merging techniques described in Chapter 7. The entire calling record can then be printed directly from your word processor with a different name and phone number on each sheet. If you're getting the list in the form of labels, you can stick individual labels on each record.

When preparing the calling report, be sure to leave a blank space directly below the address to add additional names and titles. This is particularly important when you're calling businesses, because the contact name you have may not be the decision maker.

In the middle of the calling record, the telemarketer tracks calling results. Every time the prospect is called, the telemarketer puts initials and the time and date of the call. (It's quite possible you'll be passing around prospects, so that different telemarketers may make each call.) Next to the initials, the telemarketer writes one of four codes to indicate the results of the dialing.

Calling Record

Target Information printed in this area
or a label with the information printed
and affixed to this area

Corrections, additions, or differences in ship to or bill to:

Contact _____

Title _____

Company _____

Address _____

City _____ State_____ Zip_____

Phone (___) _____ Fax (___)____ __ _____

Special Instructions: _____

ADDITIONAL CONTACTS:

Name _____ Title _____ Function _____

Name _____ Title _____ Function _____

Name _____ Title _____ Function _____

Caller	Time	Date	Result of Dialing	Call back		Notes
_____	am pm	_____	DA NA BY CB	Time _____	Date _____	_____
_____	am pm	_____	DA NA BY CB	Time _____	Date _____	_____
_____	am pm	_____	DA NA BY CB	Time _____	Date _____	_____
_____	am pm	_____	DA NA BY CB	Time _____	Date _____	_____
_____	am pm	_____	DA NA BY CB	Time _____	Date _____	_____
_____	am pm	_____	DA NA BY CB	Time _____	Date _____	_____
_____	am pm	_____	DA NA BY CB	Time _____	Date _____	_____
_____	am pm	_____	DA NA BY CB	Time _____	Date _____	_____

Record is complete:

Final Disposition _____

1. Accepted offer: _____

2. Rejected offer: _____

3. Requested additional follow-up: _____

4. Reached caling limit _____

5. Wrong number - not in service _____

6. Wrong person, no referral _____

Notes: _____
_____
_____
_____
_____

Figure 9.1: Each telemarketer should have a calling record like this to track the results of every call he or she makes.

DA: Didn't answer; the call wasn't completed

NA: Not available; the call got through, but the right person wasn't available

BY: Busy; the line was tied up

CB: Call back; the call got through to the right person, but she or he didn't have time to talk. Be sure to indicate a good time to call back.

Each calling record should also list the final disposition of the call. There are six possible outcomes to any telemarketing call:

- Accepted offer
- Rejected offer
- Requested additional follow-up
- Reached calling limit
- Wrong number—not in service
- Wrong person, no referral

In addition to tracking the result of calling each prospect, you should track the number of calls made by each telemarketer. The call tally sheet gives you a quick way to measure the numbers of calls made per hour and the response rates.

Each telemarketer receives a new tally sheet each day. At the top, the marketers record their names and the number of hours they will be calling. The telemarketers then cross off the numbers in the appropriate boxes as the day progresses. When the telemarketer dials the first number, he crosses off "0" in the Dialing box; with the second number, he crosses off "1." At the end of the day, you can simply look at the first uncrossed-off number to know how many calls each telemarketer made. The same is true of the other six boxes: *Accepted Offer, Rejected Offer, Wrong Person, Additional Follow-Up, Reached Calling Limit, Wrong Number.*

Tally Sheet	Name _____
	Program _____
	Date_____Hours calling _____
	Comments _____
	_____

Dialings

0 1 2 3 4 5 6 7 8 9 10 11 12 13 14 15
16 17 18 19 20 21 22 23 24 25 26 27 28
29 30 31 32 33 34 35 36 37 38 39 40 41
42 43 44 45 46 47 48 49 50 51 52 53 54
55 56 57 58 59 60 61 62 63 64 65 66 67
68 69 70 71 72 73 74 75 76 77 78 79 80
81 82 83 84 85 86 87 88 89 90 91 92 93 94 95 96 97 98 99
100

Additional Follow-Up

0 1 2 3 4 5 6 7 8 9 10 11 12 13 14 15
16 17 18 19 20 21 22 23 24 25 26 27 28
29 30 31 32 33 34 35 36 37 38 39 40 41
42 43 44 45 46 47 48 49 50 51 52 53 54

Accepted Offer

0 1 2 3 4 5 6 7 8 9 10 11 12 13 14 15
16 17 18 19 20 21 22 23 24 25 26 27 28

Reached Calling Limit

0 1 2 3 4 5 6 7 8 9 10 11 12 13 14 15
16 17 18 19 20 21 22 23 24 25 26 27 28

29 30 31 32 33 34 35 36 37 38 39 40 41
42 43 44 45 46 47 48 49 50 51 52 53 54
55 56 57 58 59 60 61 62 63 64 65 66 67

Rejected Offer

0 1 2 3 4 5 6 7 8 9 10 11 12 13 14 15
16 17 18 19 20 21 22 23 24 25 26 27 28
29 30 31 32 33 34 35 36 37 38 39 40 41
42 43 44 45 46 47 48 49 50 51 52 53 54
55 56 57 58 59 60 61 62 63 64 65 66 67

Wrong Number

0 1 2 3 4 5 6 7 8 9 10 11 12 13 14 15
16 17 18 19 20 21 22 23 24 25 26 27 28
29 30 31 32 33 34 35 36 37 38 39 40 41
42 43 44 45 46 47 48 49 50 51 52 53 54
55 56 57 58 59 60 61 62 63 64 65 66 67

Wrong Person

0 1 2 3 4 5 6 7 8 9 10 11 12 13 14 15
16 17 18 19 20 21 22 23 24 25 26 27 28

Comments: _____
_____
_____
_____
_____
_____
_____

Figure 9.2. At the end of each day or shift, you'll use this tally sheet to evaluate your telemarketing efforts.

The Call

Once a telemarketer reaches a prospect, he or she has to get the prospect involved immediately. The telemarketer has fewer than 30 seconds to capture a prospect's attention and interest them in what you are selling. Your offer must be simple and easy to understand. If you're selling a complex product or service, you should reconsider selling it via the telephone. Above all, make it easy for the prospect to say "yes."

Don't give the prospect lots of choices or decisions to make. You can actually get the prospect thinking positively by asking simple questions first. A discount travel agency might ask, "Are you concerned about increasing travel expenses?", "Would you like to see your travel expenses lowered by 20 percent?", finishing with, "Would you like our free audit of your travel expenses and recommendations on how to lower them?"

The entire telephone call should be scripted for your telemarketers, from the initial "Hello," to the final closing. In the script, you should include the answers to the most common objections the telemarketers will hear from your prospects so that you can be certain the questions are being handled the same way by all the telemarketers. For example, if you find prospects routinely claim your product or service is too expensive, you should have a standard answer to that particular objection. "Well, it may seem expensive at first, but the price works out to only 50 cents a day—less than a cup of coffee." Or, "This isn't one of those inexpensive valves that wears out in a couple of years. Our valve is built entirely of steel and aluminum—and should last a lifetime."

You must encourage your telemarketers to stick to the script as closely as possible. In the beginning when they are unfamiliar with the offer, they will rarely stray from the script. However, after a few hours, they'll begin to modify the words and sentence order. At this point you, or the manager of the telemarketing facility, should begin monitoring the calls to keep the telemarketers on their toes. Although it's boring for them to say the exact same thing over and over again, it's crucial for the telemarketers to be consistent so that you'll be able to fairly evaluate the results. If the telemarketers are changing words, you won't be sure whether your results are due to your offer or to the different telemarketers involved.

There are three ways to give a script to telemarketers:

1) *Printed pages:* Use your word processor to create the entire script for the telemarketers. Include the most common questions and objections and their standard answers, so that the telemarketer can refer to the appropriate answer. Unfortunately, it's easy for the telemarketer to ignore this type of script once he's got it memorized—a very likely occurrence after 10 or so calls.

2) *Flip chart script:* This method of scripting can be very effective if you need the telemarketer to ask a prospect questions. When the prospect answers each question, the telemarketer must flip to the appropriate page for the answer. Tabs are often used to make flipping pages easier.

   Let's say on the first page of the script you ask whether the prospect company uses a postage meter or not. If the answer is "Yes," the telemarketer turns over the "Yes" tab and continues with a script that focuses on the costs associated with the current type of meter being used. If the prospect answers "No," the telemarketer uses the "No" tab instead. The "No" part of the script focuses on the economic advantages of using a postage meter over stamps. The script can continue to branch, with each question leading to a different part of the flip chart.

   An advantage of the flip chart script is that it makes the call appear more customized to each customer's situation and may make the customer more inclined to hear the pitch. It is also more challenging for a telemarketer to follow this type of script. This has the combined benefit of making it more interesting work and forcing the telemarketer to stick to the script more closely.

   Of course, there are disadvantages too. It is more difficult to put together a flip chart. Although you can still type each of the pages with word processing software, it is physically difficult to put together a flip chart, particularly if you're using tabs. This effort may be prohibitive if you have to put together more than one.

3) *Computer scripting:* Although this method of scripting can be powerful, it's the most difficult to set up. Instead of printing out a script, you leave it on the computer. As the telemarketer moves through the script, he hits or clicks the appropriate keys to move to the next "page" of the script. A big advantage is that every piece

of information is already in electronic format, so that you won't have to reenter it all after the telemarketing efforts are finished.

This type of scripting forces the telemarketer to actually read the script more than any other method. However, it also requires you to have a computer available for every telemarketer and to have the ability to program such a script. Frequently, telemarketing facilities have multiple terminals, but they will often charge you extra for doing computerized scripting.

The Script Contents

Although you want to keep the script simple, you can have more than one offer ready, in case the prospect says no to your first offer. For example, when telephone company telemarketers call to offer business listings in the Yellow Pages, they first offer a display ad at the highest rates. If the prospect says no, then the telemarketer introduces the possibility of buying a smaller display ad. Finally, if the prospect continues to say no, the telemarketer offers a boldface listing for a minimal fee.

Notice, these telemarketers only offer the less expensive opportunities *if* the prospect says no. If the telemarketer convinces the prospect to buy a large display ad, she simply takes down the order information and hangs up, without ever mentioning the less expensive offers. Don't have your telemarketers list all the different offer possibilities until after they've made a sale.

A lot of people will not make a yes or no decision on the spot but will ask for additional information. A fair number of prospects will do this to politely get your telemarketers off the phone. However, there will be a percentage that really *is* interested in your offer but that doesn't like to make decisions based only on a phone call.

How you handle these people depends on whether you're calling a business or a household. Brochures and written information are generally more important to businesses, particularly since your prospect may need to show the information to someone else before he can make a buy decision. To make sure you follow up on these people properly, you should put their records in a separate pile and call them again, once they have received your literature.

On the other hand, when you're calling households, don't bother to send more information unless the prospect is already one of your customers. In the vast majority of the cases, when your follow-up package reaches the house, it's treated no differently than any other direct mail; it just goes in a big pile. The level of attention the mail will get is not worth the cost of preparing and mailing it.

Although this may be obvious, be sure your telemarketers remain courteous and polite at all times. They are likely to encounter very rude people as they make their calls, but they must not respond in kind. Whether it's an outside service or your own staff, they are representing your business. Your reputation is at stake.

Telemarketing with Direct Mail

If you have never done telemarketing, you may want to start by using it in conjunction with direct mail. The combination of the two can be extremely powerful. Let's say your direct mail alone gets a response rate of one percent and your telemarketing alone gets a response of five percent. You might think the combination of the two would result in a six percent response rate, but more often than not, it can increase your overall response rate to 15 percent to 30 percent.

If you combine the two methods, you must time your phoning carefully. Ideally, you should make your calls 10 to 15 days after you have sent out your direct mail—sooner, if you're mailing first class. With this timing, you will get the largest percentage of respondents who remember your mailing. (Surprisingly, 30 percent will say they've received your mailing even before you mail it. People don't like to appear unknowledgeable.)

The combination of direct mail and telemarketing can be particularly useful if you're marketing a somewhat complex product or service. You can use the mailing to explain the product in greater detail than you can over the phone. But, the person on the phone is ready and able to answer questions that the prospect may have and, of course, take orders.

For example, a company that is selling fax machines might initially send a brochure that describes some of the more technical aspects of a fax, along with the benefits of having one. The brochure can also show photos to make the product more concrete in the prospect's mind. The follow-up telephone call can then be used to answer questions about the fax machine and to convince the prospect on the advantages of buying now.

Telemarketing can also be a very effective method of following up on any fulfillment packages you send as a result of direct mail. By waiting to call only the direct mail respondents, you decrease your costs. You also concentrate your marketing efforts on those people who have already raised their hands to express an interest in your product.

Budgeting

T o help you decide whether to use telemarketing or not, you should estimate how much the effort will cost you and what you expect to get out of it. You should also work out a timeline planning when everything will take place. Take a look at Figure 9.3 to get a sense of a typical telemarketing timeline.

Worksheet 6 in Appendix A is designed especially to help you budget telemarketing programs. Before you begin, you should fill out the *Before* column with all your predicted expenses, calling rates, and order rates. This worksheet will help you decide whether telemarketing seems to be a financially viable option.

Telemarketing can be a very powerful tool in growing many kinds of businesses. Fame Fabrics is a small company in Georgia that manufactures industrial aprons. Its aprons are used primarily by restaurants, bars, and grocery stores, and it sells them through stocking distributors. In the beginning of 1990, it decided it needed other ways to grow its business. Because it didn't have the money to sustain an outside sales force, Fame Fabrics decided to give telemarketing a try. It hired one person to be in charge of telemarketing and prepared two other people on its staff to do occasional telemarketing. It also created a brochure to mail to interested prospects.

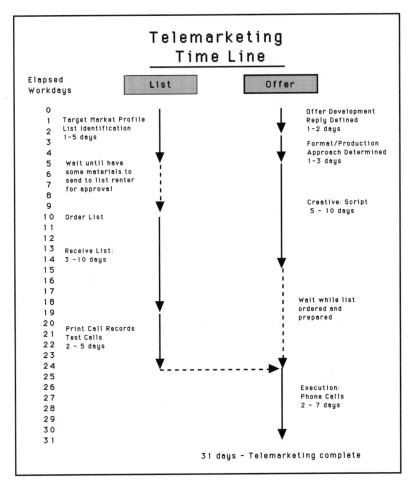

Figure 9.3: The time line for a telemarketing campaign largely depends on how long it takes to get a list.

The telemarketers would make outbound calls to potential customers. If the prospect expressed interest, they then sent along the brochure. Once the prospect received the brochure, the telemarketers would follow up the call. They also began calling their regular customers regularly, encouraging them to order more or to try stocking different aprons. In just one year, Fame Fabrics tripled its customer base—from 250 to 750 customers.

Figure 9.4: Telemarketers at Fame Fabrics sent this brochure to prospects interested in its offer.

You should consider telemarketing when you make your desktop marketing plans, particularly if you are trying to reach businesses. It's the quickest way to get yourself in front of your prospects and the quickest way to get responses to your offer. It fulfills your marketing goal to begin two-way communication with your prospects.

10

Analyze Results

We have referred to the measurability of desktop marketing over and over again in this book. The beauty of any desktop marketing program is that you can quantify the results and analyze them to determine whether you made or lost money. Most other marketing programs, such as advertising or trade shows, don't provide the same kind of measurable results that desktop marketing offers. The other programs offer intangible benefits, such as greater brand recognition or product awareness.

In this chapter, we show you how to develop the best possible desktop marketing program by testing all the elements of the program. By testing, you'll learn what modifications to the program can improve your overall results. In the second half of the chapter, we show you the mechanics of analyzing the results of any desktop marketing program. By using a spreadsheet and simple formulas, you can distill any program down to its essence—profit or loss.

Testing

T he secret to finding which desktop marketing program will best meet your needs is testing before you start and testing continuously as you go. You'll probably need to test several programs before you determine which one will generate the new customers you're looking for or which one will create the add-on sales to your existing customer base at a reasonable cost.

You can test many elements of a desktop marketing program. First and foremost, you should test the lists you're targeting. Next, you should examine the offer you're using. In addition, you should look at the creative "package," the timing of the program, and the frequency of the program. All of these elements can be isolated and tested using simple techniques. The key method in any testing process is sampling. By taking samples of your list to do different tests, you can compare the results to find the most effective desktop marketing plan.

Let's look at the testing process of a mail order gardening supply company run by Keiko Suzuki. She has a list of 3,000 customers, and she wants to contact them quarterly to sell them additional seeds, bulbs, and tools. Initially, she mails two different packages, each to 1,500 customers. This type of test is called an A/B split test, because half the list gets package A (a black-and-white catalog with 10 percent discounts) and half gets package B (a four-color catalog with no discounts). The A/B split test is one of the simplest tests you can set up. The number of testing setups is limited only by your imagination and the number of prospects you have.

In this case, Keiko gets better results with package A, which earns $1000 more than package B. (More on analyzing the results later.) Because package A did better, Keiko should now treat package A as her control package. Every quarter when she does her mailing, she should mail package A to the majority of your customers. However, she should try a new package each time to about 10 percent of the list (300) to see if she can do better than the control. Because customers are always changing, continuous testing keeps you aware of the shifts in their interest. At any point that a new package becomes more successful, it should become the control.

It's important to keep your testing within reasonable limits, particularly if you have only a small universe of names. If you had initially mailed 10 test packages to your 3,000 customers, you wouldn't have gotten conclusive results because there would have been too many variables, mailing to groups that are too small for fair statistical results. By testing two or three packages or telemarketing scripts at one time, you increase the likelihood you'll choose the right program.

You can also do testing with prospective customers. Keiko also uses direct mail to get new customers. Previously she developed a package that offers a free watering can to anyone who orders $10 or more worth of goods. With this package, she has learned that she can generally obtain a new customer at a break-even cost. Keiko decides to use this package as her control. Whenever she does mailings to generate new customers, she mails this control package to the majority of her prospects while testing alternative packages with a small percentage of her prospect list. If she ever finds a new direct mail package that does better than break even, she'll replace the watering can promotion with the new, more profitable package.

Setting Up Testing

The difficulty of testing a desktop marketing program varies depending on whether you're testing lists, offers, or creative material. If you're testing two different offers, such as 10 percent off versus 15 percent off, it will be obvious which offer any respondent originally received: the response device used will clearly state the price and discount.

Figuring out the results of list testing can be a little more difficult. Usually, when you're trying to determine the most effective lists, you should mail the same offer to all the lists. Because the offer is identical for each list, it may be more difficult to figure out to which list a respondent originally belonged.

There are tricks you can use to help you distinguish respondents from different lists. If your mailing format allows it, the simplest technique is coding. This is easiest with any direct mail format that puts the mailing address label on the response device. You can then put a different code on the labels from different lists.

For example, Keiko might mark her mailing to the subscriber list for *American Horticultist* as AMHORT and the mailing to the Burpee Seed Catalog list as BURSEE. Most list-rental companies will place a code on any labels they generate, although some may charge an additional fee for the work. They're more likely to use cryptic codes, so that it's not so obvious to the recipients where you rented their names.

You can also use codes to distinguish between different offers or variations in creativity. Big direct mailers who are mailing millions of pieces may have many, many variables to every mailing, all of which can be broken down into some code. You can even use codes with desktop marketing materials you send that encourage respondents to telephone your company. You simply have the telemarketer ask the respondents to read the code off the label. If you've ever ordered from a catalog, you're probably familiar with how the telemarketers ask you to read some code off the label.

Determining What to Test

When creating your desktop marketing testing plan, it makes sense to concentrate on those elements that will have the most impact on your results. You should test your lists first. Different list selections can improve your results by as much as 50 percent. For example, Time-Life Books may decide to use their own house lists to publicize a new series on the Civil War. However, people who have bought Time-Life's cooking series may have little interest in a series on the Civil War. They may find that renting a list from *American Heritage* or *Southern Living* magazine vastly improves their results.

Whenever possible, try to include your own customer list in your tests, because frequent mailings keep your customers in touch and can help to improve your results, since mailing to your customers is usually more profitable than mailing to prospects. However, as the Time-Life example shows, you should treat your own list as just another list source that may or may not work.

If you plan to do smaller mailings, you may run up against some problems with list rental. As we mentioned in Chapter 6, most list companies require that you rent a minimum number of names. For business lists, the minimum is generally 5,000 names, while it generally runs to 10,000 for consumer lists. Unfortunately, you can't rent 1,000 names from several different lists before you decide which list is best for you. However, if you turn to an electronic alternative such as MarketPlace Business, there's no minimum to the number of names you can use at one time. Although you wouldn't be testing different list sources, you could test lists that are made up of different types of businesses.

After testing lists, you should test your offer. A change in an offer can affect your results as much as 25 percent. Be sure to mail the different offers to similar lists so that you can tell if the difference in results is due to the offer and not to the differences in the targets. Let's say you try two different offers, a 30-day free trial versus a money-back guarantee. You should get 25 percent higher response with the 30-day free trial, because you aren't asking your prospects to put money up front. This is the type of offer variation that can make dramatic differences in your desktop marketing efforts.

Last, if you're doing direct mail, test the format and the copy and graphics of your mailing pieces. Format and copy/graphics go together, because generally you need to change the copy and graphics when you change to a different type of direct mail packages. The direct mail package you select can affect your results by 15 percent and the copy/graphics by 10 percent. Since these percentages are not very high, it should reinforce the guideline to spend most of your time working on choosing lists and creating offers, not on the "creative" aspects of direct mail.

Frequency

Another major element you should consider testing in any desktop marketing program is frequency. Successful salespeople will tell you that one of the keys to their success is never letting go of a qualified prospect. The salespeople stay in contact with known qualified prospects through personal contact, telephone selling, and the mail—until they make a sale. This same concept of repetitive contact can also be effective in desktop marketing.

Frequent direct mailings to qualified prospects can be an extremely effective method of selling commodity-type products like paper, paper clips, toothpaste, copy-machine toner, and soap. Timing is very important in selling commodity products, because it's difficult to sell toothpaste or paper clips to someone who has just bought a three-month supply. But you know they'll eventually run out of their supplies and need more. The goal of frequent mailings is to continuously remind your prospects what you can do for them, so that when they run out of supplies, they will think of you first.

You can also use frequent mailings or a combination of mailings and telephone if you're selling a larger, capital product. Because your product isn't bought often, the justification for frequent contact is different. Instead of constantly reminding the prospect of your presence, you want to help move the prospect through the decision process of buying your product. You can use frequent mailings and occasional phone calls to introduce different benefits with each mailing, gradually building up a clear-cut reason to buy your product or service.

There is no magic formula to determine how frequently you should contact a customer or prospect or how long you should wait between contacts. A lot will be decided by your initial planning phase when you determine how much you can afford to spend to acquire a sale. When you're making a strong, short-term push for a simple product, you may make contact as frequently as every week or two. You probably shouldn't keep this up beyond three months, unless you're still making money on the mailings. On the other hand, when you're selling a big-ticket item with a long sale cycle, you may want to make contact every month or two.

You may have to limit the number of contacts you make because it begins to cost more to make the mailings than you make in sales. You may find you break even after one direct mail piece and a telemarketing call. But, if you start adding another mailing, you no longer make enough new sales to cover the additional mailing costs. The key to determining the effect of frequency is to test it along with every aspect of your direct mail. You can perform multiple tests fairly inexpensively when you combine mail and telemarketing follow-ups to establish results on small samples.

Hints for Frequent Contacts

When you do frequent mailings, you don't necessarily have to change the format of your mailing every time. When you find a format that works, use it until it doesn't work any more. Magazines do this when they're trying to renew subscriptions. They will use virtually the same mailing repeatedly to get a subscriber to renew. They've done careful testing to learn exactly how many mailings to do before giving up on a former subscriber. With each mailing they do, a magazine will get fewer and fewer renewals. When the cost of an additional mailing will no longer be paid for by getting enough new subscriptions, the magazine stops mailing.

Marketers often have difficulty sending the same mailing more than once. Remember, because you've been working on the mailing for weeks, it seems incredibly familiar to you. But to your prospect, who receives dozens of pieces of mail each week, it's just another piece of mail. In fact, by the time you're absolutely sick of a repeat mailing, your prospect is probably noticing it for the first time. Some catalogers have found they can mail the same catalog to the same group 14 times per year and still get acceptable results on each mailing, simply by changing the catalog covers. This works best with business-to-business catalogs, where there are very few changes in styles or seasonality. In fact, one company that sells plastic sheet protectors has been mailing the same catalog for *23 years.*

Repeating the mailing may not be as effective if you're selling a complex product and want to facilitate the decision process over time. Instead, you should develop a series of direct mail packages to be delivered over a several-month period. In each mailing, focus on a different primary benefit. Not only will focusing on different benefits help explain your product better, but different benefits can help to attract different types of customers. Of course, just because you plan to send several mailings to each prospect, don't forget to ask for an order with every contact—you never know when you'll convince the prospect to buy.

Mike Thompson sells a water purification system to households. Because he realizes it's a complicated sell, he plans a three-step mailing to the same set of prospects. He first determines that the three primary benefits of his product are:

1) Protection from environmental poisons

2) Money savings over buying bottled water

3) Better tasting water

To avoid confusing his prospects, he focuses on one benefit per mailing. His first mailing emphasizes protecting your family from unknown poisons in the public water. This mailing captures the attention of environmentalists and parents of small children. Some of them immediately order the water filtration system.

The second mailing to the same list goes out a month later. Again, this mailing focuses on *one* benefit, but this time the benefit is the long-term cost savings of using a filtration system instead of buying bottled water. Those prospects who have already bought the water filtration system simply ignore this mailing. But it catches the eyes of several prospects who currently buy bottled water. Those who are convinced of Mike's arguments sign up to buy the system.

By the time the third mailing goes out one month later, Mike has been able to remove the initial buyers from the mailing list, decreasing the number of pieces he has to produce. The third mailing emphasizes how much better water tastes when you use the water filtration system. This mailing manages to convince a few more diehards who were already softened by the first two mailings.

Timing

You should also think about testing the timing of any direct mailing you may do. Depending on what you're offering, response rates can vary dramatically by the time of year. Table 10.1 shows how responses can vary by the month, depending on the type of mailing you're doing. Generally, responses are lowest in the summer months, no matter what you're offering. Other products and services have varied cycles. For example, mailings for investment services and tax shelters get the highest number of responses in March and April (tax payment time) and November and December (end of the fiscal year).

Table 10.1 You can see how different types of mailing fare depending on the time of year.

	Jan	Feb	Mar	Apr	May	Jun	Jul	Aug	Sep	Oct	Nov	Dec
Mail Order— except Xmas oriented (1)	126	107	98	90	89	87	100	108	103	97	103	101
Fundraising— except Xmas-oriented	105	110	115	120	105	90	65	70	115	125	105	75
Lead-getting	105	110	115	115	110	95	85	80	105	110	105	65
Application for credit card/loan	105	105	100	100	90	90	90	110	105	105	105	105
Traffic except Xmas-oriented	110	95	90	105	90	90	90	110	105	105	105	105
Any Xmas-oriented mailing (2)	90	20	0	0	0	0	20	50	100	220	400	300
Investment leads (tax shelter)	60	70	155	110	100	85	90	85	115	115	90	65
Magazine subs. except Xmas gifts	110	110	115	110	100	95	90	85	115	115	90	65
Business and farms	110	110	105	105	100	90	90	90	110	110	95	85
Institutions and organizations	130	115	110	95	90	80	75	75	120	130	100	80

1) Source for mail order only: Data compiled a number of years ago by O.I. McIntyre, Inc. (now MetroMail).

2) Index of responses assuming equal-sized mailing batches in 5 months: July through November only.

You should try your successful mailings at different times of the year to learn the seasonality of your particular business. Lesley Winn is the new marketing manager at a company that sells computer services to accounting companies. When she tried her first mailing, she sent it out in early March. Her results were absolutely dismal, with only a .02 percent response rate. However, when she did the same mailing again in

September, she got a 1.9 percent response rate and made money. When she looked at the two results, she realized her first mailing had hit the accounting businesses when they were most busy with taxes and had no time to look at anything. By scheduling the second mailing for the early fall, she was able to reach accountants when they had more time to think about her offer.

Analyzing Your Tests

All the testing in the world does you no good if you're not able to evaluate the results and figure out which method worked best. There are several steps that begin by figuring out the total cost of your desktop marketing effort. You then evaluate your response rates and compare the results from different lists or offers.

Assessing Costs

The only true measurement of the success or failure of any of the desktop marketing programs you develop will be whether you make money. In Chapter 3, you learned about the basic financial measurements you would need in order to measure the success of a program, including marketing cost per order, customer acquisition cost, and sales contact cost.

Then, as you planned your direct mail or telemarketing efforts, you budgeted the costs for production and estimated the costs for your fulfillment needs. (From Appendix A, you used Worksheet 5 to help with direct mail budgeting, Worksheet 6 for phone budgeting, and Worksheet 7 for fulfillment budgeting.) When you finish a program, you should redo each of those worksheets with the actual numbers to learn exactly how much each part of the program cost you.

However, costs are not enough to judge success; they are only the first steps. You need to measure the results of the program and learn how much money you brought in.

Measuring Results

There are three primary measurements of result in desktop marketing: response rate, cost of response, and cost of order. You can transfer Worksheet 8 in Appendix A to a spreadsheet program to help you calculate these variables.

Response rate measures how many prospects actually responded to your efforts. More importantly, cost of response measures how much it cost you to get each response. And, most important of all, cost of order indicates how much it costs you for every order you obtained.

To look at the calculations for the response rate, cost of response, and cost of order and then interpret the results, let's turn to a specific example. Elisa Stark is an insurance representative who wants to sell more life insurance policies. According to her calculations of her current marketing methods, it costs her $121 to get a new customer. Now she decides to do a direct mailing to 5,000 prospects offering the best policy for every individual's needs. The entire mailing costs her $3,000, including the cost of printing a small brochure and letter, renting a list, and postage both ways. She receives 95 responses and ultimately issues 30 life insurance policies as a result of these responses.

Number of pieces mailed:	5,000
Total cost of mailing:	$3,000
Number of responses:	95
Number of orders:	30

Elisa can now enter all the numbers in her spreadsheet and use it to easily calculate all the important measurements.

Response Rate

To calculate the response rate, Elisa divides the number of responses by the total number of pieces mailed.

Number of responses/number of pieces mailed = Response rate

In this example, it would be:

95 responses/5,000 pieces mailed = 1.9 percent response rate

Many people use a 2 percent response rate as a rule of thumb to represent a good result. However, there is no good or bad response rate, only response rates that are better or worse than you need to break even. If you make a good list selection and have an excellent offer, you can expect better than 2 percent. Offering a free subscription of a product-oriented newsletter to recent purchasers of the product is likely to get a very high response rate, maybe even 50 percent. On the other hand, if you're selling a big ticket item or are running a very inexpensive program, a response rate below 2 percent can be excellent. For some companies selling very expensive industrial products, just one sale of a $10,000 product can pay for the entire direct mailing.

Cost per Response

To get a better handle on the results, Elisa can calculate the cost per response. Cost per response is the total cost of the direct marketing program divided by the number of responses.

Cost of program/number of responses = Cost per response

For Elisa, the cost per response comes out to:

$3,000/95 responses = $31.58 per response

Because her current marketing methods generally cost her $121 to gain new customers, this price begins to look like a reasonable cost. It is certainly less expensive than making in-person sales calls.

Cost of Order

The most important measure of Elisa's success will be the cost per actual order. To calculate the number, she divides the cost of the program by the actual number of orders it generated.

Cost of program/number of orders = Cost per order

With Elisa's direct mail, the cost per order was:

$3,000/30 orders = $100 per order

$100 per order is an excellent result for Elisa. Since her current methods cost her $21 more to obtain a new customer, she's saving money by using direct mail. At this point, she also compares her cost of order to the value and worth of a customer—how much money an average customer will bring her over the customer's lifetime (as described in Chapter 3). Since each customer is worth more than $100, Elisa is very satisfied with the results of her program.

More Complex Calculations

You'll usually find that your calculations are not quite as simple as the example described above. Depending on your desktop marketing program, there may be several layers of offers and fulfillment before a sale is actually made. By using a spreadsheet program, you can more easily track the overall flow of your program to come up with a definitive result. Let's take a look at the results of a multilayered desktop marketing program and how it can be evaluated. This program includes direct mail, inbound telemarketing, follow-up direct mail, and more inbound telemarketing.

Kirpal Singh Khalsa runs a software training company in Los Angeles, California. He has just completed a desktop marketing program to sell his training services to manufacturing companies, and he wants to evaluate the overall results of the program.

In the first step of the program, Kirpal mailed an offer to 7,500 companies in the greater Los Angeles area. The total cost of the mailing alone, including letter, a MarketPlace list, brochure, and postage, is $6,225. The offer invited the prospect to attend a seminar on how software training can improve company productivity. He has found he can convert 80 percent of those who attend his seminars into customers.

Kirpal received a total of 325 responses. About 80 percent came over his inbound telemarketing line (260) and the remaining 20 percent via his mail response device. Of the respondents, only 227 were willing to sign up immediately for the free seminar. Ninety-eight wanted to be sent more information about the company and the seminar. As a result, Kirpal sent fulfillment literature to those 98, 32 of whom ultimately signed up for his seminar. Calculating the results of this mailing is a little more complicated than the first example. Kirpal sets up his spreadsheet to do the calculations.

	Responses	Sign up	More info
Total pieces mailed	7,500		
Cost of mailing (7,500x$.83)	$6,225		
Responses by phone	260	202	58
Responses by mail	65	25	40
Total	325	227	98
Initial response rate 325/7,500	4.3%		
Initial sign-up rate 227/7,500	3.0%		
Total sent fulfillment literature	98		
Cost of fulfillment (98 x $ .90)	$88		
Total to sign up (via phone)	32		
Secondary response rate 98/32	33%		
Total sign ups 227 + 32	259		
Final sign-up rate 259/7,500	3.4%		

As you can see, just calculating the response rate can be more difficult. In this case, it was a three-step process before final sign ups could be determined. In the same fashion, it is more difficult for Kirpal to calculate the cost of signing up prospects for his seminar. Not only does he have to include the cost of the initial mailing, but he also must include the cost of the fulfillment mailing and all of the incoming phone calls, whether they resulted in sign ups or not.

When he did his phone budgeting, Kirpal calculated that each incoming phone call would cost him $1.50. By multiplying $1.50 by the total number of calls—292— Kirpal comes up with a total telephone cost of $438. Now he adds up the total costs and divides it by the total number of sign ups.

Cost of initial mailing	$6,225
Cost of inbound telemarketing	$438
Cost of follow-up mailing	$88
Total program cost	$6,751
Cost per sign up 6,751/259	$26.07

It is now up to Kirpal to determine whether $26.02 is a reasonable price to pay to get prospects to attend one of his seminars. At this point, he hasn't even gotten one new customer, but he's on his way. Ultimately, he will have to take into account the cost of the seminars and how many of the seminar attendees become customers in order to carry his cost calculations all the way to the end. As you can see, calculating costs and responses can be a complex business.

Comparing Lists and Offers

Spreadsheets can be a godsend in some of the most valuable analyses you will do when you complete a desktop marketing program. We have emphasized over and over again in this book that you must test what works and what doesn't. Unfortunately, when you are testing very different programs, it can be a little like comparing apples to oranges. The calculations themselves may be very simple, but the tracking and documentation can become immensely complicated. A spreadsheet helps you to break programs into their smallest elements and come up with comparable numbers.

Comparing Lists

Comparing list results is simple if you use the same offer on all the lists. As we mentioned earlier in the chapter, you should try to include your customer list in any mailing. Worksheet 9 in Appendix A is one method of comparing the results of a customer and prospect list. Because your customers know you and respect your company, you should always achieve your highest responses from them. In fact, it's usually your current customers who will help pay for desktop marketing efforts to obtain new customers.

Lists are simpler to compare if you paid the same amount for each of them, because looking at the response rate usually tells you all you need to know. For example, Patti Curran, a caterer, rented two different test lists from the same list owner. The first list was a random sample of 10,000 households in her metropolitan area with an income above $25,000 and between the ages of 30 to 45. The other list was another sample of 10,000 households with incomes above $25,000, but the age range was between 45 and 60.

When Patti got her results, she entered them in her spreadsheet to calculate which list gave her better results:

	30–45	45–60
Number mailed	10,000	10,000
Cost per name	$.056	$.056
Cost of list	$560	$560
Remaining program costs	$6,000	$6,000
Total number of responses	110	210
Response rate (110/10,000)	1.1% (210/20,000)	2.1%
Cost per response	$59.63 (6,560/110)	$31.23 (6,560/210)

Looking at the response rate and cost per response, it is immediately clear that the 45–60-year-old list vastly outperformed the younger list. Note that a one percent increase in response rate actually represented a doubling of respondents and a halving of total costs.

Patti's analysis would have been a little more complicated if she had rented names from a source other than MarketPlace with a different fee structure. Let's say she also rented 2000 names from the customer list of a discount party store.

	30-45	45-60	Party Store
Number mailed	10,000	10,000	2,000
Cost per name	$.056	$.056	$.10
Cost of list	$560	$560	$200
Remaining program costs	$6,000	$6,000	$1,200
Total number of responses	110	210	51
Response rate	1.1%	2.1%	2.6%
Cost per response	$59.63	$31.23	$26.92

Not surprisingly, the party-store list gave Patti the highest response rate. But, in this case, the response rate doesn't tell the entire story. Although the response rate is half a percentage rate above the 45–60-year-old list, the cost per response doesn't decrease as dramatically as it did between the 30–45-year-old list and the 45–60-year-old list. Because the party store list cost more to rent, the overall cost of the mailing was higher, compromising some of the advantages of a higher response rate.

Comparing Offers

As we mentioned in Chapter 2 and earlier in this chapter, you will effect the biggest changes in your desktop marketing programs by 1) changing your target market or list, and 2) changing your offer. We've looked at using different lists. Now let's take a look at how different offers might affect Patti's evaluation of her efforts.

For her next mailing, Patti decides to test whether a free gift offer would help increase her response rate. She offers a free balloon bouquet to anyone who responds to her direct mail. Because she knows her original offer was successful, she'll use that offer as her control and will test the balloon offer on only a 10 percent sample of the mailing.

With this mailing, she mails to an additional 10,000 names in the 45–60-year-old list and to the last 3,000 from the party shop. (Unfortunately, although it's a wonderful list, the party shop only has 5,000 customers on record.) Because she has depleted the party shop list, Patti doesn't bother to include samples of that list in her test mailing. It would be useless for her to learn that it could be successful in the future, since she couldn't combine a big party shop/balloon offer in the future. Therefore, she tests only the 45–60-year-old list.

Not surprisingly, the balloon bouquet offer leads to a higher response rate. Now Patti needs to calculate whether the extra response makes up for the extra cost of the gift.

	45–60 no gift	45–60 gift	Party shop
Number mailed	8,000	2,000	3,000
Cost per name	$.056	$.056	$.10
Cost of list	$448	$112	$300

	45–60 no gift	45–60 gift	Party shop
Remaining program costs	$4,800	$1,200	$1,800
Total no. of responses	168	80	78
Response rate	2.1%	4.0%	2.6%
Cost/response—no gift	$31.23	$16.40	$26.93
Cost of gift fulfillment		$640	
Cost/response—gift	$31.23	$24.40	$26.93

The balloon bouquet more than pays for itself with increased response. Although the bouquet costs Patti $8.00, the cost per response with the gift is still $6.83 less than the mailing without the offer.

Patti should continue to keep an eye on how the balloon responders play out as clients as opposed to the nonballoon responders. There is a possibility that a lot of the balloon responders were only after the balloon bouquet and have no plans to do more catering with Patti. She should make sure that the balloon responders spend enough money with her to pay for her desktop marketing efforts. If these respondents do prove to be money makers, she should change her standard desktop marketing offer to the balloon bouquet offer and work to improve that format.

Program's Success or Failure

With your detailed analysis complete, you should take the time to evaluate the overall desktop marketing program. Worksheet 8 in Appendix A will help you to combine all of your results into one comprehensive evaluation. The worksheet is divided into three parts to summarized your direct mail results, your phone results, and your overall results.

When you are evaluating the overall results, examine what worked particularly well and what didn't work. Maybe the direct mail paid off big, but the phone follow-up costs you a lot of extra money for minimal results. Or, maybe you would have made money if you hadn't sent that expensive fulfillment package to all your undecided respondents. Because you control all the elements of desktop marketing, you can pick and choose which elements to change next time and which to keep.

CHAPTER

11

Maintain Your Customers

Up to this point, we have shown you how you can use your Macintosh to help find new customers. However, finding new customers is only the first part of a successful desktop marketing campaign. A key part of desktop marketing is *maintenance* of your customers.

Maintenance sounds dull and boring, but this chapter will show you it doesn't have to be. Maintenance refers to everything you do once a person responds—from initial billing and order fulfillment to making future sales. In this chapter, we'll first explain *what* a database is and why an electronic database is extremely valuable to any desktop marketing plans. We then explain how to plan and create your own customer database. You can then use that database to merge with other lists and databases. We show you how you can use one database to manage your desktop marketing orders, with the database doing everything from preparing shipping labels to printing invoices. For products or services that require a long selling process, we show how you can set up a lead-tracking system to monitor your sales reps' contacts with a prospect or customer. Finally, we give some guidance on planning a continuing series of marketing programs.

As you learned from calculating the values of your customer, the true money value comes from repeat purchases and larger buys. To keep those orders coming, you need to keep in touch with your customers. You'll find a database invaluable for tracking and maintaining your customers and their needs.

What Is a Database?

A database can represent a wide variety of things. If you keep a personal address book with addresses and phone numbers, you have a database. If you keep customer information on a rolodex on your desk, you have a database. For our purposes, we will use a definition from *Direct Marketing* magazine.

Direct marketing will develop and maintain a database of customer or prospects which:

- Is a vehicle for storing and measuring responses

- Is a vehicle for storing and measuring purchases

- Is a vehicle for continuing direct communication to the prospects, respondents, and customers

A customer or prospect database contains records, with each record holding all the information about a particular customer or prospect.

Each record is made up of several different fields, with each field representing a different piece of information about the record. Even when you maintain your list of customers or prospects on paper, you usually use some form of records and fields. Take a rolodex. Each card holds a single record, and each card usually holds the same fields—name, address, and phone number.

Benefits of a Database

You can duplicate these records and fields electronically almost as easily as you can on paper. However, although the initial structure of an electronic database may seem similar to a paper-based database, immense differences become apparent when you actually want to manipulate the data. With your own electronic database, you can select any customer record based on the contents of any fields you've included in the database. MarketPlace Business is a perfect example of an electronic database. With MarketPlace, you can choose businesses in one specific location or a certain type of business.

In the same way, you could use your own customer database to look for your customers by name or any other characteristic, such as products purchased, money spent, or sales territory. Working with an electronic database, you type the exact criteria you want to match and the database management software finds all the matching records. Unlike a paper-based database, you don't have to look at every record to locate the right files.

In addition to locating records easily, you can quickly rearrange the records in a database any way you want. For example, you can rearrange all the records alphabetically, or by ZIP code, or by value of purchases. In database terminology, this type of rearranging is called sorting. Sorting makes it very easy to review customers or to test different ways to categorize your customers. For example, sorting customers by sales volume lets you review the spread of sales from the best to the worst customers and gives you some guidance as to where you should draw the line between good and mediocre customers.

Finally, you can use an electronic database to help you do analysis of your customers or prospects, much as we explained using MarketPlace to do market analysis. You can count how many customers or prospects fit a specific criterion; you can add up total sales; and you can generate summary reports.

Customer Lists

nless you've just begun your business, you probably already have a list of customers. If your customer list isn't already in an electronic database package, you should make this your first database project.

There's a wide variety of database management software packages available for the Macintosh. They vary from simple databases included in integrated packages such as Microsoft Works to more advanced database management packages such as FileMaker, 4th Dimension, and Double Helix. If you are new to databases, you should probably stick to the simpler databases systems, particularly if you expect to use the database primarily to create lists and to do sorting. As you become more sophisticated and want to do more manipulations with your database, you can always migrate to more advanced, relational databases such as 4th Dimension or Double Helix.

A lot of the ultimate power of any database depends on advance planning. When planning a database, first try to imagine all the possible fields you may need for each record and all the ways you would like to use the database. Even if you don't have the data for all fields yet, it's much easier to build the database with all the possible fields. Once you have a database filled with data, it's usually more difficult to make changes.

Any customer database should contain some basic fields:

First name

Last name

Title (if a business)

Business name (if business)

Address with apt number, suite number, or mail stop

City

State

ZIP

Phone number

Product(s) purchased/Part numbers

Date of purchase

$ Amount purchased

You may have additional information depending on your product or service. For example, if you are an insurance agent, you may have fields representing the types of insurance held, for how much coverage, and expiration dates. A valve manufacturer might include type of valve, size of connectors, and the material the valve is made of (bronze, stainless steel, etc.).

If you are new to databases, you can create a simple but effective customer database using the database portion of Microsoft Works. Works combines database functionality with word processing, spreadsheet, and graphics. Works lets you sort records by the different fields and lets you select groups of records by matching criteria.

In Works, the matching capability is somewhat limited compared to other more advanced databases, in that you can't set multiple matching criteria without finding every record that meets any part of the criteria. In other words, if you try to find all the people in Wisconsin who have spent over $100 with your company, the best you can do with Works is find all the Wisconsin customers *and* a second listing of all the customers who have spent over $100. However, if you want to start simply and get a basic tool that can handle many tasks, Works is an excellent product to learn the basics of databases.

As described in Chapter 5, you can use your customer database as the basis for deciding what type of prospects you should go after. Prospects similar to your current customers are your most likely candidates. To help decide what locations you should request when you rent a list, take a count of how many customer records you have for different states, cities, or ZIP codes. Browse through the customer database to see the names and types of businesses. If you haven't been collecting such information as number of employees, age range, or income ranges in the past, maybe you can find a way to gather that information from your customers in the future.

> ### Gather Customer Information
> If you use a warranty card or service cards for your business, consider asking two or three demographic questions on the card. Although you won't get a lot of cards back—from 10 percent to 50 percent—these extra questions can help flesh out your customer database.

Use Your Customer List with Prospect Lists

Once you have your customer database in an electronic format, you can easily integrate it into any desktop marketing program you plan. It's a good idea to contact your customers whenever you're doing a marketing program. If you're contacting both your customers and prospects, you should make sure you don't have the same people on both lists. The process of looking for matching names in two different databases is called merge/purge, because you merge the two databases together and remove (or purge) the duplicate names.

If you get the prospect list in an electronic format, you can probably do the merge/purge operation with your database management software. If you plan to do the merge/purge yourself, try to get information in the same fields that you already have in your customer database to make merging easier. You can always get the list electronically if you use a product like MarketPlace, and many list rental places will give you the information in personal computer format for an additional charge. If you do get the prospect list electronically, add the records temporarily to your customer list. Most database software can locate records that are exactly the same and eliminate the duplicates.

Unfortunately, exact duplicates are rarely the case. Even if you're the only one entering information in a database, you're likely to be inconsistent. One time you might enter *Stephen Day* and the next time *Steve Day*. Or you might write *IBM* one time and *International Business Machines* the next. This makes exact matching a very difficult task, particularly when the two lists have different sources. If your list isn't too long, the best method to find duplicate records is to sort the list alphabetically and browse over it yourself. Chances are you'll be much better at recognizing duplicates than any Macintosh-based database management program.

If you have very large lists or are renting lists, you can ask a lettershop to do a merge/purge for you. Many lettershops have the most advanced matching software available and will do a much better job of finding duplicates than the software you have on your Macintosh. You may have to shop around a bit to find a lettershop that can handle a customer database that's based on a Macintosh. Many lettershops assume customer lists will come in on mainframe tape and may not have the necessary tools to convert your Macintosh information into a format they can use.

Save Money with Merge/Purge

Some rental list owners will let you purge out your own customer names from their lists *before* they calculate how many names you're renting. To do this, the list renter generally requires that a mainframe tape of their names be sent to a third party, usually a bonded lettershop. Because the lettershop is bonded, list owners trust that their names won't be added to other lists without any payment.

Once the lettershop has performed the merge/purge, it reports to you and the list rental company the number of unduplicated names. Since this can save you considerable money in list-rental fees, you should consider this option every time you rent a list.

No matter which method you use, you will never eliminate all the duplicate names in a mailing. You've probably seen that even the most sophisticated users of direct mail can't merge/purge successfully; you receive credit card offers from companies whose credit cards you already have, or subscription offers from magazines you already get. If you do a desktop marketing program for looking for new customers, you're likely to reach some of your current customers. You can specify on the mailing that the special, low-price offer is "only for new customers," but you will still get customers taking advantage of it. Generally, you're better off letting a few customers get a good deal than antagonizing them by turning them down.

Order Management Database

I f your desktop marketing program results in sales coming directly to you, setting up a database management system to handle the orders can be straightforward—and very powerful. You should set up the order management database and have it ready before you send the first piece of mail or make your first phone call. When you're developing your response device, think about what information you ultimately want in your database, because the information on the response device will be the backbone of your database.

As you plan your order management database and response device, think about what pieces of information will help you sell more later. Clearly, the most important piece of information is the name and address. A phone number is a close second, although you'll find that a fair number of consumers won't include their phone numbers if they don't want to be contacted via the telephone.

If respondents are actually buying your product, you need to know both the billing address and the shipping address. The address will probably be the same for households (unless they're giving a gift), but it can be very different for businesses. You should have fields in the database for both pieces of information, since you'll need both for fulfillment of the order.

For business marketing, you may even need space for an additional name and address for the actual decision maker. It's possible that a senior manager makes the decision to buy a product but has it shipped to a staff member *and* has accounts payable pay the bill. In the process of capturing delivery and payment information, you don't want to lose the name of the decision-making senior manager, because that's the name you'll want to use in future desktop marketing programs.

In your database, you will also need to capture what the customer has ordered, how much it costs, and how the customer is paying for it. This information is vital for quick fulfillment and billing as well as future marketing efforts.

You should also try to capture information about what marketing effort caused this new customer to contact you. If you only made an offer to one type of prospect, it's obvious where they came from. Chapter 10 discussed several ways you can code a mailing or advertising to help you distinguish where a respondent heard of your offer. Since there will always be times when the respondent has absolutely no idea where he or she heard of the offer or got your phone number, make sure your database can accept "unknown" in the source field.

Once you have the basic information, you may be tempted to try to gather additional information along with every order. Information such as type of company, company size, number of members in the household, ownership of home, and so on, seem like wonderful additions to your database. Be very careful about asking these types of questions. Every question you ask tends to decrease response rate.

A lot of people don't like volunteering more information than they feel is necessary. Customers are becoming more sophisticated and most realize you only want the information to enhance your database. In fact, if they respond via the mail, you'll find a large number of customers won't fill in the extra questions. They know the questions aren't necessary for fulfilling their orders. Try to limit your questions to one or two that will truly qualify your respondents or help you improve future marketing.

Mechanics of Using an Order Management System

All the planning of the structure of your order management system should take place hand-in-hand with the development of your response device or telemarketing script. The entire database structure should be built and ready for data when you make your first contact with prospects. Once you've made contact, there are many ways you can actually add data to an order management database.

If you have enough computers and are receiving orders over the phone, you can type in the information as it comes. The database could be set up to hold all the necessary information and can even prompt the telemarketer on what information to ask for next. If you're receiving mail responses, you may prefer to enter them into the database at the end of each day or even save them to enter them in one big batch once a week. You may find that during the major response period after any desktop marketing effort that you'll need to do data entry daily for a couple of weeks. After that, the responses will slow down enough to merit weekly entries.

If you're getting more responses than your regular staff can handle, you may consider hiring an outside service to enter the information for you. These companies are called key punchers, and they can often help you with the fulfillment of your offer as well. They can give you daily or weekly reports of the number of calls or responses that have come in and how many items they've fulfilled. If you decide to go with an outside service, make sure that you work closely with it on the database structure to ensure you'll be able to transfer the database to your Macintosh database software after the desktop marketing program is finished.

It's possible to develop a system that can handle all of your needs in one database. The same database can be used to enter the order or response, generate a purchase order or fulfillment request, print out mailing labels, create an invoice, and make summary reports on all activity.

Example of a Complete Order Management System

Edgar Lionel runs an organic lawn-care service in western Pennsylvania. He has just used direct mail to offer local homeowners four weeks of lawn care for 20 percent off. He hopes the homeowners will be so impressed by the results of this care that they will continue the service when the four weeks are over. Although he expects most of his responses to come in over the telephone, he includes a response device for mail responders.

Before sending out his mail, Ed uses FileMaker Pro, a database management software package to create a full-fledged order management database. He also wants to use the database as a measure of the success of the direct mail program. Ed first plans what information he'll need from each respondent to fulfill any orders. He needs to know their addresses and both their daytime and evening phone numbers (in case he needs to reach them during the day). He then needs the size of their yards and their current conditions (excellent, very good, good, etc.). With this information, he can generate a quote for weekly lawn-care service. Upon receiving the quote, respondents will either agree to take the offer and will set a day and time for the first appointment, or respondents will request the quote in writing and ask for further information on the service.

Ed has rented his names from a local civic organization that's willing to give it to him in electronic format. Because Ed wants to compare nonrespondents to respondents and to ease data entry time, he starts his database by bringing in the names and addresses of everyone he's mailing to. Like most database management software, FileMaker Pro allows him to import records from other formats.

With the prospect records in the database software, Ed creates two simple ways to look at his data—either one record at a time or as a complete listing. He can easily switch back and forth between either layout, depending on which is more helpful at any given time (Figures 11.1 and 11.2).

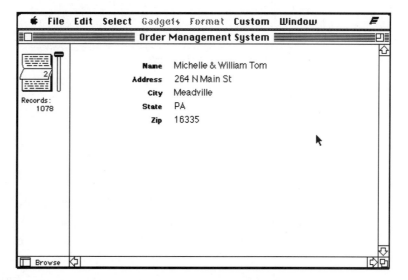

Figure 11.1: With the prospect list in FileMaker Pro, he can look at each record one at a time.

Ed plans to use this preentered data to save him data entry time. Whenever Ed receives a new response, he'll first search the database to find the prospect name that matches the respondent name. For example, if an order comes from Charlotte Hammer, 304 Main St, he can search the name field in the database for any Hammers. This searching will enable him to find basic information on most respondents, letting him track results at the same time that he's saving data entry time.

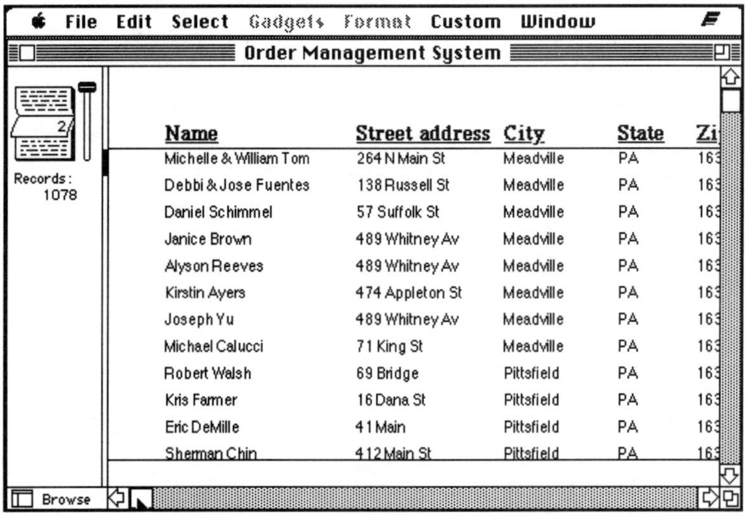

Figure 11.2: If he prefers, Ed can get a quick overview of all the records he'll be mailing to.

After entering all the MarketPlace data and laying it out, Ed creates an electronic data entry form. Once he finds the matching name and address in the database, he'll change to the Data Entry layout. First, he ties this layout to the basic database, so that it will automatically enter the name and address from the original record. Ed then designs the rest of the Data Entry form. His first field requires that he type the size of the yard. For the next field, Yard Condition, he creates a small menu with the possible choices: Excellent, Very Good, Good, Fair, and Poor. Once he's entered the yard size and made a selection of the yard condition, the next field, Quote, automatically generates a quote. To do this, Ed connects the Quote field to a table which matches the size of the yard and its condition to the appropriate quote. The remaining fields allow him to enter requests for more information, offer acceptances, appointment dates, times and directions to the acceptor's home (Figure 11.3).

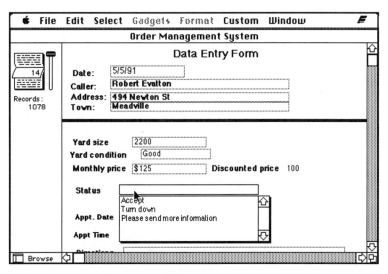

Figure 11.3: The electronic data entry form lets Ed enter all the necessary information for every response.

Next, Ed sets up the database to handle the fulfillment of information requests. To do so, he designs two more layouts, the quote layout and the mailing label layout. Each of the layouts links directly to the data from the Data Entry form. At the end of each day, he will be able to search for all the records that requested a written quote and more information. He'll then print out the matching quote forms and mailing labels to put together a fulfillment package. For those who order the service, Ed designs an invoice layout, again linking it to the Data Entry form. After he prints out the fulfillment quotes and labels, he'll be able to search for all the people who actually ordered the service. Then he can print out invoices and mailing labels to be sent directly to them.

Finally, he designs a report to display all the appointments that have been made to date, so he will be able to distribute the appointment list to his lawn care staff. He can also use this report to update the calendar the telemarketers will refer to, to insure they don't schedule too many appointments at the same time.

The efficiency of this one database amazes Ed. One person can now do the administrative work that used to take two or three people to handle. At the end of the desktop marketing program, he'll also be able to use the database to analyze the results of this efforts. He could generate reports comparing one ZIP code versus another, literature requesters versus immediate orders, and conversion rates of literature requesters. Not only will he be able to service his new customers more quickly, but he will learn a lot of valuable information that will help him gain even more customers in the future.

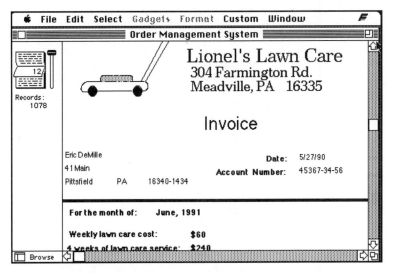

Figure 11.4: The order management system can automatically generate invoices for everyone who has ordered the service.

Lead Tracking

As you can see from Ed's example, managing your prospects and customers can be simple if they order directly from you at the main office. All the desktop marketing efforts go out of one central office and all the incoming information comes back to the same central office. All this outgoing and incoming is easy to track, using one centralized database.

Managing and maintaining your prospects and customers are more difficult if your desktop marketing goal is less tangible, i.e., to generate retail store traffic or generate leads for your sales force. With store traffic, you rarely know if customers are the target of your desktop marketing efforts or just happened to walk into your store. And, as we have mentioned before, a sales force can be very poor at following up leads. In addition, sales reps tend to be even worse at reporting back on the results of the leads. Sales reps usually don't like to admit they aren't entirely responsible for a sale, so they're less likely to admit the new customer came in as a desktop marketing lead.

In the case of store traffic and sales leads, there are some ways to track results and build a good customer list. If you are trying to increase retail traffic, include a coupon in the mailing for the respondent to use when visiting the store or purchasing the product. Counting the number of coupons you get will give you a sense of the response to your desktop marketing program. If you're willing to spend the extra time and money, you can actually attach name and address labels to each coupon, or you can gather information for your database by asking the respondent to fill out name and address information on the coupon, and then you can enter the same information into your database. Or, you can create some type of frequent buyer or store membership plan to encourage customers to sign up with you.

You need to try different techniques if you're dealing with a sales force. Because good sales reps use many different techniques to close a sale, it can be very difficult to find out what happens to the leads you send them. By creating an automated lead-tracking system, you can encourage your reps to keep track of what actions they have taken with every lead.

With a lead-tracking system, your reps can look up a prospect, write a letter, and generate a mailing label in a couple of steps. Or, the rep can look up a customer record, find the phone number and call to emphasize certain product features. All of the activities the rep takes in regard to each prospect are recorded in the lead-tracking system. When you want to learn the status of the leads you have sent, you can just ask your reps for a copy of their individual databases.

You can set up lead-tracking systems in any type of relational database, such as 4th Dimension or Double Helix. There are some other relational databases which have been developed with lead tracking in mind, so that you may find it easier to create a database within them.

Example of a Lead-Tracking System

LaVern Washington created just this type of lead-tracking system for her cellular telephone sales reps. She was tired of sending her reps leads and hearing nothing about them. She also wanted to get more information from sales reports but didn't want to swamp her reps with paperwork and prevent them from making sales.

First, LaVern took the mailing list she had created with MarketPlace Business and exported it to a text file. She exported virtually every field of information, because she was never sure what information would be useful to her sales reps. She then brought the list into CAT III, a lead-tracking software product, and created a prospect record for each person from the MarketPlace list (Figures 11.5 and 11.6).

Name List			
C•A•T® III—V1.00 by Chang Labs			
LaVern Washington@Cellular Tel			
□□□ **Work/View/Priority**			1216
W V P Account		City	St
✓ A A A		Dallas	TX
✓ A F I A Worldwide Ins Co		Dallas	TX
✓ A F Viale&son		Dallas	TX
✓ A J Marchionne Ins Agcy Inc		Dallas	TX
✓ A PH Paul		Dallas	TX
✓ A S Sandberg&co Inc		Dallas	TX
✓ A T A Insurance Agency Inc		Dallas	TX
✓ Acacia Mutal Life Ins		Ft. Worth	TX
✓ Adamo Ins Agnecy Inc		Ft. Worth	TX
✓ Adams Village Ins Agcy		Dallas	TX
✓ ADD-Men Services Inc		Ft. Worth	TX
✓ Aetna Life&casualty		Dallas	TX
✓ Aetna Life&casualty		Dallas	TX

Figure 11.5: It's simple to bring any kind of a basic list of prospects into CAT III.

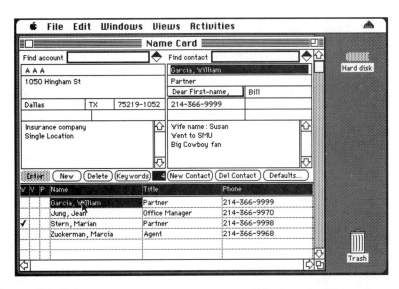

Figure 11.6: As a rep uses CAT III, he can add a lot of additional information for a single record, including multiple contacts within the same company or household.

She then sorted the list geographically, divided it into her five different sales territories, and created five subfiles. LaVern sent each subfile to the appropriate rep just as her direct mail piece went out. Once responses began rolling in, she forwarded the leads to the rep in that territory. To help the reps respond to and track the leads, LaVern had included several templates with the prospect file she sent each rep.

First, she created a standardized response letter to send to every respondent. The rep just has to search for the prospect's record and then call up the letter template (Figure 11.7). The letter automatically fills in all the proper address information and the date; all the rep needs to do is print it out. And, the rep can also quickly print out a matching mailing label.

LaVern had also added three other standard letters, including a "Thank you for the order" letter; "It's been four weeks, have you made a decision yet?" letter; and "How is the new phone working out?" letter. In all the cases, the rep only has to look up the name and call up the right letter format and all the appropriate information is filled in. However, if a rep wants to customize any of the letters, he or she can easily edit it before printing the letter. Or, if the rep doesn't like the tone of one of LaVern's paragraphs and wants to make a permanent change to the letter template, he or she has the control to do so.

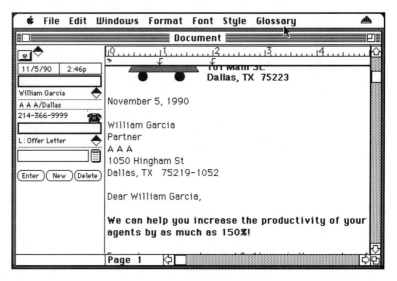

Figure 11.7: You can create a letter template that is automatically filled in with the information from any record you select.

LaVern also included a standard message pad in the lead tracking system as well. She knew how frustrating it was for reps to keep track of all their pieces of paper with information from prospect or client phone calls. With their new CAT database, the reps can quickly look up the prospect or client record and type in the gist of the call (Figure 11.8). This message file will stay linked to the appropriate client, so that the rep can easily track contacts. In the same vein, LaVern created a simple call report, so that the rep can easily fill in what happened on any given face-to-face call.

When a sale is actually made, LaVern also wanted to make it simple for the reps to create a sales order. As a result, she included a preformatted invoice and order form. Again, the rep only has to locate the appropriate name in the database and enter the order, and out comes a formatted order form.

Of course, none of the lead-tracking system so far helps LaVern with her lead-tracking problem. Fortunately, the CAT III system allows the reps to summarize all their information in series of reports. The rep can classify leads or customers into any category and select only those leads or customers that fit a specific category. The system will generate a report listing all of the clients or customers that fit the category.

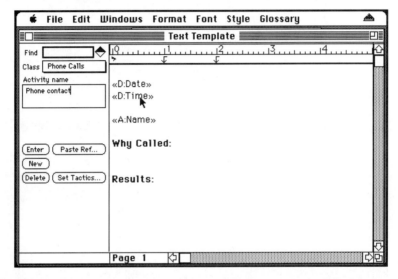

Figure 11.8: By using automation, CAT III makes it much easier for any sales rep to track the results of incoming and outgoing phone calls to clients or prospects.

Better yet, CAT III can generate an activity report, listing all the activity that has gone on for an individual client, an entire group of clients, or a specific type of activity over any number of days (Figure 11.9). Because she has the original prospects in her own file, LaVern can match the reps' information to her initial information to learn which prospects have responded. Although it isn't perfect, LaVern can now keep an eye on the productivity of her sales force while learning how to improve her desktop marketing efforts.

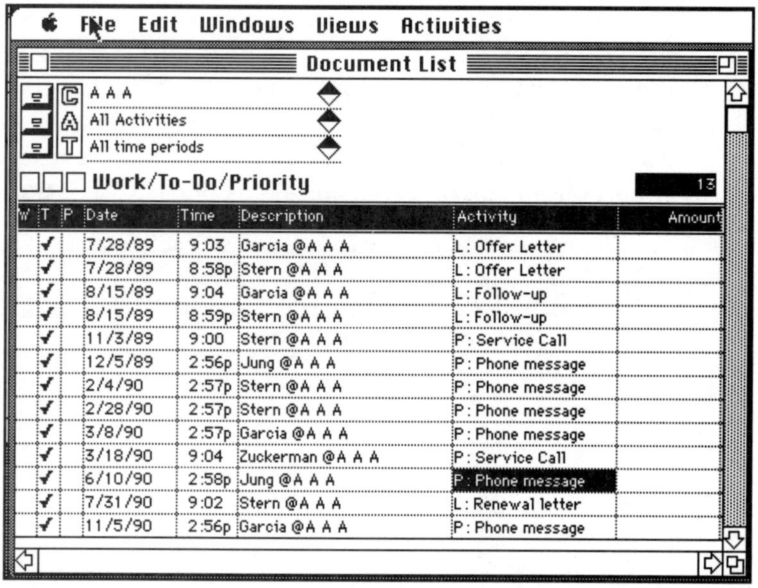

Figure 11.9: Activity reports are an excellent way for a sales rep or sales manager to keep track of the status of different leads.

Continuing Marketing Programs

Once you create your customer databases, they become one of your most valuable assets. Use these databases to encourage your customers to buy more. To help decide how to reach your customers, you should think and plan like a salesperson. A good salesperson knows you should only contact a customer when you have something to offer that will put the customer in a better position. Making contact for the sake of making contact is expensive and generally wastes money and time.

Categorizing Customers

The first rule for continued maintenance is that all customers and contacts are not created equal. Some customers are great customers; some customers are a one-time shot. An old sales rule says that 20 percent of your customers will generate 80 percent of your income. You want to be sure to focus most of your money and time on that 20 percent and keep your investment in the other 80 percent at a minimum.

A very effective approach to guide the categorization of your customers is to set up some type of scoring system for your database of customers and prospects. The most commonly used system is the A, B, or C accounts.

> *A Customers:* Customers who have bought at least $xx in the last 12 months.

> *B Customers:* Customers who have bought more than $yy but less than $xx in the last 12 months; or customers who have bought more than $xx, but not in the last 12 months.

> *C Customers:* Customers who have bought up to $yy in the last 12 months; or customers who have bought between $yy and $xx, but not in the last 12 months.

If you find that some measure other than purchase amount is important to your categorization scheme, add those to your definitions. For example, a specialty food company may find that some of its customers order gift baskets regularly throughout the year. Some of the other customers may spend the same amount of money, but they order only in November and December. Therefore, order frequency could play a major role in their desktop marketing planning—and therefore, their customer categorization scheme. Once you've decided on the dividing point for each category, you should go through your customers and rate all of your accounts.

Next, you should determine how often and what type of contact you should have with your different types of customers, keeping in mind each contact should have a purpose. Generally, A customers should be contacted most frequently, B customers the next, and C customers the least. The method of contact you use with each category may differ widely. For example, you may assign all your A accounts to sales reps to receive direct, face-to-face contact. Your B accounts might all be assigned to telesales people, to be serviced regularly via the phone. Finally, your C accounts might be handled with direct-mail efforts on an occasional basis. You can create a simple matrix to indicate how often each type of customer should be contacted and in what format (Figure 11.10).

	Phone	Mail	Visit
A	Monthly	Monthly	Monthly
B	Monthly	Monthly	Quarterly
C	Quarterly	Quarterly	Annually

Figure 11.10: Create a simple customer contact matrix to decide the level of effort you'll extend for each type of customer.

If your continuing contacts will be made via desktop marketing efforts, you should think of each contact as a separate effort in your ongoing customer programs. You should create a Program Outline and have objectives for each type of contact. This will help ensure you have purpose to each contact, instead of contacting customers just to keep in touch.

You can score prospects using a system similar to your customer scoring.

A Prospects: Inquiries that have been received within the last 90 days as a result of direct contact with a salesperson, direct mail, or telephone; or qualified leads less than 12 months old that haven't converted to customers.

B Prospects: Inquiries that are over 90 days that have received at least three additional contacts and not qualified as a lead; or inquiries from reader service; or leads that are over 12 months old that haven't converted to customers.

C Prospects: Inquiries over 180 days old that have not qualified as leads; qualified leads over 12 months old but less than 36 months old.

A software company has been doing desktop marketing to sell its software. It has used both direct response advertising and direct mail. The direct marketing offer encourages interested prospects to call an 800 number for a demo disk. The company also does outbound telemarketing to follow up on inquiries. Its prospect rating might be as follows:

A Prospects: People who have called the 800 number in the last 90 days and still expressed interest after receiving a telemarketing call.

B Prospects: People who called the 800 number between three and six months ago or have called more recently but were unsure of their interest when called by telemarketers.

C Prospects: Inquiries older than six months.

Working Your Lists

As you did for your customers, you can create a contact matrix for your prospects. You can use the same desktop marketing programs for prospects as you use for your customers, as long as you keep in mind that both customers and prospects will be a part of the program when you are developing the offer and writing the copy. Don't emphasize first-time use of your product if current customers will also be getting the mailing. Focus on benefits that are good the first and the hundredth time someone uses your product.

As you continue with your desktop marketing efforts, you should put every marketing contact into your computerized database. By doing this, you can begin using prior contact history to establish the next logical contact and marketing activity. You can combine groups of customers into marketing categories based on such measurements as recency of order, frequency of ordering, or number of orders made.

Keeping up with all your contacts and all your desktop marketing programs will mean giving a lot of attention to your database. Tracking results requires on-line storage and the flexibility to change the files each time you introduce a new marketing program.

The key database element you must keep as up-to-date as possible is the names and addresses of your prospects and customers. If one of the sources of your prospect database is MarketPlace Business, you can update your records every quarter when the new CD-ROM comes out. To do so, define a list exactly like your current database but add the data options to *include only new and changed records.* You can then buy the modified records and merge them with your database file to update your records.

If the source of your names isn't MarketPlace, use the Postal Service to help you update your records. At least once a year, you should do a direct mailing via first-class or pay the extra fee in third-class to get address corrections sent to you. You can collect all the returned envelopes after a couple of weeks and make the changes to your database.

Don't be afraid to purge prospects or customers from your database if they no longer are worth the effort. A good cutoff point can be after a C-rated customer or prospect no longer fits even the C definition. These people clearly aren't interested in your products and services and you shouldn't be wasting your money or effort to contact them.

To get the most out of your databases, you should make them accessible to as many people in your company as possible. Sales or marketing people can learn a lot by sorting and categorizing customers and prospects. Even your financial staff may be interested in looking at customers' purchasing habits.

However, although you should give a lot of people access to the database, you shouldn't allow everyone the freedom to make changes. Because accurate database information is crucial for your marketing success, you don't want it bungled unwittingly by "helpful" staff members. You should have only one or two people responsible for making any record changes. Some of the more advanced database management packages allow you to lock the database with a password, so that only the person with the password can make changes, although everyone can view the database. Of course, since you do want everyone's input on changes that need to be made, you should establish a standard form for staff members to use to indicate which records need to be modified.

We've now shown you all the steps you need to take to set up a desktop marketing program of your very own. With a modicum of analytic skills, some creativity, and a good product, you'll find you can be very successful selling your products or services direct. Always be willing to test your assumptions and your programs, because only by testing will you be able to improve yourself. Although your first attempts may not be a roaring success, use the techniques you have learned to tease out what worked and what didn't. And with flexible desktop marketing tools, changes can be made quickly and easily, so that you can go out there and try again.

CHAPTER ELEVEN

A

Desktop Marketing Worksheets

Unlike many forms of marketing, desktop marketing depends on measurement to evaluate the success and failure of any program. The worksheets in this appendix will guide you through the number crunching you will need to do, both prior to beginning your desktop marketing efforts and after you've finished.

You can photocopy these worksheets and fill them in for different programs. Better yet, copy the worksheets to a spreadsheet program and calculate the figures as directed. When you're using the worksheets, don't worry about having the exact numbers, particularly with the first four worksheets. The goal of these four worksheets is to give you an overview of your business, not to nail it down exactly. If you're planning to market an entirely new product or service, you'll initially have to estimate numbers, until you have some real numbers to go on.

By the time you complete the first four worksheets, you'll have a set of benchmarks to use: marketing cost per order, customers' acquisition cost, sales contact cost, desktop marketing requirements, and a variety of other information that will help you to spend your time and your resources more wisely. The final worksheets will help you to plan and evaluate the results of any actual desktop marketing program.

Worksheet 1) Value and Worth of Customers

T he first benchmark you must establish is how much you're willing to spend to gain a new customer. When you don't know what a customer is worth to your business, you can lose money by spending more to acquire a new customer than the customer will ultimately buy.

We will take you through the worksheet, line by line:

A) Your total sales/revenue for the year: The figure you use here should be based on the products or services you will be selling via desktop marketing. If you will be using desktop marketing for different business units or different products, you should create a separate set of worksheets for each division.

If you prefer to look at the value of your customers in terms of units of sales instead of dollars, substitute units for the dollar signs and the references to value in the worksheet.

B) Total number of customers on file: If you have a customer database, simply count how many customers you have in the database. You can count all your customers or only customers you have had for the past year or two. If you are selling to businesses, you must decide up front what level of customer you are measuring. Are you counting every individual in the corporation who buys from you, each corporate site that buys, or the corporation as a whole? It doesn't matter which you choose, as long as you are consistent for the rest of your calculations. If you're a retail operation or some other business without a customer file, do your best to estimate how many people buy from you.

C) Percent of customers who order per year: Most companies do not get orders from all their customers every year and lose some customers each year. If the numbers aren't in your customer file, just make a guess on the percentage of your total customer's order annually.

D) Total number of active customers: To calculate this figure, set up your spreadsheet to multiply Total number of customers (line B) by Percent of customers that order per year (line C). This will give you the unique number of customers, not customer orders. You may have five customers that order 300 times per year. In this case, line D will calculate to be 5.

E) Total number of order/sales per year: This is the total number of orders or sales you get in a year's time, regardless of how many customers you have.

F) Average order/sale: This is a crucial number in the desktop marketing process. You will see "average order" asked for again and again on these worksheets. Average order is one of the key leverage points of desktop marketing. You're attempting to increase the size of the average order by improving your offer and changing your customer mix to those customers more likely to place large orders.

To calculate this figure, have the spreadsheet divide *Total sales/revenue per year* (line A) by *Total number of order/sales* (line E). When you get this number, take a look at it and check it against your gut feeling about the average order size. If you find that it is too high, go back and look at the sales total. Check for any exceptionally large sales that are unlikely ever to be repeated. Drop these high sales from your totals to give you a more realistic view of your average order.

G) Average number of order/sales per customer per year: Divide Total number of order/sales (line E) by Number of active customers (line D) to calculate this value. The average number of orders will be helpful in planning how you are going to fulfill customer orders. You will be able to compare your plans for new customers with your ability to fulfill the number of orders they will generate.

H) Average revenue per active customer per year: Divide the Total sales/revenue (line A) by Total number of active customers (line D). This average is your target number for your desktop marketing programs. You can compare the customers you are bringing in with the average revenue to learn if you are bringing in better or worse customers than you expected.

I) Gross margin percentage or gross profit percentage: Gross margin is the source of overhead payments and profit. It comes directly from your profit-and-loss statement. It is total sales revenue minus the total cost of sales or cost of goods divided by total sales. If you are planning to sell different products or services, try to use the gross margin for that specific product, not an average gross margin for all your products.

Gross margin will be very important for evaluating the success of any desktop marketing program. If the gross margin of your sales equals your marketing costs, you have marketing break-even. Any sales above the break-even point will contribute to your overhead, and most importantly, your profit.

J) Annual gross margin value of a customer: To calculate the annual gross margin value of a customer, multiply Gross margin (line I) by Revenue per customer (line H). On a year-to-year basis, you shouldn't spend more than the average annual gross margin value of a customer to acquire a new customer.

K) Number of years a customer orders: This is a difficult number to come up with if you aren't in the subscription business, but it is extremely useful for determining the worth of any new customer. If you can't find the figure, just make an educated guess.

L) Lifetime worth of a customer: Calculate this number by multiplying Annual gross margin value (line J) by Number of years a customer orders (line K). You can use the lifetime worth of a customer to guide how much you are willing to spend to acquire a new customer. You should not make customer acquisition decisions based on value of the initial order. In all likelihood, you'll not make money on a new customer's first order. You must look at the expected value of a customer over a lifetime to evaluate your acquisition methods. If the acquisition cost of a customer is greater than the lifetime worth of a customer, you can take steps to increase the lifetime worth, reduce acquisition costs—or look for another business.

Worksheet 2) Salesperson Cost and Closing

Y ou should use this worksheet if you use either direct sales reps or telephone sales reps. Understanding how much these sales reps cost you provides you with a baseline of how much or how little you need to use desktop marketing to support or replace your sales force.

To get the best sense of your needs, you should enter the numbers from last year or this current year in the first column. In the second column, you should calculate what your salespeople will need to do to achieve your forecast for next year.

The assumption behind this worksheet is that you don't have a sale until a salesperson takes an order. This means your marketing costs will be amortized into your sales contacts and finally into the orders that a salesperson makes.

A) Total sales/revenue for year: In the first column, this is the same number as Line A in Worksheet 1. If you're using a spreadsheet, you can link this directly to Worksheet 1. In the second column, you need to put the level of sales you hope to do in the future.

B) Total annual marketing expenses: This number represents all your expenditures for marketing: desktop marketing, advertising, sales promotion, sales compensation (plus bonus and commissions), support staff, management costs, travel, phone, and any other item you determine to be a marketing expense. If you're selling retail, you could include the cost of your retail space and inventory carrying costs as marketing expenses, since you're using the retail floor as a sales contact point.

C) Total number of orders/sales per year: Carry this number over from line E in Worksheet 1.

D) Average order/sale: Bring this number over directly from Worksheet 1, line F.

E) Number of salespeople: A salesperson is someone who has the responsibility of asking for an order. You can calculate the worksheet using only outside salespeople, or using outside and inside salespeople, or using independent representatives. If you include independent reps, be sure you included their commissions in the marketing expenses.

F) Average sales per salesperson: To calculate this average, divide Total sales/revenue (line A) by Number of salespeople (line E). You will have some salespeople who perform above this average and others who perform below, but this number gives you a sense of what each rep is achieving. Most companies get some sales regardless of sales activity and marketing activity, but you should include all the sales for these calculations. Your goal is to increase this number by improving your salespeople or improving your marketing.

G) Cost per salesperson per year: Divide your Total annual marketing expenses (line B) by Number of salespeople (line E) to arrive at what each salesperson costs you each year. This figure is based on the assumption that every marketing activity you do, from advertising to brochures, is oriented toward making sales and bringing orders to your salespeople. The rule of thumb for the nonretail salesperson is that your cost per salesperson usually runs three times the person's compensation.

H) Average number of orders per salesperson: Set your spreadsheet to divide Total number of sales/orders (line C) by Number of salespeople (line E). The results in the second column begin to give you a sense of what each salesperson is going to need to achieve your forecasted sales goals.

If you look at the number of orders a salesperson needs to generate per year, you begin to understand why good salespeople are so protective of their time. You can also begin to understand why salespeople are generally not great at following up new "leads." They are busy trying to make their numbers, and they know new contacts don't close at the same rate as existing customers.

I) Average sales contacts per day per representative: The number of sales contacts a representative can make per day is always a matter of great debate. In a retail environment, you should look at the average over a week, or longer, since numbers can be unusually high on any given day. It is easy to track a phone representative's contacts through the use of counter or scatter sheets (see Chapter 8). An outside sales-person can usually only make from two to five contacts a day.

You need to be realistic with yourself when determining how many contacts your representatives make per day. It is probably around two to three personal contacts and three to five phone contacts.

J) Available sales days per year per salesperson: Starting with 365 days per year, you need to deduct from available selling days the following: holidays, weekends, vacation days, sick days, training days, meeting days, personal days, award or recognition days, and any other days that sales representatives are not doing what you need them to be doing—selling. When you are through, you will have between 210 and 230 days available per representative. If you are using part-time representatives, multiply the result by the percent of a day the representative works to give you the available days.

K) Number of sales contacts per year per salesperson: Multiply Average sales contacts per day (line I) by Available sales days (line J) to come up with the possible number of sales contacts for each sales-person.

This is always an interesting number; it represents the total number of sales contacts your sales rep has available to ask for orders. The only way you can get more sales contacts is to hire more representatives or increase the use of the telephone. You can, however, make each con-tact more productive.

L) Cost per contact: Divide Cost per salesperson (Line G) by Number of sales contacts per salesperson (line K) to get the cost of every per-sonal or phone contact your sales reps make. Most people find this number to be outrageously high compared to national studies. The latest report by McGraw-Hill analyzing the cost of an industrial sales call puts the number at about $250 per personal call, including the salesperson's cost and travel. Most companies find the number to be over $400, without including all the marketing costs. It is safer to include all marketing costs in your calculations if you want to understand realistically the value of a sales contact. This will help you focus on the need to qualify inquiries before you hand them over to your sales force.

M) Average sales contacts needed per order: To learn how many sale contacts your reps need to make before getting an order, divide Number of sales contacts (line K) by Average number of orders (line H). Keep in mind that this will be a calculated number based on averages to be used to guide you in your planning. The figure also includes all the contacts a salesperson makes to prospects who never order.

N) Sales cost per order: Multiply Cost per sales contact (line L) by Average sales contacts needed (line M) to find how much each order costs you. If this cost is higher than your average order (line D), you have something to worry about. If the cost is greater than your gross margin per order, you also should worry, because you aren't bringing in any money for overhead or profit.

O) Closing rate: To calculate this percentage, divide Average number of orders (line H) by Number of sales contacts (line K). This close rate is important for later planning, because it will help you set expectations for any desktop marketing programs you plan. The better your qualification of inquiries and/or the higher the requirements you used to generate traffic, the higher your close rate. Some businesses close at a 30 percent rate (about one in three). Most close at a rate in the 10 to 20 percent range (one to two in ten).

P) Sales cost rate per order: Divide Sales cost per order (line N) by Average order/sale (line D) to come up with your marketing costs as a percent of revenue. You should arrive at approximately the same result you would have had by dividing your annual marketing expenses by your annual sales.

Worksheet 3) New Customer Planning

This worksheet is designed for you to establish what you want to do in the future. You can use this worksheet for your entire business, for a subset of your business, or for a specific program.

A) Total sales/revenues (current or previous year): You used this number in Worksheet 1, line A, and Worksheet 2, Line A, first column.

B) Annual sales forecast: This is the same number you used in Worksheet 2, line A, second column.

C) Revenue per active customer per year: Take this number from Worksheet 1, line H. This assumes that you will acquire new customers at the same rate as the current, base year.

D) Number of customers lost per year: Every business loses customers through attrition. Estimate how many of your current customers you will lose next year. (It may be easier to think of it as a percentage first: "I lose 5 percent of my customers each year," and then multiply that percentage by your customer base.)

E) Sales requiring new customers: This is one of the most complicated formulas yet. It calculates how many new sales you will have to make to meet your forecasted sales increase, taking into account lost customers: Sales Forecast (line B) −[Total Sales (line A) − (Number of customers lost (line D)× Revenue per active customer (line C))]

You now are getting to the real grit of your desktop marketing planning. If this number is high, desktop marketing will have to perform extremely well. If the number is small, you can be more selective about who you want to acquire as customers.

F) New customers needed for year: Divide Sales requiring new customers (line E) by Revenue per active customer (line C), to learn how many customers you will need to reach your new sales goals. Once you know this number, you know what you have to deliver with your desktop marketing programs.

G) Sales contact closing rate: Take this number from Worksheet 2, Line O.

H) Total number of prospects needed: Divide New customers needed (line F) by Sales contact closing rate (line G). You will need to locate this many prospects to achieve your overall forecast.

If you do not use a sales force, you can eliminate lines I through K from the worksheet.

I) Number of salespeople: Transfer the same number as in Worksheet 2, line E, second column.

J) Number of new customers needed per salesperson: You simply divide New customers needed (line F) by Number of salespeople (line I).

K) Total number of prospects needed per salesperson: To calculate this number, divide Total number of new prospects needed (line H) by Number of salespeople (line I). On average, each sales rep will need this number of prospects.

L) Total marketing budget: This is the same number you used in Worksheet 2, line B, second column.

M) Percent of budget for new business: It is difficult to assess how much of your expenditures for marketing are used for current customers and for prospects. It is generally accepted that an order from a current customer can be generated at about 20 percent of the cost of an order from a new customer. The lower your customer reorder rate, the higher the amount of marketing budget you need to devote to acquiring new customers.

N) Marketing budget for prospect generation: Multiply Total marketing budget (line L) by Percent of budget for new business (line M). This is the amount of budget you should be using for programs targeted toward new customers.

O) Marketing budget per prospect: Divide Marketing budget for prospect generation (line N) by Number of prospects needed (line H). Each prospect has a cost. For most businesses, the cost ranges from $40 to $150. It's best to understand how much you're going to need to spend before you begin so that you won't be surprised when you start calculating the costs of desktop marketing programs.

P) Marketing budget cost per new customer: Divide Marketing budget for Prospect Generation (line N) by New Customer Need for Year (line F). This is what you will spend for each initial order from a new customer. If your average order gross margin is higher than this number, you may lose money on obtaining each new customer.

Q) Average sales contacts needed per order: Get this number from Worksheet 2, line M.

R) Total contacts for new customers per salesperson: Multiply Number of new customers needed per salesperson (line J) by Average sales contacts needed (line Q). This number will show you how many contacts a salesperson will need to devote to new customer acquisition.

S) Number of sales contacts per year per salesperson: Take this number from Worksheet 2, line K.

T) Percent of contacts used for new customers: Divide Total contacts for new customers (line R) by Number of sales contacts (line S). With this number, you can determine what percent of your sales reps' sales calls should be devoted to new customers. The closer the new customer contact percent is to 100, the lower your sales will be, because most sales still come from current customers.

Worksheet 4) Market Size Requirements

Y ou can push numbers around all day, but when you've finished, if the target market you're planning to attack is not big enough to support your growth plans, you will have to make some modifications. You will need either a higher average order, a higher close rate, or a different target market.

With Worksheet 4, you calculate the concentric circles of a market (see Figure A.1) The outer circle is the entire target market you can reach. The next circle indicates how many from that market will respond to your offers. Within the respondent circle is the circle of respondents who are qualified to buy your product. Finally, the inner circle represents how many will actually become customers.

Figure A.1: Think of your customers as the inner portion of the big circle representing your market.

With this worksheet, you can calculate how big each circle is, according to your needs. You can then compare the numbers with the actual size of the market by using counts in MarketPlace (see Chapter 6) or other industry sources.

You can use this worksheet for a specific program, a group or division, or a specific product line. It should match the same parameters you have been using for Worksheets 1–3.

A) Prospects needed for year: You calculated this number on Line H, Worksheet 3.

B) Responses/traffic qualified as prospects: There is a distinction between responses and a prospect. Only a certain percentage of responses is qualified to become a prospect. The tighter the selection criteria you use with a desktop marketing program, the higher the level of qualification. Setting up a procedure to screen out the unqualified is important, because you don't want to waste expensive sales contact time on unqualified prospects. A typical qualification rate is 70 percent to 80 percent.

C) Responses needed per year: Multiply Prospects needed per year (line A) by Responses qualified as prospects (line B).

D) Response rate for desktop marketing program: Not everyone within your target market will respond to a desktop marketing program. Therefore, you need to estimate what percentage will actually respond. If you have never tested your desktop marketing approach before, you will be better off if you are conservative and choose a small percentage, from .5 percent to 1.5 percent. Don't believe you have something so unique that you are going to get double-digit responses. Unfulfilled, wild expectations are big demotivators for desktop marketers. It is better to be conservative… and maybe get pleasantly surprised.

E) Number of targets needed for desktop marketing program: Divide Responses needed per year (line C) by Response rate (line D). This number will tell you how big the universe of targets must be in order to generate the number of customers you need to obtain. Check this number against the actual counts in MarketPlace or the counts from your list broker.

F) Number of programs planned: If you think you will be doing a series of desktop marketing programs over the course of the year, you should indicate here how many.

G) Targets needed for each program: You won't need to reach all your targets in one effort if you are doing multiple programs. To calculate how many you need to contact, divide Number of targets needed (line E) by Number of programs planned (line F).

Worksheet 1
Value and Worth of Customers

A. Your total sales/revenue for the year $_____

B. Total number of customers on file   _____

C. Percent of customers that order per year   _____%

D. Total number of active customers (BxC)   _____

E. Total number of orders/sales per year   _____

F. Average order/sale (A/E) $_____

G. Avg. number of orders per customer per year (E/D)   _____

H. Avg. revenue per active customer per year (A/D) $_____

I. Gross margin or gross profit %   _____%

J. Annual gross margin value of a customer (HxI) $_____

K. Number of years a customer orders   _____

L. Lifetime worth of a customer (JxK) $_____

© Tracy Emerick, 1990, USA 603-926-4477

Worksheet 2
Salesperson Cost & Closing

		Current/ Last Year	Forecast
A.	Total sales/revenue for year (line A, WS. 1)	$_____	$_____
B.	Total annual marketing expenses	$_____	$_____
C.	Total number of sales/ orders per year (line E, WS. 1)	_____	_____
D.	Average order/sale (line F, WS. 1)	_____	_____
E.	Number of salespeople	_____	_____
F.	Average sales per salesperson (A/E)	$_____	$_____
G.	Cost per salesperson per year (B/E)	$_____	$_____
H.	Average number of orders per salesperson (C/E)	$_____	$_____
I.	Average sales contacts per day per salesperson	_____	_____
J.	Available sales days per year per salesperson	_____	_____
K.	Number of sales contacts per year per salesperson (IxJ)	_____	_____
L.	Cost per sales contact (G/K)	$_____	$_____
M.	Average sales contacts needed per order (K/H)	_____	_____
N.	Sales cost per order (LxM)	$_____	$_____
O.	Closing rate (H/K)	_____%	_____%
P.	Sales cost rate per order (N/D)	_____%	_____%

Worksheet 3
New Customer Planning

A. Total sales/revenues (line A, WS. 1) $_____

B. Sales forecast (next year) (col. 2, line A, WS. 2)   _____%

C. Revenue per active customer per year (line H, WS. 1) $_____

D. Number of customers lost per year $_____

E. Sales requiring new customers B–[A–(C*D)]) $_____

F. New customers needed for year (E/C)   _____

G. Closing rate (line O, WS. 2)   _____%

H. Prospects needed for year (F/G)   _____

I. Number of salespeople (col. 2, line E, WS. 2)   _____

J. Number of new customers needed per salesperson (F/I)   _____

K. Number of prospects needed per salesperson (H/I)   _____

L. Total marketing budget (col. 2, line B, WS. 2) $_____

M. Percent of budget for new business   _____%

N. Marketing budget for prospect generation (LxM) $_____

O. Marketing budget per prospect (N/H) $_____

P. Marketing budget cost per new customer (N/F) $_____

Q. Average sales contacts needed per order (line M, WS. 2) $_____

R. Total contacts for new customers per salesperson (JxQ)   _____

S. Number of sales contacts per year per salesperson (line K, WS.2)   _____

T. Percent of contacts used for new customers (R/S)   _____%

Worksheet Four
Market Size Requirements

A. Prospects needed for the year
   (col. 2, line H, WS. 3)   _____

B. Responses qualified as prospects   _____%
   (est. 70–80%)

C. Responses needed per year (A/B)   _____

D. Response rate for desktop marketing (.5–1.5%)   _____%

E. Number of targets needed for   _____
   new customer program (C/D)

F. Number of programs planned   _____

G. Targets needed for each program (E/F)   _____

©Tracy Emerick, 1990, USA 603-926-4477

Worksheet 5) Direct Mail Budgeting

By using this worksheet, you will be able to budget your direct mail efforts both before and after you complete the mailing. The end of the worksheet asks you to estimate the type of results you expect, so that you can get a sense of whether the costs will be covered. In the Program Evaluation Worksheet, you can then compare your expectations with the actual results. When you estimate the end results at the bottom of the worksheet, estimate the final sales results, even if there will be intermediate steps involved. If there are follow-up steps either via mail or phone, you will have to include those in your ultimate success calculations.

In order to have an accurate budget for your mailing programs, you need to determine the cost for all materials used as part of the mailing, even if the materials preexist. This includes letterhead, second pages, envelopes, and brochures. If you are having materials printed especially for a mailing, you can include the cost of the portions used for the mailing. If you hire someone to design letterhead, write brochures, or prepare mechanicals, you can include the costs as an outside service or you can count the costs as overhead.

This direct mail budgeting worksheet is designed to give you results based only on your variable costs. If you include the preparation costs in the budgeting process, you might decide not to continue a program because the cost per sale is too high. However, if you were to continue the program, preparation costs would no longer be an issue, and the program might have an acceptable cost of sale.

A) Letterhead cost per page: If you use existing letterhead, simply divide your last printing bill by the quantity printed. If you had the letterhead carrier mounted or if you bought special pinholed letterhead for use in an ImageWriter, you will need to increase the cost per page by about 10 percent to account for the waste you'll experience while aligning the system.

B) Envelope cost, each: If you have carrier-mounted envelopes to be fed through your ImageWriter, your costs will be higher than if you are using single envelopes with the LaserWriter.

C) Additional inserts, each: You may elect to include some specification sheets or coupons in your package. Calculate the cost of each by dividing the total bill by the number you order. Because printers have a trade practice of overshipping and billing up to 10 percent over what you ordered, be aware of *actual* costs and numbers when you make the calculation.

D) Reply form: You may have a special reply form printed on the second page of your own stationery, or you could have a reply postcard printed on seven-point thick paper stock. You should calculate the costs as covered above. If you are using labels to address the reply card, the cost of the label should be included with the cost of the reply form.

E) Brochure: Calculate the brochure as you calculated the cost of the other printed materials in the mailing.

F) Return envelope: Calculate the cost as you calculated the other costs.

G) Postage per package: This number will be based on the weight of your package, whether you mail it first- or third-class, and whether you take advantage of some of the postal discounts available for large mailings.

H) List cost per name: If you are using your own customer files, there is no cost. If you are renting names from some other list source, the price will vary. You might consider including the cost of labels here if you're generating labels with your own list.

I) Cost per piece: Sum the material costs from Line A to Line H. This number will tell you how much each direct mail package will cost you.

J) Total pieces mailed: This is the number of pieces mailed for a specific program, even though you may mail them over several days.

K) Total materials cost: Multiply Total pieces mailed (line J) by Cost per piece (line I) to get the total cost of materials for this direct mail program.

L) Outside service or part-time labor: If you use an outside mailing house to accomplish your mailing, you will have charges for each piece, probably quoted as a cost per thousand. You will also have charges for set up or management. To make sure that all of these charges are included in your per mailing cost, they should be entered as an aggregate amount, not a piece amount. Part-time labor is often a good source of staffing for folding your mailing materials and stuffing it in envelopes. Include the total labor cost on this line.

M) Total mailing cost: Add together Total materials costs (line K) and Outside service cost (line L). Materials, list, postage, and labor are the four components of any mailing. If you have your entire mailing executed on the outside, you can put the total amount here without calculating the piece cost.

The remaining entries on this worksheet give you a sense of what type of results you will need from your mailing to break even.

N) Estimated average order size: Estimate how big you expect each sale to be that results from your direct mail effort. You can use the same average order size you calculated in Worksheet 1 or come up with another average.

O) Gross margin: This is the percentage of money you make from a sale after you subtract cost of goods. You can get this from Worksheet 1, line 1.

P) Gross margin per average order: Multiply Gross margin (line O) by Estimated average order size (line N). This number will tell you how much you will make on each order after you pay for the cost of goods or services.

Q) Number of orders needed to break even: Divide Total mailing costs (line M) by Gross margin per order (line P). This number will help you estimate how many orders you must make to break even with your marketing costs.

R) Required order rate: Divide Number of orders needed (line Q) by Total pieces mailed (line J). This number can be an excellent reality check for your numbers. If the percent is in the double digits, you should consider doing a much less expensive program.

S) Response rate: This is the percentage of people you expect to respond to your mailing, whether it is an order or a request for more information. If your program is designed to develop traffic in your store, or for lead generation, the number of inquiries is the total number of responses you can track. You can take this number directly from Worksheet 4, Line D, or come up with a new one for this specific mailing.

T) Number of responses: Multiply Response rate (line N) by Total pieces mailed (line J) to come up with the number of responses you will receive.

U) Cost per response: Divide Total mailing cost (line M) by Number of responses (line O) to learn how much it will cost you for every response you get. This number is one benchmark of desktop marketing, the cost it takes to get someone to indicate interest in your product. This cost can and should be used across all programs to compare program effectiveness. If you are using any type of fulfillment mailing, you will also need to complete Worksheet 7, Fulfillment Budgeting.

V) Total number of sales from mailing: This is the number of total sales you can attribute to this program. Total sales will seldom be a scientific number. It will include a great deal of personal judgment on your part to properly assign sales to this program. One way to make this judgment is to follow up a number of the responders—several months later—to learn what percentage ultimately bought your product or service. You can then extrapolate this percentage to all of your respondents.

W) Total revenues from mailing: This number is the money that comes in, thanks to the mailing.

X) Cost per sale: Divide Total mailing cost (line M) by Total revenues from mailing (line Q). This is another benchmark you can use to compare the effectiveness of different desktop marketing programs.

Y) Average order size: Divide Total revenues from mailing (line R) by Total number of sales from mailing (Line Q). You may find that the average order size you experience from direct mail is either smaller or larger than your sales using other means. Knowing this can be useful for planning future programs.

Z) Gross margin: This is the percentage of money you make from a sale after you subtract cost of goods. You can get this from Worksheet 1, line 1.

AA) Gross margin made on program sales: Multiply Gross margin (line U) by Total revenues (line R). This number will tell you how much you made from the direct mail program after you paid for products or services. You will use this number to see whether you have broken even, with the marketing costs of the program.

AB) Profit/loss on program: Subtract Gross margin made on program (line V) from Total mailing costs (line M). When you do this subtraction, you will know whether you made money. This is where your assessment of the program becomes essential. Sales from this program may continue for up to a year or more. You must decide if all sales are in and if the margin is accurate. If a program costs the same as its gross margin, you can extrapolate that you will have a positive return on this mailing over time if your customers continue to buy over several years. If this mailing is to old customers that you are trying to regenerate, and you do not make money, you can assume there is no point in continuing the program.

Worksheet 6) Phone Budgeting

ike the direct mail budgeting worksheet, this budget does not include any overhead or management costs. You may need to prepare one budget for telemarketing and another for telesales, because you will usually have different labor costs.

This worksheet allows you to first estimate your costs and results prior to actually doing the program to help you evaluate whether it is worth trying. You can then put in the actual results to compare and decide whether you should continue the program.

A) Hourly labor cost: The costs for telemarketers will usually be lower than the cost for telesalespeople. You can usually hire temporary employees to handle telemarketing needs, since it is entirely scripted. If you are using existing staff to make calls, your labor costs will be much higher, since they will rarely be as consistent about dialing the telephone.

B) Phone line charges: These numbers are easy to find in your regular phone bills. Take into account the geographic dispersal of the calls you are making, as this will affect the line charges. Don't mix charges for your regular business calls with the specific telemarketing calls.

C) Total variable costs: Your total variable costs are labor and phone lines. If you are using an outside service, plug that cost per hour into this line.

D) Total number of records to call: This is the number of people you plan to contact through your telemarketing or telesales program.

E) Percent of records contactable: No list will ever be 100 percent contactable, because of people moving, businesses going bankrupt, and no one there to answer the phone. You can estimate this percentage based on experience or knowledge of the list. Most likely, it will be anywhere from 60 percent to 85 percent.

F) Number of records contactable: Multiply Total number of records (line D) by Percent of records contactable (line E). This will give you the true numbers of records you can possibly reach.

G) Dialings per hour: The number of dialings that can be completed per hour will depend greatly on the experience level of your telemarketers. The general rate of dialing varies anywhere from 10 to 30 dialings per hour, partially dependent on how long the call lasts if contact is made.

H) Percent of dialings that make contact: Again, this number will vary depending on the list you are calling and when you are calling. The percent of contacts for business calls runs about 40 percent.

I) Contacts per hour: Multiply Dialings per hour (line G) by Percent of dialings making contact (line H).

J) Total telemarketing hours: Divide Number of records contactable (line F) by Contacts per hour (line I). You will probably be surprised to see exactly how many hours it will take to reach all of the people you are trying to contact.

K) Total telemarketing costs: Multiply Total telemarketing hours (line I) by Total variable costs per hour (line C).

L) Estimated average order size: Estimate of the size of each order you will get as a result of your phone marketing. Remember that it may vary from your typical average order due to a different marketing mechanism.

M) Gross margin: This is the percentage of money you make from a sale after you subtract cost of goods. You can get this from Worksheet 1, Line I.

N) Gross margin per average order: Multiply Gross margin (line M) by Estimated average order (line L). This number will tell you how much you will make on each order after you pay for the cost of goods or services.

O) Number of orders needed to break even: Multiply Total telemarketing costs (line K) by Estimated average order size (line L). This number will help you estimate how many orders you must make to break even with your marketing costs.

P) Required order rate: Divide Number of orders needed (line O) by Total number of records to call (line D). This number can be an excellent reality check for your numbers. If the percent is in the double digits, you should consider doing a much less expensive program.

Worksheet 7) Fulfillment Budget

Fulfillment for a program can be generated by phone, mail, or other media. You should calculate your fulfillment costs as part of your overall program. Include these costs when you are evaluating whether or not a program is profitable. This worksheet is designed to give you an overall evaluation of your program if you are using materials, rather than a salesperson, as a fulfillment vehicle.

Refer to Worksheet 5 for the description of most of these line items.

A) Letterhead cost per page.

B) Envelope cost, each.

C) Premium or gift cost: If you are using a premium or a gift as part of your offer, the cost should be included here. If you are giving away a sample of your product, the costs should be indicated as a fulfillment cost.

D) Reply form.

E) Brochure.

F) Return envelope.

G) Postage/freight per package.

H) Cost per name: You won't have any list rental costs when you are responding to inquiries. However, if you are using outside or part-time labor to type in your inquiries, you should enter the cost here.

I) Outside service costs, each: You may have a premium house fulfill your premiums. This is generally charged on a per-piece basis. See Worksheet 5, line L.

J) Delivered cost per piece: Sum together the items from Line A to Line I on this worksheet.

K) Total number of contacts: Estimate how many people you expect to respond to your offer requesting a fulfillment package.

L) Predicted response rate: Make your best guess at what percentage of those being contacted will respond to your offer. (You probably started thinking about this as you filled out Worksheet 5 or 6.)

M) Predicted number of inquiries: Multiply Total number contacted (line K) by Predicted response rate (line L) to calculate how many inquiries you should be expecting. Your fulfillment costs will only have to cover the number of inquiries you have, not your total contacts.

N) Total fulfillment costs: Multiply Predicted number of inquiries (line M) by Delivered cost per piece (line J) to calculate how much your total fulfillment costs will be.

Worksheet 8) Program Measurement

Each desktop marketing program that you execute should be measured and compared to your benchmarks to see if it is better or worse than your general expectations. This multilevel worksheet helps you evaluate the overall results of your desktop marketing program, including direct mail, phone, and fulfillment costs. The summary at the bottom gets you an overall program summary. The numbers should be taken from the appropriate lines in Worksheets 5–7.

The first part of the worksheet is applicable only if you did direct mail.

A) Total pieces mailed: Take this from Worksheet 5, line J, second column.

B) Total mailing costs: Take this from Worksheet 5, line M, second column.

C) Total number of responses: Record the total number of responses that came from your direct mail effort.

D) Response rate: Divide Total number of responses (line C) by Total pieces mailed (line A). This rate will tell you what percentage of prospects responded to your offer.

E) Cost per response: Divide Total mailing cost (line B) by Number of responses (line C) to learn how much it cost you for every response you got. This number is one benchmark of desktop marketing, the cost it takes to get someone to indicate interest in your product. This cost can and should be used across all programs to compare program effectiveness. If you are using any type of fulfillment mailing, you will ultimately need to take those costs into account as well.

F) Total number of sales: This is the number of total sales you can attribute to the entire program. Total sales will seldom be a scientific number. It will include a great deal of personal judgment on your part to properly assign sales to this program. One way to make this judgment is to follow up a number of the responders—several months later—to learn what percentage ultimately bought your product or service. You can then extrapolate this percentage to all of your respondents.

G) Total revenues: This number is the money that comes in, thanks to the desktop marketing program. You may also have to estimate this number.

H) Order rate: Divide Total number of sales (line F) by Total pieces mailed (line A). You can compare the actual percentage of orders to the estimate you made when you did your initial budgeting.

I) Cost per sale: Divide Total mailing cost (line B) by Total number of orders (line F). This is another benchmark you can use to compare the effectiveness of different desktop marketing programs.

J) Average order size: Divide Total revenues from program (line G) by Total number of sales from program (line F). You may find that the average order size you experience from direct mail is either smaller or larger than your sales using other means. Knowing this can be useful for planning future programs.

K) Gross margin: This is the percentage of money you make from a sale after you subtract cost of goods. You can get this from Worksheet 1, line I.

L) Gross margin on sales: Multiply Gross margin (line K) by Total revenues from program (line G). This number will tell you how much you made from the direct mail program after you paid for products or services. You will use this number to see whether you have broken even with the marketing costs of the program.

M) Money made/lost on mail: Subtract Gross margin on program sales (line L) from Total mailing costs (line B). When you do this subtraction, you will know whether you made money with just the direct mail portion of your program. This is where your assessment of the program becomes essential. Sales from this program may continue for up to a year or more. You must decide if all sales are in and if the margin is accurate. If a program costs the same as its gross margin, you can extrapolate that you will have a positive return on this mailing over time if your customers continue to buy over several years. If this mailing is to old customers that you are trying to regenerate, and you do not make money, you can assume there is no point in continuing the program.

The second part of Worksheet 8 is applicable if any part of your program uses the telephone, either inbound or outbound.

N) Total contacts made: Take this number from Worksheet 6, line F, second column.

O) Total phone costs: Take this from Worksheet 6, line K, second column.

P) Total number of responses: Write in how many of those contacted by phone responded positively to your offer.

Q) Response rate: Divide Total number of responses (line P) by Total contacts made (line N). This number will tell you what percentage of prospects respond when they are contacted via the phone.

R) Cost per response: Divide Total phone costs (line O) by Total number of responses (line P). It is worthwhile to know how much your phone costs are, when you are launching a major program using the phone in support. You may decide that multiple mail contacts that result in decisions are cheaper than one phone contact.

S) Total number of sales: Again, unless prospects are ordering directly then and there on the phone, this number can be difficult to estimate.

T) Total revenues from sales: The number will be easier to calculate if the program is entirely self-contained. Otherwise, you will have to make your best estimate.

U) Order rate: Divide Total number of orders (line S) by Total contacts made (line N). You can compare this actual rate with the rate you estimated before you began.

V) Cost per order: Divide Total phone costs (line O) by Total number of orders (line S). Cost per order can be used as a comparison number across a wide variety of desktop marketing programs to evaluate which program is most effective.

W) Money made/lost on phone: Subtract Total phone costs (line O) from Gross margin on program (line L). When you do this subtraction, you will know whether you made money on the phone part of your program. If the difference is positive, you are making money; if it is a negative number, you are not making money.

Finally, in the last part of the worksheet, you will combine all the elements of your program and decide whether or not you made money.

AA) Total contacts made: If either the mail contacts or phone contacts were a subset of another, take the largest number as your total contacts. If you mailed to some of your targets and phoned others, add the two figures together here.

AB) Total direct mail costs: Carry this down from line B on this worksheet.

AC) Total phone costs: Carry this down from line O on this worksheet.

AD) Total fulfillment costs: See Worksheet 7, line N, second column.

AE) Total program costs: Add together lines AB to AD.

AF) Total number of sales: You have this number on line F or line S of this worksheet.

AG) Total revenue from sales: You have this number on line G or line T of this worksheet.

AH) Order rate: Divide Total number of sales (line AF) by Total contacts made (line AA). This will give you the order percentage for the overall program.

AI) Cost per order: Divide Total program costs (line AE) by Total number of orders (line AF). This is one of your most crucial costs. You should compare this cost per order rate with your average rate of capturing an order. If the cost is too high, your program isn't a success.

AJ) Gross margin on sales: Carry this down from line L or line Y in this worksheet. It will tell you how much money the program made.

AK) Money made/lost on program: Subtract Total program cost (line AE) from Gross margin on sales (line AJ). This number is your ultimate decision maker. If the number is positive, your mailing is a success and the money can go toward overhead and profit. If the number is negative, you've lost money and should think about how to modify the program.

Worksheet 9) List Comparison

If at all possible, you should include your customer file in every program you run to offset the cost of acquiring new customers. Even though the list may be small compared to your potential market, your customers will almost always buy at a much higher rate than prospects. This worksheet is a simple comparison of customer-versus prospect-performance for each program you run. You can substitute the customer and prospect headings to represent any kind of list samples you are using and want to compare.

A) Number contacted: You should put here the number of people you contacted, either by phone or by mail.

B) Total program cost: Indicate the total cost of the program for each list. You may have to calculate the numbers separately by using Worksheet 8 for each individual list section.

C) Cost per target for program: Divide Total program cost (line B) by Number contacted (line A) to figure how much it cost you to contact people on each list. Generally, it will be less expensive to contact your own customers, because you won't have any list rental fees.

D) Total number of responses: If you used codes to indicate different list sources, it should be easy for you to distinguish responses from list groups.

E) Response rate: Divide Total responses (line D) by Number contacted (line A) to calculate the response rate. In most cases, the response rate for your current customers should be higher than for prospects. After running a few desktop marketing programs, you should know what type of response rate to expect from your customers.

F) Cost per response: Divide Total program cost (line B) by Total responses (line D). The cost per response is an interesting number, but it isn't key for decision making. You can use it as a benchmark to see if you are equally effective with your program execution from program to program. If your cost per response is on target, but your cost per sale is high, your problem is not in the desktop marketing program but in your ability to qualify and/or close.

G) Number of sales/closes: Try to estimate these numbers as closely as possible.

H) Sales/close rate: Divide Number of sales/closes (line G) by Cost per response (line F).

I) Cost per sale: Divide Total program cost (line B) by Number of sales/closes (line G). This is the key number for determining if your desktop marketing program is successful and for comparing it with other programs. The lower your acquisition cost of a new customer, the less you will spend for target market growth. Once you have sold to a prospect, the prospect becomes part of your customer base and should act like the rest of your customer list. If you find when you calculate cost per sale that your customer cost per sale is greater than your prospect cost per sale, put all your effort in prospecting. Some businesses find they receive no repeat business from customers; the first order is the only order.

J) Program sales: Enter all the sales for the entire program. You will have to determine a cutoff date for your program, since responses could continue to come in for a year or more. Large mail-order and direct mail companies use the "doubling day," the day when, historically, half of all responses have been received. If you plan to do many desktop marketing programs in a year, you need to develop some way to determine the success of the program before it is completed so that you will know whether you should repeat it. The sooner you can determine a successful program, the faster you can remail it.

K) Average sales for program: Divide Program sales (line J) by Number of sales/closes (line G). Looking at this number can be interesting. There are no rules here, except that customers order at a better rate than do prospects. The amount they order will be affected by how long they have been customers and how much product variety you have from program to program. If you find the average sales of this program are higher than your overall average order (calculated in Worksheet 1), go with the program. If the program average is below average, decide how you can fix it or stop the program.

Worksheet 10) Program Summary

Your effectiveness as a desktop marketer is dependent on how well you target your markets, how well you create your offer, and how well you execute your programs. By preparing a summary of each program, you will force yourself to think through the variables of each program. This worksheet is an example of the type of summary you can write to keep track of a program.

Worksheet 5
Direct Mail Budgeting

	Planned	Actual
A. Letterhead cost per page	$_____	$_____
B. Envelope cost, each	$_____	$_____
C. Additional insert, each	$_____	$_____
D. Reply form, each	$_____	$_____
E. Brochure, each	$_____	$_____
F. Return envelope, each	$_____	$_____
G. Postage per package	$_____	$_____
H. List cost per name	$_____	$_____
I. Delivered cost per piece (Add A through H)	$_____	$_____
J. Total pieces mailed	_____	_____
K. Total materials cost (IxJ)	$_____	$_____
L. Outside service or part-time labor cost	$_____	$_____
M. Total mailing cost (K+L)	$_____	$_____
N. Estimated average order size	_____	
O. Gross margin	_____%	
P. Gross margin per average order (NxO)	$_____	
Q. Number of orders needed to break even (M/P)	_____	
R. Required order rate (Q/J)	_____%	

©Tracy Emerick, 1990, USA 603-926-4477

Worksheet 6
Phone Budgeting

	Planned	Actual
A. Hourly labor cost	$_____	$_____
B. Hourly phone line charges	$_____	$_____
C. Total variable costs per hour (A+B)	$_____	$_____
D. Total number of records to call	_____	_____
E. Percent of records contactable (60% to 85%)	_____%	_____%
F. Number of records contactable (DxE)	_____	_____
G. Dialings per hour (10 to 30)	_____	_____
H. Percent of dialings that end in contact (30% to 50%)	_____%	_____%
I. Contacts per hour (GxH)	_____	_____
J. Total telemarketing hours (F/I)	_____	_____
K. Total telemarketing costs (JxC)	$_____	$_____
L. Estimated average order size	$_____	
M. Gross margin	_____%	
N. Gross margin per average order (LxM)	$_____	
O. Number of orders needed to break even (K/N)	_____	
P. Required order rate (O/D)	_____%	

©Tracy Emerick, 1990, USA 603-926-4477

Worksheet 7
Fulfillment Budgeting

		Planned	Actual
A.	Letterhead cost per page	$_____	$_____
B.	Envelope cost, each	$_____	$_____
C.	Premium or gift cost	$_____	$_____
D.	Reply form, each	$_____	$_____
E.	Brochure, each	$_____	$_____
F.	Return envelope, each	$_____	$_____
G.	Postage/freight per fulfillment	$_____	$_____
H.	Cost per name	$_____	$_____
I.	Outside service costs, each	$_____	$_____
J.	Delivered fulfillment (Add A through I)	$_____	$_____
K.	Total number of contacts	_____	_____
L.	Predicted response rate	_____%	_____%
M.	Predicted number of inquiries (KxL)	_____	_____
N.	Total fulfillment costs (MxJ)	$_____	$_____

Worksheet 8
Program Evaluation

Direct Mail	Actual	Planned
A. Total pieces mailed (col. 2, line J, WS. 5)	_____	_____
B. Total mailing costs (col. 2, line M, WS. 5)	$_____	$_____
C. Total number of responses	_____	
D. Response rate (C/A)	_____%	
E. Cost per response (B/C)	$_____	
F. Total number of sales	_____	
G. Total revenue	$_____	
H. Order rate (F/A)	_____%	_____%
I. Cost per sale (B/F)	$_____	
J. Average order size (G/F)	$_____	$_____
K. Gross margin	_____%	_____%
L. Gross margin on sales (GxL)	$_____	$_____
M. Money made/lost on mail (L–B)	$_____	$_____
N. Total contacts made (col. 2, Line F, WS. 6)	_____	_____
O. Total phone costs (col. 2, Line K, WS. 6)	$_____	$_____
P. Total number of responses	_____	_____
Q. Response rate (P/N)	_____%	_____%
R. Cost per response (O/P)	$_____	$_____
S. Total number of sales (line F)	_____	_____
T. Total revenues from sales (line G)	$_____	$_____
U. Order rate (S/N)	_____%	_____%

continues

APPENDIX A

Worksheet 8
Continued

Phone	Actual	Planned
V. Cost per order (O/S)	$_____	$_____
W. Money made/lost on phone (line L–O)	$_____	$_____

Summary

	Actual	
AA. Total contacts made	_____	
AB. Total direct mail costs (line B)	$_____	
AC. Total phone costs (line O)	$_____	
AD. Total fulfillment costs (col. 2, line N, WS. 7)	$_____	
AE. Total program costs (AB+AC+AD)	$_____	
AF. Total number of sales (line F)	_____	
AG. Total revenues from sales (line G)	$_____	
AH. Order rate (AF/AA)	_____%	
AI. Cost per order (AE/AF)	$_____	
AJ. Gross margin on sales (line L)	$_____	
AK. Money made/lost on program (AJ–AE)	$_____	

©Tracy Emerick, 1990, USA 603-926-4477

Worksheet 9
List Comparison

	Prospect	Customer
A. Number contacted (by phone or mail)	_____	_____
B. Total program costs (line AE, WS. 8)	$_____	$_____
C. Cost per target for program (B/A)	$_____	$_____
D. Total number of responses	_____	_____
E. Response rate (D/A)	_____%	_____%
F. Cost per response (B/D)	$_____	$_____
G. Number of sales/closes	_____	_____
H. Sales/close rate (G/D)	_____%	_____%
I. Cost per sale (B/G)	$_____	$_____
J. Program sales	$_____	$_____
K. Average sales for program (J/G)	$_____	$_____

©Tracy Emerick, 1990, USA 603-926-4477

Worksheet 10
Program Summary

Market _____   Media _____

Program Title _____   Date _____

  A. Market Objectives _____
     _____

  B. Program Objectives _____
     _____

  C. Program Goals _____
     _____

  D. Market Targets _____
     _____

  E. Offer (Call to Action) _____
     _____

  F. Creative Strategy _____
     _____

  G. Timing _____
     _____

  H. Fulfillment _____
     _____

  I. Contact Criteria _____
     _____

  J. Contact Qualification Process_____
     _____

  K. Contact Tracking Mechanism_____
     _____

  L. Budget _____
     _____

©Tracy Emerick, 1990, USA 603-926-4477

Using Worksheets: An Example

James Roberts' company, Clear Vision, sells window washing services to office buildings in the Southwest. His sales for the current year will be $8 million, and he would like to grow by five percent to $8.4 million by the end of next year. Because he would like to keep his sales staff level at seven sales reps, he wants to find alternative methods to get leads and make sales.

The gross margin on his company's services averages about 33 percent, depending on the various discounts and special pricing opportunities he offers. He generally budgets total marketing expenses to be at 10 percent of sales. Over the years, James has acquired 2,400 customers, of which 65 percent use him every year. His company did a total of 4,550 window-washing jobs last year, with the average job bringing in about $1,700.

James has completed Worksheets 1–4 to get a handle on his current situation, and what he will have to accomplish to grow his company as planned. To reach his growth plans, he needs 1,1171 prospects each year to ultimately convert to 878 new customers. Fortunately, when he checks the numbers for the target market, he feels confident there is room to grow.

James would like to try out a desktop marketing program to see if it can be a serious alternative for making sales, particularly to small companies. He decides to try to do a combined program in which he will mail a direct mail package, send a fulfillment package to the re-sponders, and do telemarketing as a fulfillment follow-up. He first uses Worksheets 5–7 to budget out the mailing to 4,000 prospects and pre-dict the results.

The direct mail piece will consist of a letter, brochure, an insert about his company, a reply form, and a reply envelope. James budgets the entire package out to cost $.59 a piece. Because he is generating all the materials internally, he hires a temporary, at $7 per hour, to do the folding and stuffing of the envelopes.

He expects to get about a 1.6 percent response rate, or 64 responses. He will send all the responders a fulfillment package worth $10.17. James decides to use the phone as a follow-up to his fulfillment. He again hires a temporary and prepares a script for the temporary to use when asking for orders. According to his calculations, the calls should take 13 hours to complete for a total cost of $367. He expects that about 33 percent of the responders will buy his services. Since they are smaller businesses, the average order size should be about $700, instead of his usual average of $1,758. If he can accomplish all of his predictions, James should make money on the program.

Of course, the actual program did not go exactly as he had planned. In reality, he got a 1.3 percent response rate, with only 31 percent of those responses converting to sales. The sales were also lower, running closer to $550. When he looks at the mail and the phone by themselves, the program is a great success. However, when all of the elements are combined, he comes up with a profit of only $159. Of course, the project did pay for itself, so that he feels vindicated. He has managed to make 16 new customers at the cost of $210 per order, a cost he feels is very reasonable.

James then uses Worksheet 9 to take a look at how brand-new prospects did in the program versus the 500 customers he also sent the mailing to. Not surprisingly, the customers responded much better and cost much less to make the sale. But overall, the prospects alone are still promising.

Worksheet 1
Value and Worth of Customers

A. Your total sales/revenue for the year	$8,000,000
B. Total number of customers on file	2,400
C. Percent of customers that order per year	65%
D. Total number of active customers (BxC)	1,560
E. Total number of orders/sales per year	4,550
F. Average order/sale (A/E)	$1,758
G. Avg. number of orders per customer per year (E/D)	2.92
H. Avg. revenue per active customer per year (A/D)	$5,128
I. Gross margin or gross profit %	33%
J. Annual gross margin value of a customer (HxI)	$1,692
K. Number of years a customer orders	3.5
L. Lifetime worth of a customer (JxK)	$5,923

©Tracy Emerick, 1990, USA 603-926-4477

Worksheet 2
Salesperson Cost and Closing

	Current/ Last Year	Forecast
A. Total sales/revenue for year (line A, WS. 1)	$8,000,000	$8,400,000
B. Total annual marketing expenses	$800,000	$840,000
C. Total number of sales/orders per year (line E, WS.1)	4550	4777
D. Average order/sale (line F, WS. 1)	$1,758	$1,758
E. Number of salespeople	7	7
F. Average sales per salesperson (A/E)	$1,142,857	$1,200,000
G. Cost per salesperson per year (B/E)	$114,286	$120,000
H. Average number of orders per salesperson (C/E)	650	$683
I. Average sales contacts per day per salesperson	7	7
J. Available sales days per year per salesperson	220	220
K. Number of sales contacts per year per salesperson (IxJ)	1540	1540
L. Cost per sales contact (G/K)	$74	$78
M. Average sales contacts needed per order (K/H)	2.37	2.26
N. Sales cost per order (LxM)	$176	$176
O. Closing rate (H/K)	42%	44%
P. Sales cost rate per order (N/D)	10%	10%

Worksheet 3
New Customer Planning

A. Total sales/revenues (current or previous year) (line A, WS. 1)	$8,000,000
B. Sales forecast (next year) (col. 2, line A, WS. 2)	$8,400,000
C. Revenue per active customer per year (line H, WS. 1)	$5,128
D. Number of customers lost per year	800
E. Sales requiring new customers (B−[A−(C*D)])	$4,502,564
F. New customers needed for year (E/C)	878
G. Closing rate (line O, WS. 2)	42%
H. Prospects needed for year (F/G)	2080
I. Number of salespeople (col. 2, line E, WS. 2)	7
J. Number of new customers needed per salesperson (F/I)	125
K. Number of prospects needed per salesperson (H/I)	297
L. Total marketing budget (col. 2, line B, WS. 2)	$800,000
M. Percent of budget for new business	75%
N. Marketing budget for prospect generation (LxM)	$600,000
O. Marketing budget per prospect (N/H)	$288
P. Marketing budget cost per new customer (N/F)	$683
Q. Average sales contacts needed per order (line M, WS. 2)	$2.37
R. Total contacts for new customers per salesperson (JxQ)	297
S. # of sales contacts per year per sales- person (line K, WS. 2)	1540
T. Percent of contacts used for new customers (R/S)	19%

Worksheet 4
Market Size Requirements

A. Prospects needed for the year (col. 2, line H, WS. 3)	878
B. Responses qualified as prospects (est. 70–80%)	75%
C. Responses needed per year (A/B)	1171
D. Response rate for new desktop marketing program (.5–1.5%)	1%
E. Number of targets needed for new customer program (C/D)	117,067
F. Number of programs planned	4
G. Targets needed for each program (E/F)	29267

©Tracy Emerick, 1990, USA 603-926-4477

Worksheet 5
Direct Mail Budgeting

	Planned	Actual
A. Letterhead cost per page	$.02	$.02
B. Envelope cost, each	$.05	$.05
C. Additional insert, each	$.03	$.03
D. Reply form, each	$.02	$.02
E. Brochure, each	$.10	$.11
F. Return envelope, each	$.04	$.04
G. Postage per package	$.25	$.25
H. List cost per name	$.08	$.08
I. Delivered cost per piece (Add A through H)	$.59	$.60
J. Total pieces mailed	4000	4000
K. Total materials cost (HxJ)	$2,400	
L. Outside service or part-time labor cost	$50	$48
M. Total mailing cost (K+L)	$2,410	$2448
N. Estimated average order size	$700	
O. Gross margin	40%	
P. Gross margin per average order (NxO)	$280	
Q. Number of orders needed to break even (M/P)	8.6	
R. Required order rate (Q/J)	0.2%	

APPENDIX A

Worksheet 6
Phone Budgeting

		Planned	Actual
A.	Hourly labor cost	$11.00	$11.00
B.	Hourly phone line charges	$18.00	$18.00
C.	Total variable costs per hour (A+B)	$29.00	$29.00
D.	Total number of records to call	64	52
E.	Percent of records contactable	100%	98%
F.	Number of records contactable (DxE)	64	51
G.	Dialings per hour	9	9
H.	Percent of dialings that end in contact	45%	40%
I.	Contacts per hour (GxH)	4.05	3.6
J.	Total telemarketing hours (F/I)	16	14
K.	Total telemarketing costs (JxC)	$464	$411
L.	Estimated average order size	$700	
M.	Gross margin	40%	
N.	Gross margin per average order (LxM)	$280	
O.	Number of responses needed to break even (K/N)	1.7	
P.	Required order rate (O/D)	2.6%	

©Tracy Emerick, 1990, USA 603-926-4477

Worksheet 7
Fulfillment Budgeting

	Planned	Actual
A. Letterhead cost per page	$.02	$.02
B. Envelope cost, each	$.05	$.05
C. Premium or gift cost	$9.00	$9.00
D. Reply form, each	$.02	$.02
E. Brochure, each	$.10	$.11
F. Return envelope, each	$.04	$.04
G. Postage/freight per fulfillment	$.93	$.93
H. Cost per name	0	0
I. Outside service costs, each	0	0
J. Delivered fulfillment $10.16 (Add A through I)	$10.17	
K. Total number of contacts	4,000	52
L. Predicted response rate	1.6%	
M. Predicted number of inquiries (KxL)	64	
N. Total fulfillment costs (KxJ)	$650	$529

©Tracy Emerick, 1990, USA 603-926-4477

Worksheet 8
Program Evaluation

Direct Mail	Actual	Planned
A. Total pieces mailed (col. 2, line J, WS. 5	4,000	4,000
B. Total mailing costs (col. 2, line M, WS. 5)	$2,448	$2,410
C. Total number of responses	52	
D. Response rate (C/A)	1.3	
E. Cost per response (B/C)	$47.08	
F. Total number of sales	16	
G. Total revenue	$8,866	
H. Order rate (F/A)	0.4%	0.2%
I. Cost per sale (B/F)	$151.86	
J. Average order size (G/F)	$550	$700
K. Gross margin	40%	40%
L. Gross margin on sales (GxL)	$3,546	
M. Money made/lost on mail (L–B)	$1,098	
N. Total contacts made (col. 2, line F, WS. 6)	51	64
O. Total phone costs (col. 2, line K, WS. 6)	$411	$464
P. Total number of responses	16	
Q. Response rate (P/N)	31%	
R. Cost per response (O/P)	$25	
S. Total number of sales (line F)	16	
T. Total revenue from sales (line G)	$8,866	
U. Order rate (S/N)	31%	

V.	Cost per order (O/S)	$25
W.	Money made/lost on phone (line L–O)	$3,136
	Summary	
AA.	Total contacts made	4,000
AB.	Total direct mail costs (line B)	$2,448
AC.	Total phone costs (line O)	$411
AD.	Total fulfillment costs (col. 2, line N, WS. 7)	$529
AE.	Total program costs (AB+AC+AD)	$3,387
AF.	Total number of sales (line F)	16
AG.	Total revenues from sales (line G)	$8,866
AH.	Order rate (AF/AA)	0.4%
AI.	Cost per order (AE/AF)	$211
AJ.	Gross margin on sales (line L)	$3,546
AK.	Money made/lost on program (AJ–AE)	$159

Worksheet 9
List Comparison

	Prospect	Customer
A. Number contacted (by phone or mail)	3,500	500
B. Total program cost (Line AE, WS. 7)	$2,964	$383
C. Cost per target for program (B/A)	$.85	$.77
D. Total number of responses	39	13
E. Response rate (D/A)	1.11%	2.60%
F. Cost per response (B/D)	$76	$29.46
G. Number of sales/closes	11	5
	Prospect	**Customer**
H. Sales/close rate (G/D)	28%	38%
I. Cost per sale (B/G)	$269	$77
J. Program sales	$6,206	$2,660
K. Average sales for program (J/G)	$550	550

©Tracy Emerick, 1990, USA 603-926-4477

B

Software
Options

Throughout this book, we have referred to a wide range of software for the Macintosh that can help you accomplish your desktop marketing goals. The type of software you choose to use is entirely dependent on your needs and what you decide to handle yourself.

This appendix lists a selection of software in each category we have discussed. This is by no means an exhaustive list; there are other excellent software packages available in all of the categories. To learn more about available software, you should visit your local computer software store.

Lead Generation

ead-generation software is the cornerstone of any desktop marketing effort. With lead-generation software, you get the prospect names and data you need to accomplish all the other parts of desktop marketing.

MarketPlace Business

MarketPlace provides marketing information on over 7 million U.S. businesses on a single CD-ROM. The data is provided by Dun & Bradstreet, the industry leader of business-to-business marketing information.

You can select companies based on location, type of business, and size of company by revenue and number of employees. You can then generate mailing labels, prospecting lists, reports, or export the list to other software packages.

System requirements: Macintosh Plus or above with 4MB of RAM or more. (The company recommends a Macintosh SE/30 or higher). AppleCD SC drive and hard disk.

Suggested retail price: $695.

Three quarterly updates: $195 per year.

Additional meter units: $500 for 5,000 units.

Company: MarketPlace Information Corporate, Three University Office Park, Waltham, MA 02154. (617) 894-4100.

Word Processing

Y ou can use word processing software to write copy, compose offer letters, or create telemarketing scripts. With word processing software, you can easily modify and change your copy until you get exactly what you want. Most word processors allow you to merge the names on MarketPlace lists with any text to produce personalized letters.

Word

Microsoft Word is the best-selling word processing package for the Macintosh. It is a heavyweight product with a lot of features. It's the only word processor with true style sheets that can export formatting to popular desktop publishing programs. This ability can be very useful if you plan to do most of your copywriting in your word processing software and then transfer it to your desktop publishing software.

The software also has a Table feature, which can be helpful if you create lots of tables in your writing. The structure of Word is flexible, allowing you to change the order of the menus or to assign keystrokes to represent the menu items. Unfortunately, Word is not as intuitive as some of the other word processors, so that you may not find it as easy to learn.

> **System requirements:** Mac Plus, two 800K drives or a hard disk drive.
>
> **Suggested retail price:** $395.
>
> **Company:** Microsoft Corp., 16011 NE 36th Way, Redmond, WA 98073-9717; (800) 426-9400.

MacWrite II

MacWrite II has a very easy to use interface. It probably has the easiest mail-merge setup of any Macintosh word processing package. Instead of requiring you to type out the symbols representing the field you want to merge, MacWrite II lets you select the proper field from a scrolling dialog box. This capability can be extremely helpful when personalizing letters for desktop marketing.

System requirements: Macintosh Plus or higher, hard disk recommended.

Suggested retail price: $249.

Company: Claris, 5201 Patrick Henry Drive, Santa Clara, CA 95052-8168; (408) 987-7000.

WriteNow

WriteNow is an excellent choice for a first word processor. Although it is a low-end word processing program, it can handle long documents, and can import and export a wide range of file formats. It can handle up to four columns of text, but the method used to create those columns can be difficult. The software is fast and comes with an excellent 80,000 word spell checker. You can't put boxes around text, and you can't wrap text around graphics.

System requirements: 512 Mac, 800K drive.

Suggested retail price: $199.

Company: T/Maker, 1390 Villa St., Mountain View, CA 94041; (415) 962-0195.

WordPerfect

If your office has a lot of IBM-compatible computers using WordPerfect, you might consider the Macintosh version to maintain compatibility. WordPerfect can handle columns very well and is good for macros. However, its hierarchical menu interface is more similar to an IBM interface than to a Macintosh interface. This can make WordPerfect more difficult to learn if you aren't already familiar with the IBM DOS version.

System requirements: Mac Plus, two 800K drives or a hard disk drive.

Suggested retail price: $395.

Company: WordPerfect Corp., 1555 N. Technology Way, Orem, UT 84057; (800) 451-5151.

Integrated Packages

I ntegrated packages combine several types of functionality into one software package. This makes it very easy to transfer information from one function to another. In general, integrated packages have not been a big hit for the Macintosh, because the Macintosh interface makes it so easy to cut and paste from one application to another.

Works

Works combines word processing, spreadsheet, flat-file database, communications, and drawing in one package, but each of the applications is more limited than you might find in a stand-alone package. This combination makes it very easy to draw in the middle of your text document, instead of having to cut and paste from a separate drawing package. You can also quickly cut and paste between the spreadsheet and database formats and the word processing formats. If you don't expect to have large databases or complex spreadsheets or fancy documents, you may find Works sufficient for all your marketing needs.

System requirements: Mac Plus, two 800K drives or hard disk.

Suggested retail price: $295.

Company: Microsoft Corp., 16011 NE 36th Way, Redmond, WA 98073-9717; (800) 426-9400.

RagTime 3.0

RagTime is the leading Macintosh software package in Europe, but it is just beginning to make inroads in the United State. It combines page layout, word processing, spreadsheets, and business charting in one package. The package is based on the page layout portion of the program, and everything else is done within "frames" that you draw on top of the page layout. You move the frames around to layout the page exactly how you want.

The word processing is probably the weakest part of the package, because its rulers can be difficult to control. However, because it is linked to the page layout, you control the typographic appearance of the text. The spreadsheet is quite large, and it has all the basics you need for calculation. Because RagTime has both word processing and spreadsheets, you can do calculations within your documents and can format text impressively within your spreadsheets. You can create graphs from the spreadsheet data, and you have a lot of formatting options with those graphs.

System requirements: Mac Plus or better (SE or above recommended), 1MB RAM (2MB recommended), and a hard disk.

Suggested retail price: $599.

Company: RagTime USA, 702 Marshall St., Suite 322, Redwood City, CA 94063; (800) 875-9632.

RagTime Classic

RagTime Classic is a more limited version of RagTime that includes all the principal capabilities except business charting. Each function is more limited than in the full-fledged version, but many people will find it's everything they will need.

System requirements: Mac Plus or better, 1MB RAM, hard disk recommended.

Suggested retail price: $195.

Company: RagTime USA, 702 Marshall St., Suite 322, Redwood City, CA 94063; (800) 875-9632.

Desktop Publishing/Page Layout

Desktop publishing software is designed for creating publishable pieces such as newsletters, brochures, and catalogs. The software allows you to combine both text and graphics and gives you powerful layout capabilities. You have control over the typography, including spacing, kerning, etc.

Personal Press

This is a good program for the budget-minded. Although it may be a bit slow, it has most of the key desktop publishing features including a basic word processor.

System requirements: Mac Plus or better, 2MB RAM, hard disk drive.

Suggested retail price: $299.

Company: Aldus Corp., 411 First Ave. S., Seattle, WA 98104; (800) 333-2538.

Ready, Set, Go!

This is another low-budget desktop publishing program. It comes with ready-made style sheets and the product is quite easy to use. Don't expect to be able to do a lot of graphics manipulation with the program.

System requirements: Mac Plus or better, 2MB RAM, hard disk drive.

Suggested retail price: $295.

Company: Letraset USA, Inc., 40 Eisenhower Dr., Paramus, NJ 07653; (800) 343-8973.

Publish It!

If you have only a Mac Plus or an SE, you may want to consider Publish It! It includes word-processing capabilities and simple drawing and painting tools. If you are only trying to design simple brochures or letters, Publish It! May give you everything you need at a low price.

System requirements: Mac Plus or better.

Suggested retail price: $495.

Company: Timeworks, 444 Lake Cook Rd, Deerfield, IL 60015-4919; (800) 535-9497.

PageMaker

PageMaker is the top-selling desktop publishing software package for the Mac. In spite of the complexity of desktop publishing, PageMaker has an intuitive interface that makes it very easy to learn how to combine text and graphics. PageMaker now has a Story Editor window that allows you to more easily update and change text. You can also do spell checking or word searches in this window. PageMaker will handle documents up to 999 pages long, or you can link a series of small documents together.

System requirements: Mac Plus or better (recommend SE or better), 2MB RAM, hard disk (20MB or more recommended).

Suggested retail price: $795.

Company: Aldus Corp., 411 First Ave. S., Suite 200, Seattle, WA 92104; (800) 333-2538.

QuarkXPress

Many people consider QuarkXPress more advanced than PageMaker. QuarkXPress emphasizes precision and control for every element of layout, particularly typography. However, although improvements in user interface have been made, it is more difficult to use than PageMaker.

With QuarkXPress, you can import formatted word processing files from most of the major Macintosh word processors. You can also do color separation of images within the software.

System requirements: Mac SE or better, 2MB RAM, hard disk.

Suggested retail price: $795.

Company: Quark, 300 S. Jackson, Suite 300, Denver, CO 80209; (800) 356-9363.

Spreadsheets

S preadsheets allow you to do numerical analysis, from simple addition and subtraction to advanced formulas and complex numerical models. You can use spreadsheets to examine the status of your own business, to analyze the results of your desktop marketing programs, and to assist in your analysis of new markets. Most Macintosh spreadsheet programs also have powerful graphical capabilities. They will all easily import text files from MarketPlace, either the actual lists or analysis results.

Excel

Excel is the leading spreadsheet program for the Macintosh. It has very strong statistical functions and matrix math capabilities. As with its word processing counterpart, Word, you can customize the menus in Excel and create your own dialog boxes. It is also very easy to link spreadsheets together. You can also do charting and graphics with your spreadsheet data.

System requirements: Mac Plus or better.

Suggested retail price: $395.

Company: Microsoft Corp., One Microsoft Way, Redmond, WA 98052-6399; (800) 426-9400.

APPENDIX B

1-2-3 for Macintosh

1-2-3 for Macintosh is a new version of the popular PC-based spreadsheet product. You can add popular choices to the pull-down menus and customize the appearance of the worksheet. 1-2-3 lets you build three-dimensional worksheets that allow you new methods of linking worksheets together. You can also do charting and graphics with your spreadsheet data.

System requirements: Mac Plus or better.

Suggested retail price: $495.

Company: Lotus Development Corp., 55 Cambridge Pkwy, Cambridge, MA 02142; (800) 872-3387.

Wingz

Wingz' biggest claim to fame is its impressive graphics capability. Not only do you have a lot of control over the graphs you create, you can also create 3-D charts and graphs. Wingz also includes a programming language, called Hyperscript, that makes it very easy for you to automate common functions. However, Wingz lacks an easy way to link several spreadsheets together.

System requirements: Mac Plus or better.

Suggested retail price: $295.

Company: Informix Software, Inc., 16011 College Blvd., Lenexa, KS 66219; (913) 599-7100.

Database Management

Database management software can help you to maintain customer and prospect lists. If you already have a customer database, you can transfer it to a database management software package to do customer analysis and to make follow-up marketing much easier.

There are two basic types of database management packages: flat file and relational. Flat file databases tend to be simpler to use and less expensive. Relational databases can be extremely powerful but take more effort to set up.

FileMaker Pro

FileMaker is a very popular flat-file database management package. It is simple to lay out exactly how you want your records to appear, or you can use the preformatted options that come with the software. Once you have created a layout, you can name it, so that you can quickly call it up in the future. You can easily include graphics in the database and link different files together. You can write scripts that will run through different database steps automatically with one click of the mouse.

System requirements: Mac Plus or better with 2MB of RAM.

Suggested retail price: $299.

Company: Claris, 5201 Patrick Henry Drive, Santa Clara, CA 95052-8163; (408) 727-8227.

File Force

File Force is a low-end relational database made by the same company that makes 4th Dimension. It is an excellent stepping stone to learn more about relational databases, and you can use its documentation to teach you how to create them. You can build very effective databases using File Force, but if you find yourself needing more control or more features, you may need to go to a higher-level relational database.

System requirements: Mac Plus or better, 1MB RAM, hard drive.

Suggested retail price: $395.

Company: ACIUS, 10351 Bubb Rd., Cupertino, CA 95014, (408) 252-4444.

Double Helix

With Double Helix, you create relational databases very differently than with most other databases. Instead of working out procedures in a linear way, you drag icons to create fields, do data entry design, etc. This method can be very easy to learn, although it may confuse users who are used to putting together databases in a more linear fashion. To help you spot any structural flaws in your database system, Double Helix can generate a report describing the current structure of the database.

System requirements: Mac Plus or better with 1MB of RAM, hard disk.

Suggested retail price: $595.

Company: Odesta Corp., 4084 Commercial Ave, Northbrook, IL 60062; (800) 323-5423.

4th Dimension

With 4th Dimension, you can create anything from a simple database to a very advanced application. The graphical interface makes it easy to use and to customize your database. To help you with more complex applications, 4th Dimension comes with its own debugger. You should spend a fair amount of time studying and planning your database before you start to build it with 4th Dimension, because it can be difficult to change things once a database is built.

System requirements: Mac Plus or later, 1MB of RAM with 2MB recommended.

Suggested retail price: Developing package, $795. Run-time package: 1-user $125, 2-user $225, 4-user $595.

Company: ACIUS, Inc., 10351 Bubb Road, Cupertino, CA 95014; (408) 252-4444.

Omnis 5

Along with 4th Dimension, Omnis 5 is one of the most powerful relational database software packages available for the Macintosh. If you are an experienced programmer, you will find Omnis 5 very fast and easy to use. And, if you plan to have several people on your staff entering data into the database at the same time, a database built in Omnis 5 will usually respond the best. In many cases, the database tool does not have as many features as 4th Dimension, so that a beginner programmer may have more difficulty. Also, there is no built-in debugger to help you find any programming errors.

System requirements: Mac Plus or better with 1MB or RAM. Hard disk with at least 1 MB available.

Suggested retail price: $795, $99 per additional user.

Company: Blythe Software, Inc., 1065 E. Hillsdale Blvd, Suite 300, Foster City, CA 94404; (800) 843-8615.

Specialized Software

Several different types of software can help you with the more specialized aspects of desktop marketing. Mapping software can help you to analyze information in a geographic context. Label-generation software can aid in the creation and enhancement of mailing materials. Lead-tracking software is database management software that has been customized for the purpose of tracking leads and customers.

GeoQuery

GeoQuery automatically creates "smart maps" that will accurately classify and pinpoint the location of prospects or customers based on 5-digit ZIP codes. It can import ASCII data from any database or spreadsheet and can link directly to MarketPlace data before it has been "bought." You can generate summary and list reports for standard regions or any region you define. You can display the information either as pinpoints or shade areas, based on aggregate information.

The software comes with maps of the continental United States, Alaska, and Hawaii with state boundaries and all ZIP code locations. You can also purchase additional atlas files: individual states with county boundaries, six regional United States files with county boundaries, United States with Area of Dominant Influence (ADI) boundaries, United States with Designated Market Area (DMA) boundaries, and United States with Metropolitan Statistical Area (MSA) boundaries.

System requirements: Mac Plus or better, with hard disk.

Suggested retail price: $395, state maps $100, regional maps $250, specialized maps $475.

Company: GeoQuery Corp., P.O. Box 206, Naperville, IL 60566; (708) 357-0535.

MapInfo

MapInfo will bring data in Excel spreadsheets, FoxBase/Mac or a tab-delimited ASCII file like you get from exporting a MarketPlace file. You can view the information either as text, a graph, or a map, allowing you to choose whichever mode is more useful for your analytic purpose. You can use the relational database that is created to link any record to a graphic that will appear on the map, to help you find specific types of places.

MapInfo comes with a map of the United States with state and ZIP code locations (but not boundaries). MapInfo also has a wide variety of other maps available, including StreetInfo, maps at street level detail that come with name and address ranges. It also has boundary maps for world, state, 3-digit ZIP codes 5-digit ZIP codes, block groups, counties, census tracts, 3-digit ZIP codes, counties, area codes, MCD, MSA, ADI, MA and others.

System requirements: Macintosh Plus or better with 1MB RAM (2 recommended) and hard disk.

Suggested retail price: $695.

Company: MapInfo Corp., 200 Broadway, Troy, NY 12180; (800) 327-8627.

MacEnvelope Plus

With MacEnvelope Plus, you can completely automate your mail preparation, from envelope or label design to packaging and sacking. You can use any type of graphic or font to design your label. MacEnvelope Plus can also automatically compute and place bar codes on the envelopes, which can save you money when you do bulk mailing.

MacEnvelope Plus can handle up to 100,000 addresses and can sort them on many levels. The package can import any text file or files directly from many standard Macintosh products. It can print onto any of the leading label formats, including Avery, Dennison, and Moore labels.

System requirements: Macintosh Plus or better, hard disk recommended.

Suggested retail price: $250 ($187.50 if you buy directly from SYNEX).

Company: SYNEX, 692 Tenth St., Brooklyn, NY 11215-4502; (718) 499-6293.

MacLabel Pro

MacLabel Pro can help you to print professional-looking labels very quickly. The package contains complete drawing tools so that you can easily add graphic elements to your labels, and a library of clip art is included.

You can do a print merge with an existing database of any size, either in a database management, spreadsheet, or word processing program. You can also use a MarketPlace text file with MacLabel Pro. MacLabel Pro includes preset layouts for Avery Dot Matrix and Laser Labels.

System requirements: Macintosh Plus or better.

Suggested retail price: $99.95.

Company: Avery Commercial Products Division, 818 Oak Park Rd, Covina, CA 91724-3624; (800) 541-5507.

C•A•T III (Contacts•Activities•Time)

This product combines relational database technology, word- and forms-processing, with time management functions. C•A•T stores data on your business contacts (phone, FAX, address, personal and company profiles, etc.) and can retrieve files instantly by name, date, and subject. It lets you create and store graphical forms or form letters and automatically merge them with your database information. You can import data from text files, including MarketPlace text files. You can create simple graphics within the package or bring in graphics developed in other Macintosh products.

System requirements: Macintosh 512E or better, 1MB of RAM, a hard drive.

Suggested retail price: $495.

Company: Chang Labs, 3350 Scott Blvd., #25, Santa Clara, CA 95054; (408) 727-8096.

TeleMagic

TeleMagic is a sales lead-tracking system built in FoxBase+/Mac. It allows you to easily look up customers or prospects based on serial number, name, phone number, or any other field. You can include all the fields you need to track your specific type of customer. It can generate envelopes for direct mailing, including putting bar codes onto the envelopes to save money at the post office.

System requirements: Mac Plus or better, 1MB of RAM, hard drive.

Suggested retail price: TeleMagic Professional $495, Personal TeleMagic (which lacks some features) $129.

Company: Remote Control International, 5928 Pascal Court, Carlsbad, CA 92008; (619) 431-4000.

Z-CR

If you plan to do mass direct mail efforts, it may be worth your while to subscribe to Z-CR. Z-CR is a CD-ROM that holds all the United States addresses, ZIP codes, and carrier-route numbers. You can use Z-CR to add carrier routes to any mailings you do from MarketPlace or any other databases. By adding carrier routes, you can save a considerable amount in postage costs. Because carrier routes change so frequently, the Postal Service requires that any carrier route products be sold on a subscription basis with a built-in expiration date after three months.

System requirements: Mac Plus or better, 1MB RAM, hard disk recommended.

Suggested retail price: Z-CR CD-ROM for one year $945, or Z-CR program $199 + floppy disks with carrier routes for states at $99 per floppy disk.

Company: Semaphore Corp., 207 Granada Dr., Aptos, CA 95003; (408) 688-9200.

GLOSSARY

Glossary

This glossary covers terms used in desktop marketing as well as terms used in associated marketing activities. Many of the terms are provided for your reference in order to understand the special language used by practitioners of various specialty areas.

Action devices: Items and techniques used in a mailing to initiate the response desired.

Active buyer: A buyer whose latest purchase was made within the last 12 months. (See Buyer.)

Active customer: A term used interchangeably with "active buyer."

Active subscriber: Someone who is presently committed for regular delivery of magazines, books, or other goods or services for a specific period of time.

Actives: Customers on a list who have made purchases within a prescribed time period, usually not more than one year; subscribers whose subscriptions have not expired.

Additions: New names, either of individuals or companies, added to a mailing list.

Address coding guide (CG): Contains the actual or potential beginning and ending house numbers, block group and/or enumeration district numbers, ZIP codes, and other geographic codes for all city delivery service streets served by 3,154 post offices located within 6,601 ZIP codes.

Address correction requested: An endorsement which, when printed in the upper left-hand corner of the address portion of the mailing piece (below return address), authorizes the United States Postal Service to provide the known new address of a person no longer at the address on the mailing piece. There is a fee for this service.

A.D.I. (Area of Dominant Influence): Broadcaster's method of defining a market within its reach.

A.I.D.A.: The most popular formula for the preparation of direct mail copy. The letters stand for get attention, arouse interest, stimulate desire, ask for action.

Alphanumeric: A contraction of "alphabetic" and "numeric." Applies to any coding system that includes letters, numbers (digits), and special symbols such as punctuation marks.

Audience: The total number of individuals reached by promotion or advertisement.

Average order size: A simple arithmetic formula used to establish the average order size. The total revenue generated from a program, divided by the total number of orders, will establish the average order size.

Back end: The activities necessary to complete a mail order transaction once an order has been received and/or the measurement of a buyer's performance after he or she has ordered the first item. It can also be used to define the measurement of prospects who became leads and their performance in purchasing.

Bangtail: Promotional envelope with a second flap that is perforated and designed for use as an order blank.

Beat-the-champ: A process where you establish a baseline or best performing promotion as the champ. You then continually test other promotions in hopes of finding a new champ. Also known as Control.

Bill enclosure: Any promotional piece or notice enclosed with a bill, an invoice, or a statement not directed toward the collection of all or part of the bill, invoice, or statement.

Bought list: A MarketPlace list that has been paid for with units from your meter.

Bounce-back: An offer enclosed with mailing sent to a customer in fulfillment of an offer.

Branches: Local company offices.

BRC (business reply card): An addressed reply form that carries a postage payment guarantee or requires no envelope. It must be printed on .007 inch thick stock to pass postal regulations.

BRE (business reply envelope): A preaddressed envelope with a postal payment guarantee, to hold a reply form.

Break even: The point in a business transaction when income and expenses are equal.

Broadcast media: A direct response source that includes radio, television, and cable TV.

Brochure: A pamphlet, with especially planned layout, typography, and illustrations. Term is also loosely used for any promotional pamphlet or booklet.

Building a list: MarketPlace option that selects names from the CD-ROM that match the criteria defined by the user.

Bulk mail: A category of third-class mail involving a large quantity of identical pieces that are sorted and classified before delivery to a post office.

Business list: Any compilation or list of individuals or companies based upon a business-associated interest, inquiry, membership, subscription, or purchase.

Buy list: A MarketPlace term for passing a user-defined list through the software meter, allowing the customer to use the list for mailings, telemarketing, or marketing analysis purposes.

Buyer: Someone who has purchased from a company.

C/A: Change of address.

Carrier route: Grouping of addresses based on the delivery route of each letter carrier. The average number of stops is 400 but may range from 100 to 2,500 to 3,000. In total, there are about 180,000 carrier routes in the United States.

Cash buyer: A buyer who encloses payment with order.

Cash rider: Also called "cash up" or "cash option," wherein an order form offers installment terms, but a postscript offers the option of sending full cash payment with order, usually at some savings over installment price.

Catalog: Any promotion that offers more than one product. Frequently, a catalog is a book or booklet showing merchandise with descriptive details and prices.

Catalog buyer: A person who has bought products or services from a catalog.

Cell(s): In list terminology, a statistical unit or units. A group of individuals selected from the file on a consistent basis.

Census tract: Small geographical area established by local committees, and approved by the Census Bureau, which contains a population segment with relatively uniform economic and social characteristics with clearly identifiable boundaries averaging approximately 1,200 households.

Cheshire label: Specially prepared paper (in rolls, fanfold, or accordion-fold) used to produce names and addresses to be mechanically affixed, one at a time, to a mailing piece.

Circulars: General term for printer advertisement in any form, including printed matter sent out by direct mail.

Cleaning: The process of correcting and/or removing a name and address from a mailing list, because it is no longer correct or because the name is to be shifted from one category to another. The term is also used in the identification and elimination of duplicate names on a house list.

Clip art: Art and graphics that have already been designed and converted to electronic format. The art is combined in collections, often with a specific theme, and sold for anyone to use.

Closed-face envelope: An envelope that is addressed on its face and does not have a die-cut window.

Cluster selection: A selection routine based upon taking a group of names in a series, skipping a group, and taking another group, (i.e., a cluster selection on an nth name basis might be the first 10 out of every 100 or the first 125 out of 175); a cluster selection using limited ZIP codes might be the first 200 names in each of the specified ZIP codes.

Coding: 1) Identifying devices used on reply devices to identify the mailing list or other source from which the address obtained; 2) a combination of letters and numbers used to classify characteristics of an address.

Collate: 1) To assemble individual elements of a mailing in sequence for inserting into a mailing envelope; 2) a program which combines two or more ordered files to produce a single ordered file. Also the act of combining such files. Synonymous with merges as in Merge/Purge.

Commission: In the list-rental business, this is a percentage of the sale, by prior agreement, paid to the list broker, list manager, or other service arm for their part in renting a list.

Compiled list: Name and addresses derived from directories, newspapers, public records, retail sales slips, trade show registrations, etc., identifying groups of people with something in common.

Compiler: Organization which develops lists of names and addresses from directories, newspapers, public records, registrations, etc., identifying groups of people, companies, or institutions with something in common.

Comprehensive: Complete and detailed layout of a printed piece. Also: "comp," "compre," or "mechanical."

Computer compatibility: Ability to interchange the data or programs of one computer system with another computer.

Computer letter: Computer-printed letter that includes personalized, fill-in information in predesignated positions.

Computer personalization: Printing of letters or other promotional pieces by a computer using names, addresses, special phrases, or other information based on data appearing in another file, usually a database file. The objective is to use the information in the data file to tailor the promotional message to a specific individual.

Computer record: All the information about an individual, company, or transaction stored in a data file.

Computer service bureau: An internal or external facility providing general or specific data processing services.

Consumer list: A list of names (usually, home addresses) that has been compiled, or is based on a common inquiry, membership, subscription, or buying activity.

Contact: Each time a target is reached by mail, phone, or in person. Multiple contacts may be necessary to accomplish a single sale.

Continuation: The next step after a list test. If the test proved responsive within established financial parameters, the list should be reordered.

Continuity program: Products or services bought as a series of small purchases, rather than all at one time. Generally based on a common theme and shipped at regular or specific time intervals.

Continuous form: Paper forms designed for computer printing that are folded and sometimes perforated, at predetermined vertical measurements. These may be letters, vouchers, invoices, cards, etc.

Contributer list: Names and addresses of persons who have given to a specific fund raising effort. (See Donor list.)

Control: A baseline package or program against which other packages or programs can be measured.

Controlled circulation: Distribution of a publication at no charge to individuals or companies on the basis of their titles or occupations. Typically, recipients are asked from time to time to verify the information that qualifies them to receive the publications.

Controlled duplication: See Merge/purge.

Conversion: 1) Process of changing from one method of data processing to another, or from one data processing system to another. Synonymous with reformatting. 2) To secure specific action such as a purchase or contribution from a name on a mailing list or as a result of an inquiry. 3) First-time subscriber renewal.

Co-op mailing: A mailing of two or more offers included in the same envelope, with each participating mailer sharing mailing costs according to some predetermined formula.

Cost per inquiry (C.P.I.): A simple arithmetic formula derived by dividing the total cost of a mailing or an advertisement by the number of inquiries received.

Cost per order (C.P.O.): A simple arithmetic formula derived by dividing the total cost of a direct marketing campaign by the number of orders received. Similar to cost per inquiry, except based on actual orders rather than inquiries.

Cost per thousand (C.P.M.): Refers to the total cost per thousand pieces of any part or the entire direct mail program.

Coupon: Part of an advertising promotion piece intended to be filled in by the inquirer or customer and returned to the advertiser.

Customer: An individual who has purchased product(s) or service(s) from you.

Data: A representation of facts, concepts, or instructions in a formal manner suitable for communication, interpretation, or processing by manual or automatic means.

Data field: One of the types of information attached to each record in a database: for example, annual sales or ZIP code.

Database: A collection of records or information. For the purposes of desktop marketing, a database holds names and marketing information on customers or prospects, as well as having the means to store further information and to extract information as needed.

Database management software: Software that allows you to organize, sort, and manipulate data records on your computer.

Deadbeat: One who has ordered a product or service and, without just cause, hasn't paid for it.

Decoy: A unique name especially inserted in a rented mailing list by the list owner to verify use.

Demographics: Socioeconomic characteristics pertaining to geographic unit (county, city, sectional center, ZIP code, group of households, education, ethnicity, income level, etc.)

Desktop marketing: Desktop marketing is the active pursuit, targeting, and maintenance of customers using a personal computer and a wide selection of software tools such as lead generation, word processors, database management, lead-tracking tools, spreadsheets, and desktop publishing.

Desktop publishing software: Software designed to create publishable materials, such as flyers, ads, or brochures. The software gives you control of layout of text and graphics and the overall appearance of the final version.

Dimensional mailings: Large three-dimensional mailings; generally packages or thick letters that have a tendency to be put on the top of a prospect's mail pile.

Direct mail advertising: Any promotional effort using the Postal Service, or other direct delivery service, for distribution of the advertising message.

Direct response advertising: Advertising, through any medium, designed to generate a response by any means (such as mail, telephone, or telegraph) that is measurable.

DMA: Direct Marketing Association, a trade association for direct marketing.

DMA Mail Preference Service: See Mail Preference Service.

Donor list: A list of persons who have given money to one or more charitable organizations. Synonymous with Contributor list.

Doubling day: A point in time established by previous experience when 50% of all returns to a mailing will have been received.

Dummy: 1) A fictitious name with a mailable address inserted into a mailing list to check on usage of that list, similar to Decoy. 2) See Mechanical. Dupe (Duplication): Appearance of identical or nearly identical names more than once on a file.

Duplication elimination: See Merge/purge.

Editing rules: Specific rules used in preparing name and address records that treat all elements in the same way at all times. Also, the rules for rearranging, deleting, selecting, or inserting any needed data, symbols, and/or characters.

Establishment: A single location where business is conducted or where services or industrial operations are performed.

Expiration: A subscription that is not renewed.

Expiration date: The date a subscription expires.

Expire: A former customer who is no longer an active buyer.

Field: One of the types of information attached to each record in a database. Also the reserved area in a database management system that serves a similar function in all records of the file.

File maintenance: See List maintenance.

Fill-in: A name, address, or other words added to a preprinted letter.

First-time buyer: Someone who buys a product or service from a specific company for the first time.

Fixed field: A way of laying out or formatting list information in a compute file that puts every piece of data in a specific position relative to every other piece of data, and limits the amount of space assigned to that data. If a piece of data is missing from an individual record, or if its assigned space is not completely used, that space is not filled (every record has the same space and the same length.) Any data exceeding its assigned space limitation must be abbreviated.

Flat-file database: A flat-file database has a rigid structure consisting of a series of records with the same number of fields (which may or may not contain data). It differs from a relational database in that it isn't set up with tables which you can link together.

Former buyer: Someone who has bought one or more times from a company but with no purchase in the last twelve months.

Frequency: The number of times an individual has ordered within a specific period of time. (See Monetary value and Recency.)

Front end: Direct marketing activities that occur prior to getting an order or contribution.

Full print: When the addressee, salutation, and all of the body copy are generated by the computer printer one at a time.

Function addressing: Addressing an envelope or letter according to the functional duties an individual performs rather than the title or name. It is used when mailing to business lists when there is no individual name.

Geo code: Symbols used to identify geographic entities (state, county, ZIP code, SCF, tract, etc.).

Geographics: Any method of subdividing a list based on geographic or political subdivisions (ZIP Codes, sectional centers, cities, counties, states or regions.)

Gimmick: Attention-getting device, usually dimensional, attached to a direct mail printed piece.

Guarantee: A pledge by the seller guaranteeing satisfaction and specifying the terms by which the seller will make good that pledge.

Headquarters: The center of a company's operation or administration. In MarketPlace, parent companies appear in this data field.

Hot-line list: The most recent names available on a specific rental list, that are no older than three months. Companies renting lists should specify whether the "hot-line" list is weekly, monthly, etc.

House list: Any lists of names owned by a company as a result of compilation, inquiry, or buyer action, or acquisition, that is used to promote that company's products or services.

House-list duplicate: Duplication of name and address records between a company's own lists and any other list the company is mailing to.

Indicia: Imprint on the outgoing envelope to denote payment of postage.

Influencer: In the business-to-business environment, a person who is involved in the buying decision process but not the decision maker. They can influence the decision but not make it themselves.

Inquirer: One who has asked for literature or other information about a product or service. Unless otherwise stated, it is assumed no payment has been made for the literature or other information.

Insert: Refers to a promotional piece inserted into an outgoing package or invoice.

Installment buyer: Someone who orders goods or services and pays for them in two or more periodic payments after their delivery.

K (Kilobytes): Used in reference to computer storage capacity, means 1,000 bytes of storage.

Key Code (Key): A group of letters and/or numbers, colors, or other markings, used to identify a specific mailing in order to measure the effectiveness of specific media, lists, advertisement, offers, etc.

Label: Piece of paper containing the name and address of the recipient that is applied to a mailing for address purposes.

Layout: 1) Artist's sketch showing relative positioning of illustrations, headlines, and copy. 2) The positioning of subject matter on a press sheet for most efficient production. 3) The designing of database management data structures and reporting formats.

Lead: A prospect that has been qualified and turned over to sales for contact and closing.

Letterhead: The design on a letter that identifies the sender.

Lettershop: A business organization that handles the mechanical details of mailings such as addressing, imprinting, collating, folding, and preparing for mailing according to postal regulations. Most lettershops offer some printing facilities and many offer some degree of creative and other direct mail-related services.

Lifestyle: Categorization of consumers based on where they live, the types of things they do, the things they buy, etc. There are several different lifestyle categorization schemes.

Lifetime value: Measurement of the long-term dollar value of a customer, subscriber, donor, etc. This figure is essential when evaluating initial costs to bring in a customer against the lifetime proceeds.

List: Names and addresses of individuals and/or companies having common interests, characteristics, or activities.

List broker: A specialist who makes all necessary arrangements for one company to use the list(s) of another company. A broker's services may include most, or all, of the following: research, selection, recommendation, and subsequent evaluation.

List buyer: Technically, this term should apply only to someone who actually buys mailing lists. In practice, however, it is used to identify anyone who rents mailing lists for one time use.

List cleaning: See Cleaning.

List compiler: See Compiler.

List exchange: A barter arrangement between two companies for the use of mailing list(s). This may include: list for list, list for advertising space, or list for a comparable value—other than money.

List maintenance: Any manual, mechanical, or electronic system for keeping name and address records (with or without other data) up-to-date at any specific point in time. See Update.

List manager: Someone who, as an employee of a list owner or as an outside agent, is responsible for the use, by others, of a specific mailing list. The list manager generally serves the list owner in several or all of the following capacities: list maintenance (or advice thereon), list promotion and marketing, list clearance and record keeping, collecting for use of the list by others.

List owner: Someone who, by promotional activity or compilation, has developed a list of names having something in common; or someone who has purchased (as opposed to rented, reproduced, or used on a one-time basis) such a list from the developer.

List rental: An arrangement whereby a list owner furnishes names to a mailer, with the privilege of using the list on a one-time basis only (unless otherwise specified in advance). For this privilege, the list owner is paid a royalty by the mailer.

List royalty: Payment to list owners for the privilege of using their names on a one-time basis.

List sample: A group of names selected, usually randomly, from a list in order to evaluate the responsiveness of that list.

List segmentation: See List selection.

List selection: Characteristics used to define smaller groups within a list or database (essentially, lists within a list). Although very small, select groups may be very desirable and may substantially improve response.

List sequence: The order in which names and addresses appear in a list. While most lists today are in ZIP code sequence, some are alphabetical by name within the ZIP code, others are in carrier sequence (postal delivery), and still others may (or may not) use some other order within the ZIP code. Some lists are still arranged alphabetically by name and chronologically, and in many other variations or combinations.

List sort: Process of putting a list in specific sequence or no sequence.

List source: The media used to acquire names: direct mail, space, TV, radio, telephone, etc.

List test: Part of a list selected to try to determine the effectiveness of the entire list. See List sample.

List user: Someone who uses names and addresses on someone else's list as prospects for his product or service; similar to Mailer.

Load up: Method of offering a buyer the opportunity to buy an entire series at one time, after the customer has purchased the first item in that series.

M: Refers to a 1,000 measurement unit, as in CP/M cost per thousand.

Magnetic tape: A computer storage device primarily for mainframe and minicomputers that electronically records and reproduces defined bits of data. Processing via computer tape is restricted to sequential processing of the information.

Mail date: The date by which a rental list user is obligated to have mailed a list. No other date is acceptable without specific approval of the list owner.

Mail merge: Combining a database of names and addresses with a text file, such as a cover letter, to create personalized mailings.

Mailer: 1) A direct mail advertiser who promoted a product or service using lists. 2) A printed direct mail advertising piece; 3) a folding carton, wrapper, or tube, used to protect materials in the mail.

Mailgram: A combination telegram-letter, with the telegram transmitted to a postal facility close to the addressee and then delivered as first-class mail.

Mailing list: See List.

Mailing machine: A machine that attaches address labels, inserts printed pieces into envelopes, affixes postage to pieces, and otherwise prepares pieces for mailing. They are usually found in lettershops.

Mail-order buyer: Someone who orders, and pays for, a product or service through the mail. Generally, an order telephoned in response to a direct response advertisement is considered a direct substitute for an order sent through the mail.

Mail Preference Service (MPS): A service of the Direct Marketing Association wherein consumers can request to have their names removed from, or added to, mailing lists. These names are made available to both members and nonmembers of the association.

Mapping software: Software that allows you to bring in data with some type of geographic content (usually ZIP codes) and will then accurately place the data on a ready-made map.

Master file: File that is of a permanent nature or regarded in a particular job as authoritative, or one that contains all subfiles.

Match: A direct mail term used to refer to the typing of personalized addresses, salutations, or comments onto letters in which other copy has been imprinted by a printing process.

Match code: A code determined either by the creator or the user of a file for matching duplicate records contained in another file.

Match fill: After the body copy of a letter has been typeset and preprinted by a printer, the process of using computer printing to add an address, salutation, and perhaps some specific information in the body of the letter to simulate a personal letter.

MB (Megabyte): Used in reference to computer storage capacity, meaning a million bytes of storage.

Mechanical: A mock-up giving a preview of a printed piece, showing placement and nature of the material to be printed.

Merge/purge: A method by which names and addresses from two or more lists are matched (usually by computer) in order to eliminate or limit extra mailings to the same name and address.

Meter: MarketPlace has a software meter that is installed on a computer hard disk to allow users to "buy" a list before using it. The meter can be filled with meter refills in 5,000 unit increments.

MicroVision: A lifestyle categorization schema developed by Equifax, Inc. MicroVision describes each ZIP+4 in the United States by modeling more than 100 variables, including credit-related data and comprehensive demographic information, to create 48 unique market segments that share common interests, purchasing patterns, and financial behavior.

Monetary value: Total expenditures by a customer during a specific period of time, generally 12 months.

MSA (Metropolitan Statistical Areas): A United States Government designation for areas that comprise one or more counties containing a city of at least 50,000 population, or an urbanized area of at least 50,000 with total metropolitan area population of at least 100,000.

Multiple buyer: One who has bought two or more times over two or more time periods; also called a Multibuyer or Repeat buyer.

Name: Single entry on a mailing list.

Name acquisition: Technique of soliciting a response to obtain names and addresses for a mailing list.

Name-removal service: Portion of Mail Preference Service offered by the Direct Marketing Association wherein a consumer is sent a form which, when filled in and returned, constitutes a request to have the individual's name removed from all mailing lists used by participating members of the Association and other direct mail users.

NECMAs (New England County Metropolitan Areas): NECMAs designate county-based urban regions in New England, because MSAs in New England are actually defined in terms of cities or towns rather than counties. MarketPlace uses NECMAs in New England to offer consistent metro data across the United States.

Negative option: A buying plan in which a customer or club member agrees to accept and pay for products or services announced in advance at regular intervals unless the individual notifies the company, within a reasonable time after each announcement, not to ship the merchandise.

Nesting: Placing one enclosure within another before inserting into a mailing envelope.

Net name arrangement: An agreement whereby a list owner agrees to accept adjusted payment for less than the total names rented to a list user, usually to make up for names that duplicate the list user's customers names. Such arrangements can be for a percentage of names shipped or names actually mailed (whichever is greater) or for only those names actually mailed (without a percentage limitation).

Nixie: A mailing piece returned to a mailer by the Postal Service because of an incorrect, or undeliverable, name and address.

No-pay: Someone who hasn't paid (wholly or in part) for goods or services ordered.

North/south labels: Mailing labels that read from top to bottom and can be affixed with Cheshire equipment.

Novelty format: An attention-getting direct mail format.

Nth name selection: A fractional unit that is repeated in sampling a mailing list. For example, in an "every 10th" sample, you would select the 1st, 11th, 21st, 31st, etc., records.

OCR (Optical character recognition): Machine identification of printed characters through use of light sensitive devices.

Offer: The terms promoting a specific product or service.

One-time buyer: A buyer who has not ordered a second time from a given company.

One-time use of a list: An intrinsic part of normal list use, list reproduction, or list exchange agreements in which it is agreed that the mailer will not use the names on the list more than one time without specific prior approval of the list owner.

Optical scanner: An input device that optically reads a line of printed characters and converts each character into its electronic equivalent for processing. It can also be used to convert pictures, photographs, or other graphical images to an electronic format that can be used in software packages.

Order-blank envelopes: An order form printed on one side of a sheet, with a mailing address on the reverse, The recipient simply fills in the order, folds it, and seals it like an envelope.

Order card: A reply card used to initiate an order by mail.

Order form: A printed form on which a customer can provide information to initiate an order by mail. It is designed to be mailed in an envelope.

Package: A term used to describe all of the assembled enclosures, parts, or elements of a direct mailing effort.

Package insert: Any promotional piece included in a product shipment. It may be for different products (or refills and replacements) from the same company or for products and services or other companies.

Package test: A test of part, or all, of the elements of one mailing piece against another.

Paid circulation: Distribution of a publication to individuals or organizations that have paid for a subscription.

Peel-off label: A self-adhesive label attached to a backing that is attached to a mailing piece. The label is intended to be removed from the mailing piece and attached to an order blank or card.

Penetration: Relationship of the number of companies, individuals or households on a particular list (by state, ZIP code, SIC, etc.) compared to the total number possible.

Per Inquiry (P.I.): A payment method in the direct marketing industry. The user agrees to pay for media services based on a per-lead or per-sale basis.

Personalization: Individualizing of direct mail pieces by adding the name or other personal information about the recipient.

Phone list: Mailing list compiled from names listed in telephone directories.

Piggy-back: An offer that hitches a free ride with another offer.

Positive option: A method of distributing products and services incorporating the same advance notice techniques as Negative option, but requiring a specific order each time from the member or subscriber. Generally, more costly and less predictable than Negative option.

Postal Service Prohibitory Order: A communication from the Postal Service to a company indicating that a specific person and/or family considers the company's advertising mail to be pandering. The order requires the company to remove from its own mailing list and from any other lists used to promote the company's products or services all names listed on the order. Violation of the order is subject to fine and imprisonment. Names listed on the order are to be distinguished from those names removed voluntarily by the list owner at an individual's request.

Postcard: Single-sheet self-mailers on card stock.

Postcard deck: Offerings from many different companies printed on 3x5 cards, gathered together in an envelope or cellophane wrapper, and mailed to a specific list. The card deck is extremely easy to respond to, because each card also serves as its own business reply card.

Postcard mailers: Booklet containing business reply cards that are individually perforated for selective return, to order products or obtain information.

Premium: An item offered to a buyer, usually free or at a nominal price, as an inducement to purchase or obtain for trial a product or service offered via mail order.

Premium buyer: Someone who buys a product or service to get another product or service (usually free or at a special price), or who responds to an offer of a special product (premium) on the package or label (or sometimes in the advertising) of another package.

Presort: Refers to presorting of mail to carrier route by ZIP codes and preparing it to specifications established by the United States Postal Service. Properly executed, the mailing receives a discounted postal rate.

Program: 1) A sequence of steps to be executed by the computer to solve a given problem or achieve a certain result; 2) a sequence of direct marketing activities that identifies a direct marketing effort to sell products or generate leads.

Prospect: 1) A responder to a desktop marketing program, considered to be a potential buyer for a given product or service and who has not previously made such a purchase. 2) A group of targets that meet your predetermined qualification criteria and are included in ongoing marketing programs.

Prospecting: Using direct marketing to get leads for further sales contact.

Publisher's letter: A second letter enclosed in a mailing package to stress a specific selling point. Also called a buck slip or lift memo.

Purge: The process of eliminating duplicates and/or unwanted names and addresses from one or more lists.

Questionnaire: A printed form to a specified audience to solicit answers to specific questions.

Recency: The latest purchase or activity recorded for an individual or company on a specific customer list. See Frequency and Monetary Value.

Record: The collection of information about a single business establishment or household.

Reformatting: Changing a magnetic tape format from one arrangement to another, more usable format. Synonymous with Conversion.

Relational database: Information in a relational database is stored in tables, which can be linked together through a common field, such as customer name or account number.

Renewal: A subscription that has been renewed prior to expiration or within six months thereafter.

Rental: See List rental.

Repeat buyer: See Multiple buyer.

Reply card: A sender-addressed card, included in a mailing on which the recipient may indicate his response to the offer. Synonymous with Order card.

Reply-O-Letter: One of a number of patented direct mail formats for facilitating replies from prospects. It features a die-cut opening on the face of the letter and a pocket on the reverse. An addressed reply card is inserted in the pocket, and the name and address shows through the die-cut opening. It can be used with ImageWriters.

Reproduction right: Authorization by a list owner for a specific mailer to use that list on a one-time basis.

Response rate: Percent of returns or inquiries from a mailing.

Return envelopes: Addressed reply envelopes, either stamped or unstamped, included with a mailing.

Return on investment (ROI): The evaluation of return on invested capital. In desktop marketing, often loosely described as the return (income) based on the dollars expended in a desktop campaign.

Return Postage Guaranteed: A legend imprinted on the address face of envelopes or other mailing pieces when the mailer wishes the Postal Service to return undeliverable third-class bulk mail. A payment equivalent to the single piece, first-class rate must be made for each piece returned. See List cleaning.

Return requested: An indication that a mailer will compensate the Postal Service for the return of an undeliverable mailing piece.

Returns: 1) Responses to a direct mail program; 2) returns of products shipped to customers on free or limited trials that are not purchased.

RFMR: Abbreviation for recency–frequency–Monetary–Value ratio, a formula used to evaluate the sales potential of names on a mailing list.

Roll out: To mail the remaining portion of a mailing list after successfully testing a portion of that list.

Rough: Dummy or layout in sketchy form with a minimum of detail.

Royalties: Sum paid per unit mailed or sold, for the use of a list, imprimatur, patent, etc.

Running charge: The price a list owner charges for names that are run or passed through the computer, usually for some type of analysis. When such a charge is made, it is usually to cover extra processing costs.

Salting: Deliberate placing of decoy or dummy names in a list to trace list use and delivery. See Decoy or Dummy.

Sample buyer: Someone who sends for a sample product, usually at a special price or for a small handling charge, but sometimes free.

Sample package: An example of the package to be mailed by the list user to a particular list. Such a mailing piece is submitted to a list owner for approval prior to commitment for one-time use of the list. Although a sample package may, due to time pressure, differ slightly from the actual package used, the list owner agreement usually requires the user to reveal any material differences when submitting the sample package.

SCF (Sectional Center): A Postal Service distribution unit comprising different post offices whose ZIP codes start with the same first three digits.

Selection criteria: Definition of characteristics that identify segments or subgroups within a list.

Self-mailer: A direct mail piece mailed without an envelope.

Seven point: The minimum paper thickness (.007 inches) the United States Postal Service allows for use as a post card for mailing purposes.

Sheet-fed forms: A standard cut form for use in LaserWriter printers. Also referred to as cut-sheet forms.

Shopper Type: One of the selection criteria in MarketPlace: Household. It categorizes households into one of nine types of shoppers.

S.I.C. (Standard Industrial Classification): A United States Department of Commerce system that organizes all types of business in the United States economy. Each business establishment is classified according to its primary activity. For a complete SIC manual contact any Government Printing Procurement Office or contact: National Technical Information Service, 5285 Port Royal Road, Springfield, VA 22151, order # PB 87-100012.

SMSA (Standard Metropolitan Statistical Area): Major metropolitan areas as set forth by the government that are used by the print publications to define and compare markets. See also ADI.

Software: A set of programs, procedures, and associated documentation concerned with operation of a data processing system.

Solo mailing: A mailing promoting a single product or a limited group of related products. It usually consists of a letter, brochure, and reply device enclosed in an envelope.

Source code: Unique alphabetic and/or numeric identification for distinguishing one list or media source from another. See Key code.

Source count: The number of names and addresses in any given list, for the media (or list sources) from which names and addresses were derived.

Split test: Two or more samples from the same list—each considered to be representative of the entire list—used for package tests or to test the homogeneity of the list.

Step up: The use of special premiums to get a mail order buyer to increase his or her unit of purchase.

Stock art: See Clip art.

Stock formats: Direct mail formats with preprinted illustrations and/or headings to which a company can add its own copy.

Stopper: Advertising slang for a striking headline or illustration intended to attract immediate attention.

Stuffer: Advertising enclosures placed in other media, e.g., newspapers, merchandise packages, mailings for other products, etc.

Subscriber: Individual who has paid or has qualified to receive a periodical or some other ongoing service.

Syndicated mailing: Mailing prepared for distribution by firms other than the manufacturer or syndicator.

Tag: To mark a record in a database with a definitive criteria that allows for subsequent selection or suppression.

Tape layout: A simple "map" of the data included in each record and its location.

Tape record: All of the information about an individual or company contained on a specific magnetic tape.

Target: A household or business selected as the recipient of some form of marketing effort.

Teaser: An advertisement or promotion planned to elicit curiosity about a later advertisement or promotion.

Telemarketing: Using the telephone as a marketing medium staffed with scripted communicators.

Telephone Preference Service (TPS): A service of the Direct Marketing Association for consumers who wish to have their names removed from national telemarketing lists. The name-removal file is made available to subscribers on a quarterly basis.

Telesales: Using the telephone as a marketing support tool, staffed by communicators or sales people that have product knowledge and some selling skills.

Test panel: A term used to identify each of the parts or samples in a split test.

Throwaway: An advertisement or promotional piece intended for widespread free distribution. Generally printed on inexpensive paper stock and most often distributed by hand to passers-by or from house-to-house.

Tie-in: Cooperative mailing effort involving two or more advertisers.

Till Forbid: An order for continuing service that is to continue until specifically cancelled by the buyer.

Title: A designation before or after a name to more accurately identify an individual. (Prefixes: Mr., Mrs., Dr., Sister, etc.; suffixes: M.D., Jr., President, Sales Manager, etc.)

Title addressing: Addressing an envelope or letter according to the title of the desired recipient when mailing to a business list, rather than to an individual name.

Tip-on: An item glued to a printed piece.

Token: An involvement device, often consisting of a perforated portion of an order card designed to be removed from its original position and placed in another designated area on the order card, to signify a desire to purchase the product or service.

Traffic builder: A direct mail piece intended primarily to attract recipients to the mailer's place of business.

Trial buyer: Someone who buys a short-term supply of a product, or buys the product with the understanding that it may be examined, used, or tested for a specified time before deciding whether to pay for it or to return it.

Trial subscriber: A person ordering a publication or service on a conditional basis. The condition may relate to delaying payment, a right to cancel, a shorter than normal term, and/or a special introductory price. Unbought list: A MarketPlace list that has not been paid for with units from the meter.

Unit of sale: Description of the average dollar amount spent by customers on a mailing list.

Universe: Total number of individuals that might be included on a mailing list; all of those fitting a single set of specifications.

Update: Recent transactions and current information added to the master (main) list to reflect the current status of each record on the list.

Up front: Securing payment for a product offered by mail order before the product is sent.

Variable field: A way of laying out database information that assigns a specific sequence to the data but doesn't assign it specific positions or lengths. While this method conserves space, it is generally more complicated to work with.

Verification: The process for determining the validity of an order by sending a questionnaire to the customer.

White mail: Incoming mail that is not a form sent out by the advertiser; all mail other than orders or payments.

Window envelopes: Envelopes with a die-cut portion on the front that permits viewing the address printed on an enclosure. The "die-cut window" may or may not be covered with transparent material.

ZIP Code: A group of five digits used by the United States Postal Service to designate specific post offices, stations, branches, buildings, or large companies.

ZIP code sequence: Arranging names and addresses in a list according to the numeric progression of the ZIP code in each record. This form of list formatting is mandatory for mailing bulk third-class mail, based on the sorting requirements of the Postal Service.

ZIP+4: A group of nine digits used by the United States Postal Service to designate one side of a block. There are currently over 28 million ZIP+4s in the United States.

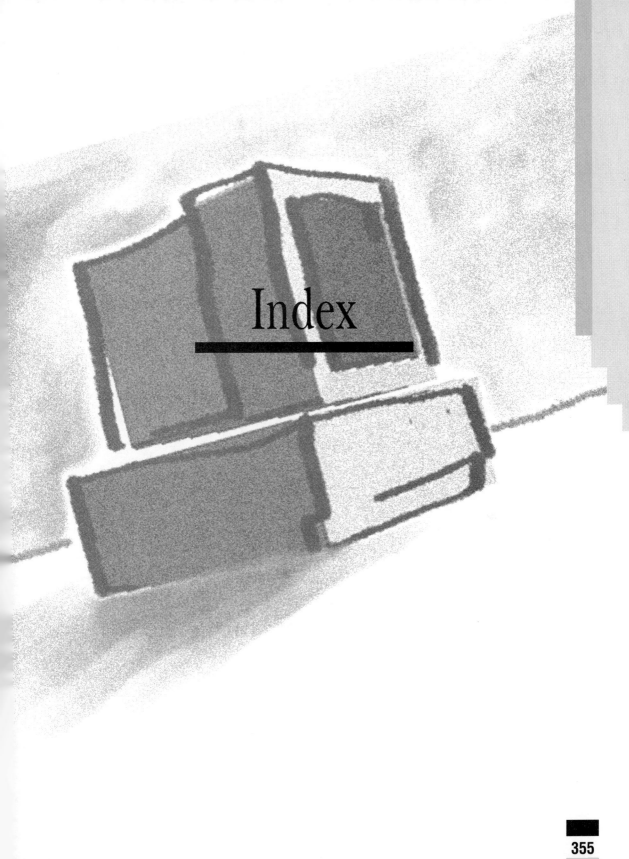

Index

Q-R

X-Z